The
ULTIMATE
book of
IMPOSTORS

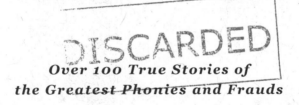

Over 100 True Stories of
the Greatest Phonies and Frauds

IAN GRAHAM

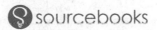

Published by Sourcebooks, Inc.
P.O. Box 4410, Naperville, Illinois 60567-4410
(630) 961-3900
Fax: (630) 961-2168
www.sourcebooks.com

Library of Congress Cataloging-in-Publication Data

Graham, Ian.
  The ultimate book of impostors : over 100 true stories of the greatest phonies and frauds / Ian Graham.
       pages cm
  Includes bibliographical references and index.
  (pbk. : alk. paper) 1. Impostors and imposture--History. I. Title.
  HV6751.G73 2013
  364.16'3--dc23

                                        2013031145

Printed and bound in the United States of America.
VP 10 9 8 7 6 5 4 3 2 1

To Ormeau Road public library in Belfast,
Northern Ireland, where I learned to love books.

CONTENTS

TO BE...
OR TO BE SOMEONE ELSE

T hat is indeed the question. When I was a youngster, I was a sucker for horror stories. One that stayed with me is "The Ohio Love Sculpture" by Adobe James. In just seven pages it tells the story of an art collector who stumbles across the most magnificent sculpture he has ever seen—three reclining nudes. He has to have it. He offers more and more money, but the stubborn sculptor won't sell. Eventually the collector manages to trick the sculptor into giving up his stunning creation. But before he can pick it up, the sculptor is involved in an incident that brings the police to his home, where they make a chilling discovery:

The artist isn't a sculptor, he's a taxidermist!

This story sowed the seed in my mind at a young age that people are not always what they seem. Decades later, this same idea led me to write this book. The idea of mistaken or deliberately falsified identity is common in fiction, but you don't have to go to the trouble of dreaming up fictitious impostors. As you'll see in this book, there is no shortage of the real thing. History is littered with examples of people who pretended to be someone else.

You may wonder why on earth so many people would risk so

much—their lives, families, careers, freedom—simply to put on a different face. In most cases, their various motivations can be boiled down to just four things, the four E's:

- ► Envy
- ► Ego
- ► Escape
- ► Espionage

Envy of other people's wealth or social status has driven many impostors to claim to be the heir to a kingdom or an aristocratic title. This was especially easy in past times: before DNA testing and photo IDs, how would you know whether someone really was the Earl of this or Duke of that, or a royal prince? A pretender with the right fashion credentials and a regal bearing, coupled with the gift of the gab and bags of confidence, was indistinguishable from the real thing to most people. Add the support of a Machiavellian manipulator, such as a kingmaker, and you're a winner. At least, you hope you're a winner. Many a pretender who failed to convince those more powerful than he ended his days at the point of a sword or in the merciless hands of an executioner. For example, when a woman who pretended to be Margaret, Maid of Norway and daughter of King Erik II of Norway, in the thirteenth century was exposed as an impostor, she was burned at the stake and her husband was beheaded!

Since then, envy of wealth for its own sake has driven some criminals to use fake identities to steal large sums of money or valuable property. Most of them are known for one false identity, but a few are serial impostors who moved seamlessly from one identity to another to suit their needs.

Fantasists boost their ego by becoming someone else with a more interesting, exciting, or exotic life than their own. They seek attention and approval. This group includes the bogus pilots, spies, and war heroes whose false identities command respect and admiration. And of course one of the quickest and easiest ways to escape from the consequences of crime is to adopt a false identity.

At times when there was no such thing as social mobility, some people tried to escape the limits of the class they were born into by becoming someone else. Others escaped the social straitjacket of their time by switching gender, usually from female to male. Women with an ambition to serve as a soldier or sailor in past centuries could do so only by appearing to be men. Some of them served for years without being found out.

Some people have adopted false identities perfectly legally. They are the undercover police officers and secret service agents who infiltrate groups for the purposes of surveillance or espionage. Deep-cover agents sometimes live for years under a false identity, gathering intelligence for law enforcement and national defense agencies.

Beyond these four reasons, there are numerous other motives for wanting to adopt a false identity. For instance, a handful of professional entertainers created a stage persona so successful and so convincing that they started living the role offstage too. Their fans got a shock when the truth of these entertainers' lives was revealed after death.

In most cases, impostors adopt fictitious *false* identities, but sometimes they steal the identities of real people, alive or dead. Stealing a real person's identity has advantages—they have a real life history with facts that can be verified by anyone who gets suspicious. However, one obvious disadvantage is that if the real person is still alive, he or she may turn up and expose the impostor. One way to get around this is to steal the identity of someone who has died. This was the method used by the assassin in Frederick Forsyth's book, *The Day of the Jackal* to obtain a birth certificate, which he used to apply for a passport in the dead boy's name. But of course anyone who takes the trouble to investigate the impostor is likely to discover evidence of the death. Two real impostors who copied this method were discovered when background checks revealed that they had died years earlier!

You might think imposture would be virtually impossible today, with our photo-ID, online credit checks, official certificates and licenses, fingerprints and DNA databases to confirm identity. However, the very existence of some of this identity documentation can actually make it more difficult to detect an impostor. Convincing forgeries of official certificates are sometimes taken at face value and no other checks are made. Bogus pilots and doctors continue to foil lax authorities by using fake documents.

The dictionary definition of *impostor* is clear—an impostor is someone who assumes a false identity for the purpose of deception or fraud. But sometimes real life is not as clear cut. Is someone who exaggerates his military service an impostor? Probably not. But someone who wears a uniform or military decorations he isn't entitled to, even without adopting a false identity, is a different matter. Military and ex-service organizations aggressively seek out impostors in uniform.

At first thought, impostors might seem to be universally reprehensible—tricksters, thieves, and fraudsters without a redeeming feature. But as you read their stories, I hope you will find, as I did, that a few of them are worthy of understanding and sympathy. They adopted false identities simply to get by in a world that would otherwise have rejected them for reasons of gender or race. For example, the name Mata Hari conjures up ideas of spying, prostitution, and exotic dancing, but Mata Hari chose her lifestyle as a way to survive the considerable setbacks and difficulties in her life that might have destroyed a lesser woman. She overcame everything that was thrown at her and not only survived, but also prospered—a rare achievement for a woman on her own in the early 1900s. Chief Buffalo Child Long Lance invented a Native American backstory that made him more acceptable in a society that would otherwise have excluded him. Marvin Hewitt adopted several false identities of high-flying scientists to enable him to achieve his ambition to teach physics, which by all accounts he did very well. These are just a few examples of impostors who certainly deceived people but seem to have done no harm.

Of course, all of the impostors featured in this book are failures, because we know about them. For every impostor who has been discovered and exposed, no one knows how many others have been successful.

So as you read these amazing, hilarious, and bizarre stories, ask yourself this...

**Can you be sure your partner, friend, or coworker
really is the person you think he or she is?**

It may seem unlikely, but it is perfectly possible to be branded an impostor when you're nothing of the sort. If your partner suddenly looks at you as if you're a total stranger, he or she could be suffering from a condition called Capgras syndrome. A sufferer is convinced that a friend or relative has been replaced by an identical impostor. It sounds like the plot of a film like *The Invasion of the Body Snatchers,* but it's real. It can be triggered by neurological disorders or brain injuries.

chapter

1

SERIAL OFFENDERS

Most impostors are content with one false identity, but a few have moved from one identity to another and then another and another, changing their name and occupation many times. When the danger of discovery loomed before them, their solution was not to surrender or go underground but to reinvent themselves as someone else yet again. Some of these serial offenders created multiple identities for the purpose of fraud. Each new disguise kept the hounds of the law at bay until the next payday. Others seem to have simply enjoyed being different people and fooling everyone around them.

Some serial impostors carefully researched each of their false identities to make themselves all the more believable. The most famous, Frank Abagnale, researched his role as a doctor so thoroughly that a hospital where he became a familiar face offered him a job. He also worked as a lawyer and sociology professor. When he posed as a doctor, he didn't treat any patients, but another serial impostor, Ferdinand Demara, did. Posing as a navy doctor, but without any medical qualifications, he pulled teeth and carried out surgical procedures on wounded men with just a medical textbook to guide him.

Demara's other false identities included a monk, a psychologist, a teacher, and even a prison warden.

Michael Sabo is reported to have assumed more than one hundred false identities over three decades, including airline pilots and military officers, to steal around $10 million. When Steven Spielberg was planning to make his film, *Catch Me If You Can*, Sabo was his first choice as a subject on which to base the plot. However, Sabo was a wanted man and couldn't participate, so the film was based on Frank Abagnale's life instead.

One of the most extraordinary cases of recent years involved a man going by the name of Clark Rockefeller, who triggered a nationwide manhunt in the United States when he disappeared with his daughter. As we'll see in a moment, even his false identity was not what it seemed.

THE ROGUE ROCKEFELLER

Many Americans now know exactly who the infamous impostor Clark Rockefeller is. But when Rockefeller was arrested for kidnapping his own daughter, his wife asked the police an extraordinary question about him—*Who is he?*

Sandra Boss got to know and fell in love with a man she thought was Clark Rockefeller, a member of *the* Rockefeller family. He was living the life of a Rockefeller in New York, and she was a high-flying management consultant and Harvard Business School graduate. They married in 1995. Their daughter, Reigh, was born in 2001, but Sandra was becoming increasingly unhappy. She said her husband had changed—he had become argumentative, abusive, and controlling. He was no longer the man she had married. By then, they were living in the small town of Cornish, New Hampshire. Rockefeller had made enemies in the community after a series of disagreements with residents. In 2006, he reluctantly agreed to move to Boston so that Sandra could be closer to her new workplace in the city and could spend more time at home, but things didn't improve and she finally decided to leave. Both parents filed for custody of their daughter.

During the divorce proceedings, Sandra's father remembered Rockefeller saying at one point that his mother's name was Mary Roberts, but later he claimed that his mother was a former child actor called Ann Carter. When Carter was contacted about this, she denied having any connection with anyone called Clark Rockefeller. Sandra had already begun to suspect that he might not be who he said he was, so she hired a private detective to investigate her husband. The detective discovered that there was no record of Clark Rockefeller before 1994 but couldn't get to the bottom of his real identity. When he was challenged with this, "Rockefeller" offered to drop his custody claim in return for a million dollars. He finally settled for $800,000. Sandra moved to London with Reigh and agreed to her ex-husband having three supervised visits with her every year.

She insisted on the meetings being supervised, because she was afraid he might try to kidnap the girl. And, during a visit in Boston on July 27, 2008, that's exactly what happened. As "Rockefeller" walked along a Boston street with the seven-year-old he called Snooks, he suddenly bundled her into a waiting car and sped off before the social worker chaperone following them could stop him. A few streets away, he switched to a cab and then to another car. By the time the police arrived, he was long gone. They searched the surrounding area but couldn't find any trace of him. When officers tried to build a picture of his life by searching the usual databases, they found nothing. They discovered that Clark Rockefeller had no social security number, driver's license, credit cards, tax records, or passport. When the Rockefeller family was contacted, they said they'd never heard of him. When the police questioned his friends, they found he had told each of them a different story about where he was planning to go, but none of the stories was true. His disappearance was very well planned. The police had no idea where he'd gone or even who he really was.

When his picture was publicized by the FBI, people who knew him in Wisconsin, California, Boston, and New York contacted the police, naming him as Christopher Chichester and Clark Rockefeller.

Interestingly, Crowe had been pulled over by police while he was driving a pickup truck. They had no idea who they'd gotten. By the time the Department of Motor Vehicles discovered that the truck actually belonged to the missing Jonathan Sohus, Crowe and the truck had disappeared. He tried to sell the truck, but the buyer became suspicious and called the police. However, he managed to get away again. He disguised himself by dying his hair and growing a beard.

They were also contacted by people from Connecticut who had known him as a television producer called Christopher Crowe. But they were no closer to finding him until callers from Baltimore identified the wanted man as their new neighbor, Chip Smith. Within hours, agents were staking out his house. They wanted to make sure he couldn't use Reigh as a hostage to get away. They tricked him into leaving the house by phoning him and telling him that his boat in a nearby marina had sprung a leak and was taking in water. As soon as he came out, he was arrested. Reigh was found unharmed inside the house.

Fingerprints taken from a friend's house cracked the mystery of his identity. The prints belonged to a man called Christian Karl Gerhartsreiter. His identity was confirmed by his brother, Alexander, in Germany. He was born in Siegsdorf, West Germany, in 1961 and grew up nearby in Bergen. He traveled to the United States in 1978 on a tourist visa. Then he managed to get a place at the University of Wisconsin–Stevens Point. A few months later, he transferred to the University of Wisconsin at Milwaukee. By then he'd decided that he wanted to stay in the United States, and a surefire way of achieving it was to marry an American. In 1981, he married Amy Janine Jersild, enabling him to get a green card. He left her the day after the wedding and dropped out of college soon afterward. He turned up next in California, where he changed his name. He had already shortened it to Chris Gerhart, but now he wanted something that sounded less German. He chose Christopher Mountbatten Chichester and set up home in San Marino. The word got around that he was related to Lord Louis Mountbatten, a member of the British royal family who

4

had been murdered by the Provisional IRA (Irish Republican Army) in 1979.

Gerhartsreiter's trial began in May 2009. His lawyers admitted everything he was accused of but pleaded insanity. They said he had been pushed over the edge by the loss of his daughter. They said he believed that his daughter had contacted him telepathically and begged him to rescue her. Expert witnesses for the defense testified that he suffered from a personality disorder. The prosecution accepted that he was suffering from a personality disorder but insisted that he was still able to tell right from wrong. His meticulous planning of his daughter's abduction so as to evade arrest was evidence of this. So he was bad, not mad.

Gerhartsreiter did not give evidence. The jury retired after twelve days. On June 12, after discussing the case for a week, they found him guilty of kidnapping and assault but, amazingly, not guilty of giving a false name to police. He was sentenced to four to five years in prison for kidnapping, to be served concurrently with two to three years for assault—he had shoved Reigh's social worker chaperone to the ground during the kidnapping, leaving him bleeding and suffering from a concussion.

A Sinister Turn

While Gerhartsreiter was serving his prison sentence, his story took an even more sinister turn. When he was arrested, he had been linked to the mysterious disappearance of a couple in the 1980s. In 1994, a homeowner in San Marino, California, dug up his backyard to build a swimming pool and unearthed a human skull. A further search discovered the rest of the skeleton. In 2010, the remains were identified as those of Jonathan Sohus, whose mother had owned the property. Sohus, a twenty-seven-year-old computer engineer, and his wife Linda had disappeared in 1985. Linda has never been found, but she is presumed dead. Sohus had been killed by three heavy blows to his head, which smashed his skull to pieces. The skull was so badly damaged that it had to be sent to a Department of Defense facility in Hawaii to be reconstructed. The weapon could have been something like a baseball bat. The body had been dismembered, and the pieces had been wrapped in plastic and packed in a fiberglass box.

In the early 1980s, the property was a guesthouse. One of the guests at the time of the Sohuses' disappearance was a man called Christopher Chichester. Police later learned that Chichester had borrowed a chainsaw around the time of the disappearance. In the late 1980s, they traced him to Connecticut, where he had been living as Christopher Crowe.

The police were able to connect Gerhartsreiter to the murders in a very unusual way: Gerhartsreiter had attended the University of Wisconsin–Milwaukee in 1980–81, and Jonathan Sohus's skull was found in a University of Wisconsin–Milwaukee bag bearing a logo that was used only between 1979 and 1982. Now the police knew that Christopher Chichester, Christopher Crowe, and Christian Gerhartsreiter were the same person. On March 15, 2011, a judge ruled that Gerhartsreiter should stand trial for the murder of Jonathan Sohus.

The trial opened in Los Angeles in March 2013 with Gerhartsreiter's lawyer branding the twenty-eight-year-old murder case old, cold, and still untold, because his client was not guilty. He accepted that Gerhartsreiter was a con man, but this didn't mean he was a murderer too. He suggested that Sohus's missing wife, a robust six-foot-tall, two-hundred-pound woman, could have murdered her husband. Prosecution and defense lawyers questioned and cross-examined witnesses for three weeks. Gerhartsreiter himself did not give evidence.

The jury retired April 10, 2013, and took only six hours to find Gerhartsreiter guilty of first-degree murder. Gerhartsreiter fired his legal team and represented himself at a presentencing hearing in July. He claimed he had discovered a new lead suggesting that John Sohus had been murdered by his wife, and he attempted to request a new trial. However, the judge was unconvinced and sentencing went ahead in August. Gerhartsreiter will serve twenty-seven years to life. Hopefully the many disguises of Christian Karl Gerhartsreiter have now run their course. For the next few years, his only alias will be inmate 2800458.

A RUNNER TRIPS UP

Most impostors avoid attracting attention, blending in with everyone around them to become invisible. But one impostor's outstanding talent made him a little too noticeable.

Alexi Indris-Santana was the ultimate collegiate track star. When he ran, very few people could catch him. Princeton University was particularly pleased to have secured the young athlete as a student. He had the potential to be one of their greatest long-distance runners. Then a Yale student recognized him at an Ivy League track meet in 1991 as a student he had known by a different name, Jay Mitchell Huntsman, in high school in Palo Alto, California, several years earlier. At the time, he'd been a memorable student at Palo Alto as well because of his circumstances—Huntsman said his parents had been killed in a car accident in Bolivia. And he was an outstanding runner.

In fact, Santana and Huntsman were actually James Hogue, born in 1959 and brought up in Kansas City. He attended the University of Wyoming but left without graduating. In 1980, he moved on to the University of Texas but didn't graduate there either. In 1985, he changed his name to Jay Huntsman and enrolled in high school in Palo Alto. The principal thought he looked older than the sixteen years he claimed—and was right. Hogue was actually ten years older than his fellow students. When a reporter ran some background checks on the mysterious runner, the only Jay Huntsman he could find in San Diego, where Huntsman claimed to have been born, had died in infancy. The obvious implication was that "Huntsman" had stolen the dead child's identity. When Hogue learned that his fraud had been discovered, he suddenly dropped out of high school and disappeared.

He got a job as a coach at a cross-country training camp in Vail, Colorado, having told his new employer that he had a doctorate in bioengineering from Stanford University, where he had also worked as a professor. Once again, his outstanding running ability drew attention. But a runner recognized him and tipped off the staff. They checked with Stanford, which couldn't confirm Hogue's claims. When confronted, he simply left.

In an apparently unrelated incident shortly after Hogue left Vail, a bicycle builder's shop in San Marco, California, was broken into and $20,000 of bicycle frames and tools were stolen. The shop was owned by Dave Tesch, who had met Hogue when they were both working at the Vail training camp. Hogue worked at Tesch's shop for a short time. A few months later, a cyclist in Utah contacted the police to say that he had seen Hogue with a wrench engraved with Tesch's name. It was one of the stolen tools. The police tracked Hogue down and arrested him. When officers opened a storage locker used by Hogue, they found Tesch's tools and bike frames inside. He was found guilty of the theft and sentenced to one to five years in prison. Released in 1989 after serving ten months, he skipped parole and disappeared. A fugitive warrant for his arrest was issued.

Hogue, now going by the name of Santana, was accepted to Princeton in 1988. His application for one of 1,200 places at Princeton had stood out from the other 14,000 the university received that year because he had no high school diploma and he claimed to be entirely self-taught while working as a cowboy on the Lazy T Ranch in Utah. The press clippings and race results he sent with his application also caught the eye of Princeton's track coach, Larry Ellis. Ellis was so keen to have Santana that he sent him a round-trip ticket to visit Princeton. When the university's runners saw him on the track, they were convinced that he was the real deal and they wanted him on their team.

When interviewed for admission, Santana impressed the admissions panel with the depth and breadth of his knowledge, especially in science and history. He was accepted. When he started classes in 1989, other students reported that he seemed to be able to do well without trying very hard. He was a straight-A student. He avoided socializing with his roommates or even talking to them and was always vague about his past. His fellow students never felt that they got to know him.

The Camera-Shy Athlete

Despite his undoubted athletic ability, Santana often disappointed on the track. He would put in blistering performances in training but pull up with mysterious injuries before meets, especially the biggest events that attracted a lot of fans and reporters. When he was finally recognized by the Yale runner and Princeton found out he was a phony, they acted fast. Santana was pulled out of a geology class and arrested. His fellow students were stunned to see him being handcuffed and taken away by detectives. They were even more shocked when they learned that he wasn't twenty years old as they thought but thirty-two! When he stood trial, he was found guilty of defrauding the university to the tune of $30,000. He served nine months in jail plus one hundred hours of community service and five years' probation. He was also ordered to pay more than $20,000 in restitution.

After his release and with yet another false identity, he secured a job as a guard at one of Harvard University's museums. A few months later, staff noticed that several gemstones on display had been replaced by cheap fakes. Hogue was arrested and charged with thefts amounting to $50,000. He was arrested again in 1996 when he was spotted hanging around at Princeton, which violated his parole conditions. This led to yet another term of imprisonment. A couple of years later, he cooperated in the production of a film about his life called *Con Man*, released in 2002. By then, he was living in Colorado.

In 2007, he was back in court following a police search of his home in Telluride, Colorado, and a rented storage locker nearby that uncovered more than seven thousand stolen items worth over $100,000. He had taken them from homes where he'd been working as a repairman. When he was arrested in Tucson, Arizona, he seemed to have been preparing to take on yet another false identity, as a doctor this time. He accepted a deal that limited his penalty to no more than ten years imprisonment in return for pleading guilty to one charge of theft.

Have we finally heard the last of James Hogue? Don't bet on it!

Interestingly, Hogue/Santana had to defer his admission to Princeton for a year because he was still in prison for the bicycle theft. Of course, he didn't tell Princeton that he was in prison. He spun them a yarn about his mother falling seriously ill in Switzerland and having to go to her bedside.

THE CHAMELEON'S TALE

Given our natural protective instincts, seeing a distressed child is more likely to elicit our help than our suspicion. A French serial impostor nicknamed the Chameleon used this simple observation to his advantage again and again.

On June 8, 2005, the principal of the Jean Monnet College in Pau, southwestern France, sent for one of her students. When the boy arrived, police officers grabbed the fifteen-year-old and handcuffed him.

The boy, Francisco Hernandez Fernandez, had been found alone in a nearby town, Orthez, after a phone call to the police from someone who had spotted him. He claimed he had run away from an abusive relative with whom he had been living in Spain after the rest of his family died in a car accident. The boy was placed in a local children's home. When he started attending school, he quickly became popular with the other students. He was a fast learner and readily helped the others with their work.

Then the school administrator told the principal about a television program she'd seen, featuring a serial impostor called Frédéric Bourdin, who had perpetrated an extraordinary imposture in the United States in the 1990s. She said that Bourdin bore a remarkable resemblance to their star student, Francisco. When the principal checked, pictures of Bourdin did indeed look very like Francisco, so she called the police.

The fifteen-year-old Francisco Hernandez Fernandez turned out to be the thirty-one-year-old serial impostor Bourdin. He had a long and very odd history of impersonating children to get into children's schools, hospitals, orphanages, and shelters in countries across Europe. His motive appeared simply to be the desire to find a home and a loving family.

The Barclay Escape

In 1997, on the point of being exposed as an impostor, Bourdin carried out his most audacious and risky pretense yet. While he was at a

Bourdin was born in Paris in 1974 to a French mother and an Algerian father who had left unaware that his partner was pregnant. His early home life was somewhat chaotic. The young Bourdin is said to have invented exotic stories to cover his difficult circumstances. He explained his father's absence by claiming he was a secret agent. His teachers described him as imaginative and artistic. However, he was also beginning to exhibit disruptive and sometimes criminal behavior. By the age of twelve, he was in a juvenile crime unit. He ran away and invented his first false identity. He hit on the idea of simply turning up somewhere, apparently sick or suffering from amnesia, whereupon he would be taken to a local hospital or children's home and cared for. When he thought he was close to being found out, he moved on and used the same technique somewhere else.

children's home in Linares, Spain, the twenty-three-year-old Bourdin had been challenged to prove he was the teenager he claimed to be or else his fingerprints would be taken and given to the police for checking. He came up with an extraordinary plan. He rang the National Center for Missing and Exploited Children in Alexandria, Virginia, and, posing as the children's home director, he claimed that a child found in the area appeared to be American. Then he described himself and asked if they had details of any missing person who matched the description.

The most likely candidate was a boy called Nicholas Barclay, who had disappeared from San Antonio, Texas, three years earlier at the age of thirteen. Bourdin asked for everything they had on Barclay and the information was duly faxed to him. When he saw the boy's photograph, he thought he could impersonate him. He rang the missing persons center back and confirmed that the boy in Spain was Barclay. Then, assuming the identity of a Spanish police officer, he rang the detective in San Antonio who was dealing with the case and, using information he had been given by the center, convinced the officer that Barclay had been found. He concocted a story to explain Barclay's disappearance involving a kidnapping by pedophiles, who had then taken him to Europe.

Barclay's family started calling Bourdin from America, convinced that the missing Nicholas Barclay had been found alive. Barclay's sister traveled to Spain to collect him. He was sure he would be found out, but she accepted him as her missing brother. He set about learning everything he could about the family. He studied family photographs and paid close attention to stories about past events. He was finally part of a real family. He stayed with his "sister" Carey, her husband, and their teenage son. The family wasn't well off. They lived in a trailer home, and Bourdin slept on the floor. He started school and, as usual, did well.

Then the extraordinary events of the Nicholas Barclay case came to the attention of a popular investigative television show called *Hard Copy*. They wanted to know what had happened to Barclay and they wanted proof, so they hired a private investigator. When he arrived at the trailer home with a camera crew to talk to Nicholas Barclay, he was a little surprised when Barclay readily agreed to record an interview. Despite a confident performance from Barclay, the investigator was suspicious. He cleverly advised the cameraman to get a close-up of the boy's ear. He had heard that ears were almost as good as fingerprints for identification. When he compared the image of Barclay's ear with photographs of the missing boy, their ears didn't match. Whoever the boy was, he wasn't Nicholas Barclay.

The boy's eyes were the wrong color too. The real Nicholas Barclay had blue eyes, but Bourdin's were brown. Bourdin had already realized this and claimed that his eyes had been treated with chemicals by the people who kidnapped him to change their color. The investigator consulted an ophthalmologist, who said it couldn't be done. He passed his findings on to the police. Meanwhile, Bourdin was beginning to break under the constant pressure of living as someone else within the Barclay family. He was suspended from school for missing classes and arrested for speeding. After slashing his face with a razor, he was placed in a psychiatric unit.

Exposure

The FBI was also looking into Nicholas Barclay by then. The agent who interviewed him when he arrived in the United States from Spain had been suspicious of him. Bourdin had bleached his hair to match the photograph of Nicholas Barclay. By the time the agent interviewed him, his dark roots were visible. A psychiatrist who had interviewed Bourdin about his alleged kidnapping told the agent he thought the boy was probably French or Spanish but definitely not American. Fearing that he might be a foreign spy or even a terrorist, the CIA was informed too. His fingerprints were taken and checked with Interpol in case he had a criminal record in Europe. He did. By the time the results came back, he had admitted to the private investigator that he was Frédéric Bourdin. He was arrested and tried for perjury and obtaining false documents. On September 9, 1998, he was sentenced to six years in prison.

Then in 2006, Bourdin's life took a surprising and dramatic turn. A girl who saw him on a television program was so moved by his story that she tracked him down and met him. A year later, they were married and he was holding down a regular job. Soon afterward, his wife gave birth to a daughter, followed in due course by two more children. Bourdin finally had the family he had craved all his life, and he'd achieved it as himself, not as an impostor playing a part.

> At the end of his sentence, Bourdin was deported back to France, where he resumed his normal lifestyle. He pretended to be a boy called Léo Balley, who had disappeared eight years earlier. In 2004, he was deported from Spain when he was discovered masquerading as a teenager under the name of Ruben Sanchez Espinosa, claiming that his mother had been killed in the Madrid bomb attack in March of that year. It looked like he was incapable of simply being Frédéric Bourdin.

THE MAN WHO WAS NEVER BORED

On August 27, 1960, two men walked into the Dunwoodie Motel in Yonkers, New York, with guns drawn. They expected the sixty-nine-year-old night porter to hand over the cash, but he threw the cash box to the floor, leapt over the front desk, and rushed at the two gunmen. It was an act of astonishing bravery that cost him his life.

The night porter went by the name of Stanley Clifford Weyman, but that wasn't his real name. He was born Stanley Jacob Weinberg on November 25, 1890, in Brooklyn. When he graduated from high school in 1909, his ambition was to be a diplomat, a doctor, and a lawyer—all three! However, it wasn't to be. After high school, he had to find a job and earn a living, so he worked as a clerk in a small real estate company. But he left after a few months when his employer declined to take his suggestions for expanding the business. Then he worked in a camera shop, but the owner refused to pay him after his first month on the grounds that he hadn't done anything worth paying for, and then fired him! As he left, he took an expensive camera with him in lieu of wages. It was the first of many crimes he is known to have committed—so many that it is quite difficult to disentangle all the transgressions and identities that make up the eventful life of Stanley Jacob Weinberg.

After a series of dead-end jobs, he seemed to lose hope of ever making anything of himself, so he simply became someone else with better prospects. He chose to be the newly appointed U.S. Consul General to a North African state. Then he organized a send-off banquet for himself at the Hotel St. George and invited a host of influential people. Dozens of them were taken in by the printed invitations they received and they turned up. The evening went well. A few of the dignitaries were even persuaded to make a short speech wishing their departing diplomat good luck in his new posting. Weyman had the bills sent to his father!

Soon afterward, the police caught up with him for the theft of the camera. It resulted in the first of many, many appearances in court. He received a suspended sentence and was put on probation. After the excitement of being, or at least pretending to be, a diplomat, life at home with his parents sent him into a deep depression. On the advice of a doctor, his father took him to a sanitarium where he spent the next six months. Weyman described his stay there as a happy time, probably because of all the attention he received from the psychotherapists.

When he left the sanitarium, he found a job as a reporter with the *Brooklyn Daily Eagle* newspaper. Everything was going well for him until he stopped reporting to the police under the terms of his probation order. He was arrested and brought back to court. The judge sent him to the Elmira Reformatory. During his time there, he became so depressed that he was transferred to the hospital. Unfortunately, when he was released, the newspaper didn't want him back.

For his next adventure, he became Lieutenant Commander Ethan Allen Weinberg of the Romanian Army, Consul General for Romania. He thought a fitting thing for a Romanian Consul General to do was to inspect a U.S. Navy battleship, so he phoned the U.S. Navy Department and arranged it! On the appointed day, he boarded a launch that took him out to the USS *Wyoming* in the Hudson River. At the end of the tour, he invited the officers to a lavish dinner at the Astor Hotel in Times Square. When he made the arrangements, he told the hotel to send the bill to the Romanian Consulate in Washington.

On the day the dinner was to be held, the hotel, eager to take

> Weyman was soon locked up at Elmira again for a parole violation. After another spell in the hospital, he was released again, and once again he violated parole. Committing an offense and then violating parole was to be a common feature of Weyman's life.

advantage of the publicity potential, announced the event in the *New York Times*. When detectives saw the newspaper, they recognized the host's name straightaway. Federal agents gate-crashed the dinner, and the guests were treated to the sight of the Consul General being cuffed and led away.

He was free a year later and promptly reinvented himself as a French naval officer with the extraordinary name of Royal St. Cyr. As St. Cyr, he attended a string of prestigious dinners. Then he dressed as an admiral in the U.S. Navy and went on another official tour, this time at the

Brooklyn Armory. After a spell behind bars for impersonating a naval officer, he turned up in Lima, Peru, where he worked as a physician and sanitation expert for an American company. When the company discovered he was an impostor, they recalled him to New York and fired him.

In July 1921, he heard that Princess Fatima of Afghanistan had arrived in the United States saying that she wanted to meet President Harding. However, she stood little chance of having her wish granted, because the United States was avoiding any contact with the newly independent Afghanistan at the request of Britain, which wanted to sign a treaty with the country before it established diplomatic relations with other major world powers.

Weyman spotted an opportunity. If Princess Fatima wanted to see the President, then he would make her wish come true. He called to see her in her suite at the Waldorf Astoria in the guise of State Department Naval Liaison Officer Rodney Sterling Wyman and offered to arrange a meeting with President Harding. In fact, there was no such position as the State Department Naval Liaison Officer, but no one seemed to know that and they didn't check. Amazingly, he succeeded in arranging a meeting between Princess Fatima and Secretary of State Charles Evans Hughes, and then, on July 26, 1921, with President Harding himself. Eventually, the State Department realized it had been duped and asked one of its special agents to investigate the man behind the scam. They knew his name was Rodney Sterling Wyman, so they asked the New York police to arrest him. Of course, Wyman didn't exist, but one lead led to another, and they ended up at the home of Stanley Jacob Weinberg. He was sentenced to another two years in prison for impersonating a naval officer.

On his release, he went straight, but not for long. He successfully applied for a job as an accountant but mysteriously disappeared after six weeks. Then the company started receiving bills charged to them by U.S. Navy Captain Sterling C. Wyman. Of course, it was Weyman. A few months later, he was working as the private secretary to Dr.

Adolf Lorenz, a Viennese physician who was visiting the United States. When photographs of Dr. Lorenz with his new secretary, Dr. Clifford Weyman, appeared in a newspaper, one of Princess Fatima's sons recognized Weyman and alerted the authorities. He was arrested and consigned to the Atlanta Penitentiary.

On August 23, 1926, the famous film star and sex symbol Rudolph Valentinow died from peritonitis. Valentino's mistress, actress Pola Negri, was grief-stricken. Weyman decided to help her. Claiming to be Dr. Sterling Wyman, a physician and friend of Valentino, he went to see Negri in her suite at New York's Ambassador Hotel. He told her that "Rudy" would have wanted him to take care of her and volunteered to stay with her until she was fully recovered. She gave Weyman an adjoining room. When Negri went to see Valentino's body, which was lying in state at Campbell's Funeral Church on Upper Broadway, Weyman escorted her through the crowds of adoring movie fans who had gathered outside. He even issued press statements to the newspapers, which eventually realized that Dr. Wyman was actually the Stanley Clifford Weyman they had been writing stories about for years. When they told Negri about his imposture, she refused to make a complaint because she said he'd been the best doctor she'd ever had!

> While Weyman was serving time in the Atlanta Penitentiary, he studied law and actually passed the bar exam, which qualified him as an attorney in Georgia. In a way, he had achieved his childhood ambition of becoming a diplomat, doctor, and lawyer.

The Negri affair had given newspapers an excuse to raid their thick files on Weyman and run articles reviewing his career as an impostor. He made headlines again in 1928 when he gate-crashed an event welcoming the Bremen Flyers, three men who had just made the first east-west flight across the Atlantic Ocean to New York. In the middle of the ceremony, Captain Stanley Wyman of the United States Volunteer Air Service burst in and took over. He gave a speech welcoming the men and then personally escorted them to the train waiting to take them to Washington, DC. Some of the reporters and photographers who recorded the event instantly recognized Weyman as the same man who had posed as Pola Negri's physician. The police took no action this time, probably out of embarrassment, because police officers at the event had accepted Captain Stanley Wyman without question and even helped him to escort the Flyers to their train.

He was still reporting to the police regularly to satisfy his parole conditions, but he suddenly stopped in February 1930. As a result, Weyman was arrested and sent to Sing Sing for seventeen months. He spent another ten months in Sing Sing in 1932 for the same reason. He managed to hold down a job until 1935, when reporters recognized him and ran yet more stories about him. He resigned to spare his employer from adverse publicity, and then his life took a turn for the worse. Later in 1935, he was picked up for vagrancy and sentenced to four months in a workhouse.

In 1954, Weyman was in court yet again. This time he had obtained home loans amounting to more than $8,000 fraudulently. He was found guilty and sentenced to eighteen months in prison. When he was released, he was hired as a meeter and greeter at a restaurant, and he proved to be very popular with the customers. After a while, he confessed his past convictions to his employer, who nevertheless kept him on.

Weyman managed to go straight and stay out of trouble for the next eight years. However, in 1943, he got into very serious trouble indeed. In the midst of World War II, he was arrested by the FBI for teaching draft dodgers how to fake mental illness so the military would reject them. He was put on trial for violating the Selective Service law and found guilty. At the age of fifty-three, he was potentially facing a maximum sentence of thirty-five years and fines up to $70,000. Instead, he was sentenced to seven years and fined $17,500. He served five years.

Eventually, Weyman took a night porter's job at the Dunwoodie Motel. The man who had rubbed shoulders with presidents and princesses finally seemed to be at peace with himself when the two armed

Weyman's ability to get to important and reclusive people was recognized by Emile Gauvreau, the editor of the *Evening Graphic* newspaper in New York. Gauvreau wanted an interview with Queen Marie of Romania, who was visiting New York. She had shut herself away from reporters at the Ambassador Hotel. Gauvreau challenged Weyman to get the interview for him. And of course, he did it. Smartly dressed as a government official, he gave his visiting card to one of the secret service agents guarding an elevator reserved for the Queen's use and swept past them. His clothes, confidence, and the card identifying him as an Undersecretary of State convinced them he was genuine.

When he got into the Queen's suite, he asked her if everything was satisfactory for her. She assumed he worked for the hotel management. He flattered her and asked her all sorts of questions about her views on America, American men, American women, hairstyles, fashion, and so on, and she was happy to chat with him. Gauvreau got his interview.

robbers burst in. And at that moment, he did the bravest thing he'd ever done in his life. As he rushed the gunmen, he was shot in the abdomen and the head. The robbers grabbed $200 in cash, but they didn't get the bulk of the money in the cashbox, which was found on the floor behind the counter, still locked.

Weyman was once quoted as saying, "One man's life is a boring thing…I lived many lives. I'm never bored." He certainly led an interesting and eventful life. His various colorful impostures and impersonations did little harm and he didn't use them to line his own pockets. He appears to have simply enjoyed being someone rather grander than his real self for a while.

DRIVEN TO TEACH

Impostors are often driven people, usually driven to steal money or convince everyone they're more important than they really are. But one impostor was driven by the unusual desire to teach.

Marvin Hewitt was fascinated by science, mathematics, and

electronics. He read widely about them in public libraries, going far beyond the level of his class at school and even his teachers. He became so bored with classes that he left school at the age of seventeen without a diploma. He had a burning desire to study mathematics and physics but no qualifications that would enable him to go on to college. So he had to make do with working as a laborer.

During World War II, while he was working as a warehouseman for the Signal Corps, he heard about a military school that was looking for a teacher. He got the job with the help of a falsified educational record. After some initial nervousness, he soon settled into his new career.

When the school closed at the end of the war and he had to find a new position, he took on his first false identity. He looked through some college handbooks and picked a name he liked the sound of. The man was an aerodynamicist. With his new name and credentials, Hewitt successfully applied for a job as an aerodynamicist at an aircraft factory. He had no difficulty with the work, but his false name proved to be a problem. He hadn't done enough research. The man whose identity he'd stolen was quite well known, so it quickly became clear that Hewitt would be exposed as an impostor sooner or later. After a few weeks, he left.

He phoned colleges to see if any of them needed a physics teacher. It turned out the Philadelphia College of Pharmacy and Science had a vacancy. When they asked him for his details, he was ready with a new identity. This time he was Julius Ashkin, a real scientist who had worked at the Los Alamos and Argonne National Laboratory. While the real Ashkin was about to take up a teaching post at the University of Rochester, Hewitt started work as Ashkin, teaching calculus, algebra, and trigonometry. The work came easily to him. He enjoyed it and his classes scored well.

A tragedy in his family almost resulted in his exposure. His father, a police officer, was shot dead by a car thief. Newspapers wanted photographs of the dead officer's family. His family didn't know he was working under the name Ashkin, and his employer didn't know his real name was Hewitt, but just one photograph with either name would have exposed him as an impostor.

Hewitt had to take time off work and hide from the cameras and reporters. He realized he'd have to leave Philadelphia. He admitted his deception to his girlfriend, Estelle, who stuck by him and married him soon afterward. After honeymooning in Chicago, they went on to Minnesota, where Hewitt, still calling himself Ashkin, had found a job at a teachers' college. He soon became bored with the simple work he was teaching and decided that a job at a university would be more challenging and rewarding. Still masquerading as Ashkin, he was hired by St. Louis University's physics department, where he taught nuclear physics and advanced mathematics.

Meanwhile, the real Julius Ashkin carried on with his research, unaware of his alter ego. Hewitt had to keep a watch on the learned journals to spot papers published by Ashkin in case Hewitt's fellow academics wanted to discuss them with him. Research papers listed him as being at the University of Rochester, where the real Ashkin still worked. Hewitt explained this by saying the work the paper was based on was done while he was at Rochester. When he discovered that friends of the real Ashkin attended events at the nearby Washington University, he decided to move elsewhere.

The staff at the University of Utah thought themselves lucky to engage the services of the accomplished Julius Ashkin. They'd checked his credentials and phoned laboratories and universities where he, or rather the real Ashkin, had worked. Everything seemed in order. Oddly, the one place they didn't call was Rochester. If they had, Hewitt would have been exposed immediately. Utah hired him as a full professor. He now held a more senior position than the real Ashkin!

Then an extraordinary coincidence almost sank him. One of the administrative staff at Utah announced that she knew Ashkin from Rochester. Hewitt prepared to be exposed, but it turned out that the woman had only ever spoken to Ashkin by phone and had never seen him in person. It was an uncomfortably close shave, and another was to follow soon afterward.

A Bizarre Twist

Hewitt received a letter from the real Ashkin, saying that he knew someone was impersonating him and he wanted it to stop. However, in a bizarre twist, instead of threatening to expose the impostor, he recognized that the impostor must be a genuinely accomplished theoretical physicist and he offered the man time to extricate himself from the situation voluntarily. While Hewitt was mulling it over, wondering what to do, he was called in to see the university's president, who told Hewitt that he'd received an anonymous letter from the University of Rochester saying that Utah's Ashkin was an impostor. After an initial denial, Hewitt gave up and told the truth. Utah, not wanting any bad publicity, gave him the option of staying at Utah while he gained the degrees he had falsely claimed to have. They had no doubt that he would make the grade. Alternatively, as his colleagues were bound to find out what he'd done, he could transfer to another university and take his degrees there. In fact, he ran. He headed back to his mother's home in Philadelphia.

The famous Harvard astronomer Harlow Shapley heard about Hewitt and contacted him. The two men met, and Shapley was impressed with Hewitt's undoubted understanding of advanced theoretical physics. He wanted to introduce Hewitt to J. Robert Oppenheimer at Princeton,

Back in Philadelphia, unemployed, Hewitt had to find work to support his twin children. He went back to his first love, physics, and took on the identity of a physicist called Clifford Berry. Soon he was on his way to the New York State Maritime College in the Bronx. Although he was making a living, he was bored by the basic physics and mathematics he was required to teach, so he started looking for a job in industry that might make better use of his abilities. He was so confident of getting a new job that he resigned from his teaching post. However, most of the industrial jobs he eyed in nuclear physics, aerodynamics, and electrical engineering involved classified government and military work, which required security clearance. Hewitt knew he wouldn't pass a security check. Eventually, he had to give up and go back to teaching.

but the fear of public ridicule was too much for him, and he resigned himself to a life of obscurity. However, by the beginning of 1950, he felt able to think about going back to teaching, though not in physics. He decided on electrical engineering. He contacted an employment agency as Johns Hopkins graduate and former RCA research director George Hewitt. He backed up his application with forged references. In no time, George Hewitt was on his way to Fayetteville to take up a new job at the University of Arkansas College of Engineering. Once again, the ever-faithful Estelle was at his side. When he arrived, he was alarmed to hear that one of his students had attended St. Louis University, but he was in luck. The student had not been there when Hewitt was masquerading as Julius Ashkin. He started publishing his own research papers and began to build a reputation for himself. The dean of the college bragged to visitors about his star member of staff. Unfortunately, one of the people he spoke to was an RCA talent scout looking for promising engineers. When the dean mentioned the former RCA research director who was working for him, the talent scout didn't recognize the name George Hewitt. The truth came out and Hewitt lost his job.

The End of the Road

A few years later, going by the name Kenneth Yates, a real physics PhD from Ohio, he went to work at the University of New Hampshire in Durham. Hewitt, always alert to any potential risk of exposure, became convinced that one of his students was watching him. He was right. The student, Wayne Overman, had done one simple thing that the university authorities had neglected to do. He had looked up Kenneth Yates in publicly available registers and discovered that the real Yates was working for an oil company in Crystal Lake, near Chicago. Overman passed on his suspicions to the university. As before, Hewitt was challenged and resigned, but this time the news got out and he found his story in the papers. Oddly, Hewitt was relieved. He said that once the story became public, he knew it had to stop. It was all over.

The Glenn L. Martin Company heard about him, and, even knowing his past history, they were so impressed with him that they offered him a job as a design specialist in their earth satellite program. He was back in research again, legitimately at last.

The students Hewitt taught had done well. The academics he'd worked with regarded him as a brilliant physicist. And he did all of this while being largely self-taught. Imagine what he might have achieved if he'd had the advantage of a college education.

THE QUEEN OF OHIO

When banks learned that Cassie Chadwick was the illegitimate daughter of the billionaire philanthropist Andrew Carnegie, they tripped over each other to lend her money. She made, and spent, millions of dollars before the banks found out the truth about her.

Chadwick started life as Elizabeth Bigley. As a child, "Betsy" was said to be a bit of a daydreamer. She was born in Eastwood, Ontario, Canada, on October 10, 1857. Her criminal career began in her teens, when she was arrested for check forgery, but she was released on the grounds of insanity. Soon after this, she moved to Cleveland, Ohio, to join her sister.

In Cleveland, she adopted the first of several false identities, setting up a business as a clairvoyant called Madame Lydia DeVere. In 1882, DeVere married Dr. Wallace S. Springsteen. By then, she had run up a string of debts that her new husband knew nothing about. When her creditors saw a notice of her marriage in the local paper, they went looking for her and demanded payment. Springsteen settled her debts, but he also threw her out and divorced her after just eleven days of marriage. She knew a winning formula when she saw one. She quickly transformed herself into Madame Marie LaRose, another clairvoyant, and married a farmer called John R. Scott in 1883. Her second marriage lasted for four years before Scott outlived his usefulness to her and *she* filed for divorce.

It wasn't long before she was in court again. Posing as a fortune-teller called Lydia Scott, she was convicted of forgery and imprisoned in a Toledo penitentiary. When she was paroled, she became Cassie Hoover and set up a brothel in Cleveland. By then she had a son, Emil. In 1897, she married for a third time, to Dr. Leroy Chadwick, a wealthy man. The couple lived in a grand house on Euclid Avenue, Cleveland, known locally as Millionaires' Row.

A Billionaire's Daughter?

The scam for which Chadwick is most notorious began with a trip to New York City. She came back to Ohio with a promissory note for $2 million signed, apparently, by the wealthy philanthropist Andrew Carnegie. Chadwick told one of her husband's friends that she was Carnegie's illegitimate daughter and that he was willing to pay handsomely to keep her quiet. She said she already had $7 million in promissory notes from him and she was in line to inherit $400 million when he died. This information leaked out to Cleveland's businesses and banks, which were keen to get a slice of her fortune. She took full advantage of their greed and gullibility! Over the next eight years, she took out loans amounting to more than $10 million, using the Carnegie promissory notes as security. The banks were happy to let her repayments and interest mount up in the belief that the Carnegie family would settle her debts. Chadwick spent and entertained lavishly, earning herself the nickname "the Queen of Ohio."

The scale of her fraud was uncovered in 1904 after she took out a loan for $190,000 from a Massachusetts banker, Herbert B. Newton. Unlike the other lenders, Newton wanted his money back. When Cassie failed to pay him, he reported her to the police and started legal proceedings. The banks began looking at the loans they had made to her. On closer inspection, the promissory notes they had accepted were found to be forgeries. When Andrew Carnegie was questioned, he denied knowing Chadwick or writing any of her promissory notes. When Chadwick was arrested on December 7, 1904, she was wearing a money belt containing $100,000 in cash!

Her husband filed for divorce and then hurriedly left for a tour of Europe to avoid the scandal. She was charged with conspiracy to bankrupt a federally chartered bank, the Citizen's National Bank of Oberlin, Ohio. When customers discovered that Chadwick had borrowed $800,000 from it, the bank suffered a run that forced it out of business. Chadwick was found guilty and sentenced to fourteen years plus a fine of $70,000.

Chadwick served her sentence in the Ohio State Penitentiary in Columbus, which allowed her to bring her furniture and trunks full of clothes with her. The prison warden was said to have charged admission to the many reporters and other visitors who were keen to talk to her.

Her health had started to deteriorate during her trial, and it continued to worsen in prison. During one visit by her son, Emil, she collapsed and was taken to the prison hospital. She never left. She died there on her fiftieth birthday, October 10, 1907, less than two years after she entered the prison.

THE GREAT IMPOSTOR

When Dr. Robert French was summoned to the abbot's office at a Benedictine college near Seattle, he suspected nothing. But upon arriving, he was greeted by a stranger who said, "Good to see you, Ferdinand." The stranger was an FBI agent—and Dr. French was really Ferdinand Waldo Demara Jr. Demara was instantly arrested and put on trial for his life.

Ferdinand Demara was born on December 12, 1921, in Lawrence, Massachusetts. His father had been a movie projectionist in Providence, Rhode Island. When he made enough money to open his own movie theater, he chose Lawrence as the location for his new business. Soon, he had a chain of movie theaters. However, he lost everything during the Depression when his son, who was known as Fred, was just eleven years old. Young Fred hated being poor. He ran away from home when he was sixteen and entered a Trappist monastery in Rhode Island. After two years, he moved on to the Brothers of Charity in Boston. They sent him to a retreat in Montreal and then to a Brothers of Charity home for boys near his birthplace in Lawrence.

Demara was a diligent teacher and guardian of the fourth grade boys in his care, but he found the home's rules petty and illogical. One day in 1941, he could stand the straitjacket of inflexible regulations no longer. He stole the school's station wagon and left. On impulse, he joined the U.S. Army. The ink was barely dry on his recruitment papers when he realized he'd made a terrible mistake. For a man who had spent years in the company of genteel and courteous monks and priests, army life and the habits, morals, and coarse language of soldiers came as a terrible shock.

Becoming Anthony

He was sent to Keesler Field Air Force Base in Biloxi, Mississippi, for basic training. There, he found numerous ways to beat the system and avoid his duties. And he adopted his first false identity. He went AWOL from the base under the name of another soldier, Anthony Ingolia. He went to Ingolia's home in New Orleans and stole some of his personal records and documents. Then, using a forged army travel order, he took a train to Louisville, Kentucky, changed into civilian clothes, and entered a Trappist monastery there as Anthony Ingolia. When he was recognized by one of the other monks, he fled to another monastery near Des Moines, Iowa. When he spotted a letter from the bishop's office in Anthony Ingolia's home city, New Orleans, he wondered if it might be about him. He stole it before anyone else could read it. It revealed that the theft of the real Anthony Ingolia's documents had been discovered and the authorities had made the link between Ingolia and Demara.

He left immediately for a seminary in St. Louis, where he waited until his family could send him some money. As soon as it

> Ferdinand Waldo Demara Jr. used so many false identities over so many years that he was known as the Great Impostor. His alter egos included monks, a psychologist, doctors, teachers, and a prison warden!

Devastated by his failure to be selected for medical training, Demara decided to get the required background one way or another. He stole official stationery from his commanding officer's desk. Then he found someone with the background he needed and used the stolen stationery to request a copy of the man's grades. Finally, he doctored the documents by substituting his own details. He used the package of forged documents to support his application for a commission. While he waited for it to grind through the system, he used his expertise in forgery to set up several other false identities, including that of a Dr. Robert Linton French—more of him later.

arrived, he left Anthony Ingolia behind and went home to Lawrence, Massachusetts, as Fred Demara. By then, his family was aware of what he had done. His father insisted that he should turn himself in to the police. As Robert Crichton noted in his 1959 biography, *The Great Impostor*, Demara left home with every intention of going to Boston to do just that, but by then the United States had entered World War II following Japan's attack on Pearl Harbor, and Demara decided that serving a spell of imprisonment would be a waste of his talent. Instead of going to the police, he traveled to New York and joined the U.S. Navy under his real name.

Predictably, he didn't like the navy any more than he'd liked the army. After training, he was assigned to a destroyer, the USS *Ellis*, and served in the stormy, freezing north Atlantic. Desperate to get out of the navy, he successfully applied to medical school. He proved to be a first-class student, but despite scoring highly in all the tests he took, he was rejected for more advanced training because he didn't have the necessary educational qualifications.

Killing Fred Demara

While he was on leave from the navy, he stole stationery from a rectory near his home. Then he visited Cardinal O'Connell's residence in Boston and stole more stationery there. On his return to his naval base in Virginia, his application for a commission was finally being considered. When he heard that his background was going to be checked, he realized that his fraud would be discovered. His solution was to fake his death.

He left a pile of his clothes and a suicide note at the end of a pier and disappeared into the night. Fred Demara was dead. So he used one of his standby false identities and became ex–naval officer and psychologist Dr. Robert Linton French. He bounced around a few different monasteries, teaching science, before finally settling in St. Martin's, a Benedictine abbey college near Seattle. Here, as Dr. French, he claimed to be a doctor of medicine, whose approach to treatment was that anyone who is seriously ill, you send to the hospital; the rest will get better whatever you do for them, so anything you do will make you look like a good doctor. It worked most of the time, but he almost came to grief when he was confronted by a seriously ill monk. He failed to take even the most basic steps to help the man while he waited for an ambulance to arrive. Onlookers were puzzled, but somehow he got away with it.

Unlike the other monks, who had little contact with the outside world, Demara actively cultivated friendships in the local community. Bizarrely for a monk, he was appointed a deputy sheriff, which enabled him to carry a gun and put a siren on his car!

His unconventional behavior and rumors of heavy drinking prompted the abbot to write to institutions where Dr. French had lived and worked in the past. Then, while the abbot was away attending a conference and mentioned Dr. French, he heard worrying stories about an impostor with the same name. When he returned to the abbey, replies from Dr. French's past employers had arrived, confirming his worst fears.

"Good to See You, Ferdinand..."

One day, the unsuspecting doctor was summoned to the abbot's office. There, he was met by the abbot, the local sheriff, and two other men. One of these strangers greeted Dr. French with "Good to see you, Ferdinand." They were FBI agents. They arrested Demara immediately for desertion from the navy and threw him in jail.

The penalty for desertion during wartime was death. Demara took the risky decision to defend himself in court. He explained that he had deserted to escape from the company of coarse, foul-mouthed sailors and pleaded guilty with mitigating circumstances. He was sentenced to six years, but this was reduced to eighteen months because of his good behavior and positive attitude. At the end of his sentence, he was dishonorably discharged from the navy.

Following his success defending himself in court, he decided to study law. However, a convicted criminal could not become a lawyer. Of course, that didn't deter Demara in the least. His solution was to enroll at law school under yet another false name—Cecil Hamann, a real teacher in Lexington, Kentucky, with a PhD in biology from Purdue University.

However, he found his law course so boring that he left. In Alfred, Illinois, he presented himself as Dr. Hamann at yet another religious order, the Brothers of Christian Instruction, who were happy to accept the distinguished doctor. While he was working for them near Grand Falls, New Brunswick, Canada, he met Dr. Joseph Cyr. Cyr wanted a license to practice medicine in the United States. Demara offered to help him, but of course he would have to borrow Dr. Cyr's credentials, which Cyr readily handed over. When Demara returned to Alfred, the college he had been organizing there was up and running. He expected to be made its first rector but was disappointed to find that he was to be a lowly biology teacher. He was so angry that he stole one of the college's cars and left, eventually traveling to St. John, New Brunswick, where he joined the Royal Canadian Navy as Dr. Joseph Cyr in March 1951.

War Service

By then, Canadian forces were fighting in the Korean War, so the navy was very happy to have the services of such an experienced doctor. Despite having fake documents and no surgical experience, he was commissioned as a surgeon-lieutenant and sent to work at a navy hospital in Halifax, Nova Scotia.

He managed to cope with routine procedures and minor illnesses without giving himself away. After a couple of months, he was assigned to the aircraft carrier, HMCS *Magnificent*. The ship's medical officer was immediately suspicious of him. Demara, who by then had met and fallen in love with a navy nurse named Catherine, immersed himself in medical books to make up for his lack of knowledge. He wanted to tell Catherine the truth about himself, but he couldn't. It made him so unhappy that he volunteered to be sent to Korea. He was assigned to a destroyer, the HMCS *Cayuga*. As soon as he went onboard, he was rushed to see the captain, who had fallen ill. The captain's face was badly swollen because of infected teeth. Demara shot the captain's face full of Novocaine and yanked two teeth out. The captain was very pleased with his treatment, and Demara had survived another close call without being exposed.

When the *Cayuga* reached Japan, a naval press officer heard about Dr. Cyr's surgical work on the captain and various wounded soldiers and thought it would make a great story. He wrote articles about the "doctor's" successful exploits. When these were released in Canada, the real Dr. Joseph Cyr started receiving phone calls from the press asking him about his service in Korea. At first, he thought the mix-up must be a coincidence, but the details of the Korean War Dr. Cyr seemed suspiciously similar to his own. When he made inquiries, he was sent a copy of Dr. Cyr's photograph and immediately realized the truth. The man he knew as Brother John Payne of the Brothers of Christian Instruction, otherwise known as Dr. Cecil Hamann, had made off with his credentials *and* identity!

When the *Cayuga* reached Korean waters, it bombarded targets on the coast and gave cover to South Korean warships. At first, Demara had little to do, but one day a boat brought a cargo of wounded Koreans out to the *Cayuga*. Without any surgical experience, Demara operated on several of the men. As the ship pitched and rolled in a storm, he removed shrapnel from their wounds, tied off blood vessels, and sewed them up. The men were shipped out a day or so later.

Life after Death

The navy investigated and confirmed the fraud. When the captain of the *Cayuga* got wind of this and challenged Demara, the latter vehemently produced the documents and certificates that proved he was Dr. Cyr and reminded the captain that the navy had assessed them as genuine.

Then he seems to have suffered some sort of breakdown. He helped himself to the ship's rum supply, drinking so much that he had to be evacuated with suspected alcohol poisoning. He was returned to Canada, and while he was being held under arrest, the navy discovered that Dr. Cyr or Dr. Hamann was also Dr. French, who was Fred Demara. After a brief board of inquiry, he was discharged from the navy and escorted to the border, from where he traveled home to Lawrence, Massachusetts, drinking heavily on the way. He arrived penniless, only to find that the newspapers were keen to pay for his story. *Life* magazine paid him $2,500 for an interview, and in an astonishing act of benevolence, Demara gave most of the money to his parents. For the next few years, he tried to go straight, but time and time again, someone would recognize his name as that notorious fraud and impostor who was in *Life* magazine and so it would be time to move on again.

Maximum Security

Somewhere along the way, the credentials of a man called Ben W. Jones fell into his possession. He used them to find work at a hotel in Houston and then as a guard at a large prison in Huntsville, Texas. He was sent to work at the prison farm. Armed guards on horseback kept watch on the prisoners working in the fields, but he managed to get himself transferred from guard duty to become a recreation officer. He made such a success of it that he was moved into the maximum security part of the prison. His experiences, albeit fraudulent, of the church, psychology, medicine, and military forces equipped him well for the job. He dealt with the prisoners more humanely than the guards they were used to and was rewarded with their cooperation. He was quickly promoted to the rank of assistant warden in maximum security.

Just before Christmas 1956, boy scouts brought books and magazines to the prison for the inmates. While one prisoner was looking through a copy of *Life* magazine, he came across the article about Fred Demara and instantly recognized him as assistant warden Jones. He showed the article to a guard. Jones was summoned to see the head of the Texas prison system, O. B. Ellis. Ellis showed him the *Life* article and asked if he was Demara. He denied it. While the prison service managers investigated Jones, he loaded up his car and left. By the morning, his face was already in local newspapers. The authorities caught up with him in Key West, Florida, where he had given away his whereabouts by cashing a check, and arrested him for a string of offenses including imposture, embezzlement, fraud, drunkenness, and vagrancy. He was terrified of being extradited to Texas and perhaps having to serve time in the same Huntsville prison where he had worked, but Texas didn't want him back. His mother paid for all the bad checks he had passed, so most of the charges against him were dropped. After being released from jail on the condition that he would leave the state, he returned home to Lawrence to find that his father had died.

The Final Arrest

After a short stay in Lawrence, his wanderlust returned. He left home and worked for a time at a children's home in Massachusetts and then at a school in Brooklyn. While there, he heard about a small school in North Haven, an island off the coast of Maine, which was looking for teachers. Using stolen official stationery and forms, he established a new identity as Martin Godgart. He got a job in the island's school and made a good impression with the children, the other teachers, and the local people. But on St. Valentine's Day, 1956, two Maine state police officers took a Coast Guard cutter out to North Haven and arrested the popular teacher. They had discovered that he was not Martin Godgart when, as a result of a tip-off, they compared Godgart's fingerprints to those of Ferdinand Demara supplied by the Royal Canadian Mounted Police. Demara pleaded guilty and was given a suspended six-month

Demara had a small acting role as a surgeon in a 1960 horror film called *The Hypnotic Eye,* and he was played by Tony Curtis in a film made in 1961 about his life called *The Great Impostor.* He is said to have been paid $4,000 for the film rights to his story. Ironically, the movies were probably shown in theaters that were once run by his late father.

jail sentence and two years' probation. A group of people from the island visited him and asked him to come back to the school, but he refused.

Demara once again bounced from place to place, but illness eventually forced the Great Impostor to stop work in 1980. In the same year, he administered the last rites to a dying friend—the film star Steve McQueen. Eventually, complications of his diabetic condition resulted in him having his legs amputated. He died from heart failure on June 7, 1982, at the age of sixty.

THE SKYWAYMAN

On December 16, 2002, actors Tom Hanks and Leonardo DiCaprio joined director Steven Spielberg in Los Angeles for a night at the movies. They were attending the premiere of their latest film, *Catch Me if You Can,* based on the life of a real serial impostor and forger, Frank Abagnale.

Abagnale started inventing false identities to get by as a teenager living on his own in New York. The sixteen-year-old had run away to the Big Apple in 1964 to get away from an unhappy home life. He soon discovered that it was impossible to earn a living wage if he was honest about his age. So he altered his driver's license to make himself ten years older. Even with higher pay, he still found it difficult to make ends meet. His solution? Keep writing checks, even though he didn't have the money. He cashed the checks in stores and hotels. After a couple of months, he figured it wouldn't be long before he was caught…unless he could come up with another moneymaking scheme.

He decided to create a false identity and open a new bank account in his false name. Then he could start writing checks all over again. To make himself more trustworthy, he reinvented himself as an airline pilot called Frank Williams. He managed to trick Pan Am out of a uniform, supposedly to replace one that had been stolen. Then he forged a Pan Am ID card and pilot's license, researching aircraft, airlines, and the jargon pilots use

> Abagnale has said that many of the details, names, dates, and places that feature in his story have been changed to protect other people and for dramatic effect in the book and film based on his life, so it's impossible to know how much of the story is true, exaggerated, or invented.

until he knew his new identity inside out. He even dated stewardesses to pick their brains on airline procedures.

He discovered that pilots could take free flights with any airline if seats were available, called deadheading. Still in his teens, he used this to operate his check scam all over the country and abroad too. By the time his bad checks got back to the banks and the fraud was discovered, he'd already moved on.

The law finally caught up with him in Miami. When he landed at the end of one of his free flights, police officers were waiting for him. The airlines had realized that Frank Williams wasn't a pilot or even a Pan Am employee. The police handed him over to the FBI, but the persuasive young man managed to talk his way out of custody and left town on the first flight out. He headed to Atlanta, Georgia, and rented an apartment there. Still going by the name Frank Williams, he obviously couldn't be a pilot anymore in case someone checked his details with Pan Am. So, Frank Williams became a doctor: a pediatrician.

> Early on in Abagnale's new disguise as a pediatrician, he nearly came to grief when, by coincidence, one of his neighbors turned out to be a doctor who asked some awkward questions, but he muddled through.

Doctor Frank

Dr. Frank Williams became a familiar face at a local hospital, where he used the library to educate himself in pediatrics. He became so well

After Atlanta, Abagnale made for Louisiana when, posing as a commercial pilot with a law degree from Harvard, he heard that there were vacancies for lawyers on the state attorney general's staff. How hard could it be to pose as a lawyer? He forged the documents he needed and sat the bar examination. After just a few weeks reading up on his new profession, he passed the bar exam and went to work for the attorney general. Unfortunately, he encountered a genuine Harvard law graduate, who was immediately suspicious of him. Fearing imminent exposure, he left.

known that he was even asked to join the staff when they were short of doctors—not to treat patients, thankfully, but to ensure that the minimum number of doctors were on duty to satisfy the state regulations. He was paid so well for helping the hospital out that he stopped writing bogus checks for a while.

As soon as his stint at the hospital came to an end, he thought it was time to move on before someone got around to checking out his medical credentials more carefully.

On his way to San Francisco, he stopped at a city called Eureka. He hadn't intended to stay for long, but a pretty girl changed his plans. He'd always had an eye for the ladies, and as a pilot or a doctor, he was never short of attractive companions. To make some money, he became pilot Frank Williams again for just long enough to cash a handful of forged Pan Am checks at local banks. Unfortunately, he inadvertently used a check with his name and his father's New York address written on the back. He had to get it back. By the time he realized what had happened and phoned the bank, they'd already discovered it was a fake and called the FBI. In a brilliant show of split-second creative imagination, he claimed he was calling back from the FBI and an agent would be at the bank in a few minutes to collect the check. Agent Bill Davis duly arrived on cue and was given the check. He didn't even have to show any ID. Why would he? The FBI had already told them he was coming. Frank had his incriminating check.

Unknown to Abagnale, FBI agents had been tracking his movements from the trail of abandoned rental cars, scammed hotels, and dud checks he'd left behind. And they were getting closer. They missed him at the bank in Eureka by just a few minutes. They nearly caught him in San Francisco after he was affected by an uncharacteristic outbreak of honesty. He'd fallen in love yet again. The object of his affection was an airline stewardess. In a moment of madness, he confessed everything to her. She was devastated by the tale of deception and criminality. The next time Frank went to visit her, there were two police cars parked outside her house. It was time to move on again. Within a few hours, he was in Las Vegas.

Making a Mint

After a chance meeting with someone who worked for a check printing company, Frank bought the same equipment that they used for printing checks. He could now print as many checks as he wanted instead of producing each one by hand. He passed dozens of them in hotels and bars and left Las Vegas with tens of thousands of dollars in his bags. Next stop Chicago, where he tried a new scam. He stole a pile of blank deposit slips from a bank, printed his own bank account number on them, and returned them to the bank. When someone filled in one of these slips, the deposit was diverted to Abagnale's account. A few

Abagnale pulled off each new stunt brilliantly. One involved banks in three cities. First, he opened a bank account in New York with a small cash deposit. Then he flew to Philadelphia and opened an account there with a BIG check drawn on his New York account. There wasn't enough money in the New York account to cover the check, but this wouldn't be discovered for a few days. Meanwhile, he flew to Miami and told a bank there that he needed $15,000 in cash urgently, but he didn't have a bank account in Miami. He offered them a check for $15,000 from his Philadelphia account, which, when they checked, had a big enough balance to cover the check, although the cash wasn't actually in the account yet (and never would be). The Miami bank then issued him with one of its own checks made out to cash and he cashed it the next day.

days later, he was $40,000 better off. He made almost as much running the same scam in Hawaii.

By 1967, his ill-gotten gains amounted to half a million dollars. He'd used his check scams all over the country until he thought they had probably run their course. He flew to Mexico City, leaving most of his fortune behind, tucked up in safety deposit boxes in several cities, and bounced around for a while.

After a brief run-in with state troopers in the U.S. and a narrow escape from the FBI again, a brand new scam occurred to Frank. He found out where a local bank got its guards' outfits and got one for himself. Then he bought a replica pistol and rented a station wagon. When the bank closed and all the staff had gone home, he parked outside and put a notice on the night safe saying that it was out of order and customers should give their money to the guard. As the local shops closed, dozens of shopkeepers arrived, read the notice, and handed over their takings to the smartly uniformed armed guard. Then he made for the airport with tens of thousands of dollars in his luggage and flew to Istanbul.

Believe it or not, Abagnale had only entered his second decade after all this. At the grand old age of twenty, he decided that it was time to retire from his life of crime before the law caught up with him. He needed to find a place where he could settle down unknown. He

On his way to Acapulco, Abagnale cashed a check to help out a stewardess. He really wanted to get his hands on the stewardess's genuine Pan Am check. It cost him a couple of hundred dollars, but he made a lot more than that from it. After passing thousands of dollars in dud checks around Mexico, he left for London and then moved on to Paris. There, he met an Air France stewardess whose father was a printer. He showed the printer the Pan Am check he'd gotten in Mexico and asked if he could print 10,000 of them for him. He could. Abagnale passed dozens of the fake checks in and around Paris. Then he returned to New York with fake Chase Manhattan checks he'd had printed in France.

While Abagnale was in Turkey, he realized that a whole aircrew would be less suspicious for his scams than a pilot traveling on his own, so he decided to get himself a crew. He went to the University of Arizona as a Pan Am recruiter and held interviews. The next day, he had eight stewardesses. He told them they were to go on a promotional tour of Europe before starting work with the airline, kitted the girls out with uniforms and fake ID cards, and paid their hotel bills with fake Pan Am checks. The checks were always made out for amounts greater than the bills, so hotels all over Europe gave him change in cash. The girls enabled him to pass many more checks than he could have done if he'd been on his own. The tour netted more than a quarter of a million dollars for him. Of course, soon after their return to the United States, the girls discovered they'd been conned.

needed a town without an airport or big hotels, so he'd be unlikely to bump into anyone he'd scammed. He chose Montpellier in France and moved there as Robert Monjo, a writer. After a few months, he had settled into his new life when, while shopping, he was confronted by a posse of armed police officers. They knew exactly who he was. He'd been spotted by chance by an Air France flight attendant who reported her sighting to the police. After a two-day trial, he was sentenced to a year in prison.

From Hell to Hotel

His new home was a tiny, dark, damp, stinking, bare stone cell in a seventeenth-century prison building. He spent months in the cell with the nauseating stench of an overflowing latrine bucket, soiled with his own waste, infested with lice, with no light, no washing facilities, and an inadequate diet. After six months, he was taken to Paris in chains and finally allowed to wash, shave, and cut his shoulder-length hair. The next day he was handed over to the Swedish police at Orly Airport. A string of countries were queuing up to extradite him for trial and the Swedes happened to be the first in line. He was so ill that he had to be hospitalized for a month as soon as he arrived in Sweden. In court, he admitted to his crimes and was sentenced to six months in prison. Compared to his time in France, the Swedish prison was like a hotel. It was warm, clean, and bright, and he was fed well. However, he heard that on his release he would be handed over to Italy, where prisons were said to be scarcely better than the French dungeon he'd barely survived.

Hours before he was due to be extradited, a Swedish judge threw him a lifeline. The judge persuaded the U.S. authorities to revoke his passport. This was a game-changer, because it meant that he couldn't be extradited. Without a passport, he could only be deported to his home country. The same night, he was on a plane to New York.

He had promised the judge in Sweden that he'd learned his lesson and his life of crime was over, but his resolve weakened as the plane approached the United States and the certainty of many years in prison hit him. A few minutes before landing, he vanished! FBI agents searched the plane from nose to tail, but they could find no trace of him. He had gone to the lavatory and stayed there. As the plane taxied in, he pulled out the toilet unit, squeezed down into the compartment below it, and then dropped out of the plane through the hatch on the outside that covered the toilet drain. Then he simply ran to the nearest road and hailed a cab!

He caught a train to Montreal, Canada, where he had some money hidden in a safe-deposit box. Then he planned to go to Brazil, because it had no extradition treaty with the United States. However, while he was waiting for a flight from Montreal, he was spotted and arrested by the Mounties, who handed him over to the FBI at the border.

When he was delivered to a prison in Georgia to await trial, the guards thought he was an undercover prison inspector, so, true to form, he figured out a way to use it to his advantage. He planned one of the most brazen prison escapes ever attempted. He got a friend to pose as a writer and arrange an interview with a genuine prison inspector. She came away from the interview with the man's business card, which she passed on to Abagnale during a prison visit. She also gave him a fake card printed with an FBI agent's name and phone number. Then Abagnale admitted to a guard that he was indeed an inspector and showed him the real inspector's business card. He told the guard it was vital that he contact an FBI agent with some information he had been given by other prisoners. He gave the guard the fake FBI card and the guard phoned the number on it. The phone was picked up by Abagnale's friend on the outside. Abagnale fixed a meeting outside the prison to pass on the information. Then, when the car pulled up as arranged, the guards let Abagnale walk out to it. Of course, he got in and the car sped away into the night, leaving some pretty angry and red-faced guards behind.

The Perfect Plan

While he was trying to lie low in Washington, DC, he was recognized by someone. His motel was soon surrounded by police officers. He got away again by identifying himself to the officers as an FBI agent and simply walking through the police line to freedom! A few weeks later, he was arrested in New York and handed over to the FBI. Frank Abagnale finally stood trial. He was tried on eight sample charges to represent the hundreds of offenses he'd committed.

He was found guilty and sentenced to seven concurrent ten-year terms plus two years for his escape—a total of twelve years. He served about five years. After his release in 1974 at the age of twenty-six, he had a series of dead-end jobs, but every time his employer learned about his past, he was fired. Then he came up with the perfect plan.

He told a local bank about his criminal past and offered to use his vast experience to train the bank's staff in how to spot fraudulent checks. His talks proved to be so successful that other banks asked him to help them too. It was the beginning of a new career as a

> Pan Am estimated that Abagnale had flown more than a million miles on 250 flights to 26 countries at the airline's expense to carry out his various check frauds!

security consultant. In no time, hotels and airlines were asking for his help. He even helped to train FBI agents. Ironically, in the end, his legitimate career made him a millionaire.

FRAUD ALERT: BRAZEN BLUFFERS

Throughout history, bluffers have adopted false identities to gate-crash events and bluff their way into places denied to most people. Here are a couple of the most interesting ones:

■ Barry Bremen (1947–2011) bluffed his way into numerous sporting events by impersonating baseball players, professional golfers, a World Series umpire, a team mascot, and even a Dallas Cowboys cheerleader, complete with a wig, hot pants, and shaved legs! He also managed to get onstage at the 1985 Emmy Awards show and even gave an award acceptance speech. Bremen was arrested for this and fined $175. For the most part, his stunts were treated as lighthearted and harmless. However, gate-crashers at high-profile events were taken a lot more seriously after tennis star Monica Seles was stabbed by an intruder during a match in Hamburg in 1993. As a result, security at crowd-pulling events all over the world was stepped up significantly. Bremen brought his activities to an end soon after this.

■ Highly secure military and civilian sites have always been no-go areas for bluffers and gate-crashers, especially those attempting to breach NASA's normally airtight security. But in 1998, Jerry Allen Whittredge, a forty-eight-year-old man from Galveston, Texas, made it through before being arrested and taken to court for penetrating NASA's defenses. He claimed to have been selected as an astronaut and to have worked for the CIA. He also claimed to have won the

Congressional Medal of Honor. None of it was true, of course, but he was so convincing that he managed to get inside secure NASA and military sites, received training on a navy flight simulator, and obtained confidential space shuttle technical information. He even managed to get into mission control during a shuttle mission.

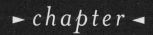

►chapter◄

2

GENDER BENDERS

Most impostors stick to the same gender, but a few have fooled people into thinking they were men when they were actually women, or vice versa. Most were women motivated by a desire to serve a greater purpose in society than was available at the time. For example, for a long time, women were forbidden from enlisting in the armed forces during wartime or were limited to working as nurses and in other noncombat positions. A few women refused to accept these traditional roles, so they disguised themselves as men and went to war as front-line soldiers and sailors.

Joan of Arc famously dressed as a man to lead the French army against the English in the fifteenth century. Her male clothing was a key element in the heresy case against her and the brutal death sentence that was ultimately passed on her. During the Civil War, hundreds of women are thought to have served in the Union and Confederate armies. They were mainly poor, working-class women.

In the seventeenth and eighteenth centuries, there was another way for women to break out of their traditional role in society without joining the army or navy—as pirates! During this age of exploration and colonization,

It was relatively easy for women to enlist in military forces up to the end of the nineteenth century if they looked passably masculine. Recruits were subjected to physical examinations, but these were usually limited to spotting obvious disabilities. If you had a full complement of arms and legs, good vision, and could fire a musket in the right direction, you were in. Once in uniform, soldiers and sailors lived, fought, and slept in the same clothes for months on end, so discovery was unlikely.

European ships were crossing oceans and returning laden with gold and silver. They were prime targets for pirates, including a few female ones. Often women pirates wore men's clothes but didn't hide the fact that they were women. On the wild open seas, there was a little more freedom to be your "true" self. But others masqueraded as men.

Women went to war or became pirates for a variety of reasons. Some of them were as patriotic as any man and wanted to fight for the same reasons. Others wanted to serve alongside their husbands or lovers. Yet others were motivated by nothing more than the promise of regular pay or the prospect of making a fortune as a pirate instead of living in poverty at home. A private in the Union Army during the Civil War earned $13 a month, which was double the pay a woman could expect to earn in civilian employment at that time.

There are hundreds of examples of women, and a few of men, who falsified their gender. In the following pages, we'll look at a few of the most interesting ones.

Mary Read lived as a man from her childhood. When her brother died, she was disguised as the dead boy to trick his grandmother out of financial support. And she carried on dressing as a man. She served as a soldier but revealed her gender to another soldier, whom she married. When he died, she went to sea as a man, and when her ship was captured by pirates, she became a pirate herself and served alongside another female pirate, Anne Bonny, under Captain "Calico Jack" Rackham.

ALL THAT JAZZ

When seventy-four-year-old jazz musician Billy Tipton collapsed on January 21, 1989, medics were at his side a few minutes later. They quickly discovered something that even his ex-wives and adopted children claimed not to know—Billy Tipton was a woman!

Dorothy Lucille Tipton was born in Oklahoma City on December 29, 1914. Her parents divorced when she was only four years old, and she went to live with an aunt in Kansas City, Missouri. At school, she had a talent for music and a particular interest in jazz. She played saxophone in the school orchestra and excelled at the piano. She wanted to join the school's jazz band, but it was an all-male group. Girls need not apply.

Tipton returned to Oklahoma City when she was eighteen and completed her senior year at Connors State College High School, where she was finally able to join the school band. By that time, the oil industry had arrived and the town was booming. There was a constant demand for musicians in the

> Tipton described being inspired by seeing a pianist called Lovie Austin in a Pittsburgh theater. Austin is regarded as one of the best female jazz blues piano players of the day.

clubs and bars, but few of them were women. Women were seen as trouble, and they spoiled the uniform look of the all-male bands. Tipton tried in vain to find work.

She figured that if men stood a better chance of finding employment, then she'd become a man. She bound her chest tightly with a sheet and slicked back her short hair into a boyish style. And it worked. She got a job as a saxophone player and pianist with a band. Her father and aunt were furious and cut off contact with her. She was on her own now, making her own way in life, supporting herself as male musician Billy Tipton.

In 1935, Tipton was on the road with an eight-piece band called the Banner Playboys. Many of the musicians "he" played with said they knew he was a woman. The Banner Playboys evolved into a series of new bands, including the eleven-piece Banner Cavaliers, which attracted increasing publicity on local radio stations.

Full Time Billy

In 1941, Billy settled in Joplin, Missouri, in the Ozarks with his female partner, called Non Earl. He now started living as a man offstage as well as onstage. He played and sang at the Cotton Club in Joplin with George Mayer's band. None of the other musicians knew he was a woman. The band often played comedy routines that required them to act. Paradoxically, Tipton would often take women's parts, so he was a woman masquerading as a man acting a woman's part in comedy routines! By all accounts, the audiences loved his comic female characters and never knew they were the ones being duped.

> Billy briefly wore a dress for the last time in 1939. When his career took a dip, he went to live in Enid, Oklahoma, and played whatever spots he could get in local clubs. Enid was a Bible Belt town that wouldn't have tolerated a cross-dressing musician. Within a year, he was male Billy again for good and on the road with a big band.

In 1942, the George Mayer band broke up, and the twenty-seven-year-old Tipton seized the opportunity to start his own band, the Billy Tipton Quartet. The following year, his relationship with Non Earl broke up. Within a few months, Tipton was introducing an attractive young singer called June to friends as his wife.

Moving On

In 1944, Tipton and June suddenly moved sixty miles away from Joplin and he took a job as a radio station pianist in Springfield, Missouri. He is thought to have felt uncomfortable with the 40,000 troops at Camp Crowder on Joplin's doorstep at a time when young men not in uniform were coming under increasing suspicion.

After only a couple of months, the Tiptons moved on again amid rumors about Billy's gender. They moved to Corpus Christi, Texas, to work for his old bandleader, George Mayer, again. However, Corpus

Christi wasn't much better than Joplin. Instead of thousands of soldiers, Corpus Christi was a navy town with thousands of sailors on its door-step. Fistfights between sailors in the clubs where Billy played were common. He often had to dodge flying glasses and stools. After two years, he returned to Joplin.

Although Billy had worked constantly and was outwardly very suc-cessful, working musicians like him didn't earn much. He'd had to borrow money for the move to Corpus Christi. When he returned to Joplin, he had to drive a cab for a while to make ends meet.

By the end of 1946, he was on the road with a band again, but June was no longer with him. He had already met the next woman in his life, Betty Cox. Billy was thirty-two by then and Betty was just eighteen. When Billy moved to San Angelo, Texas, to join yet another new George Mayer band, he asked Betty to come with him and she said yes. By the time they returned to Joplin in 1948, the big band era was coming to an end, but there was still a demand for trios and quartets playing in small clubs. Billy picked up work wherever he could. Then one night, a band-leader called Russ Carlyle heard Billy playing sax and hired him on the spot. Coincidentally, another of Carlyle's musicians, Lew Raines, had lived in Enid and remembered a jazz piano

When America entered World War II in 1941, Tipton risked facing questions about why he wasn't in the forces, but he had an answer ready. When he was only sixteen months old, he'd been seri-ously injured in a car accident. The car, driven by his father, was hit by a train. Billy's grandmother died in the accident and Billy suffered cuts, a broken arm, and abdominal injuries. For the rest of his life, he claimed that the bindings hiding his breasts were actually ban-dages that protected his crushed ribs and abdominal injuries.

player there called Dorothy Tipton. He put two and two together and realized that Billy was Dorothy masquerading as a man, but he didn't give her away.

About this time, George Mayer asked Billy to join a new band that was to tour the Pacific Northwest club circuit. It was 1949, and Billy jumped at the chance to move to new pastures where he wouldn't be recognized. He played in bars and clubs full of miners and cowboys.

In 1951, Mayer moved to Hawaii. Billy could have gone with him, but he chose to stay behind in Portland, Oregon, and form his own band, the Billy Tipton Trio. While they were performing a radio spot in Santa Barbara, California, in 1954, they were heard by a talent scout for Tops Records and offered a recording contract. At about this time, Betty left to be with her sick father. Billy replaced her straightaway with a new partner named Maryann.

Star Billing

In 1958, Tipton had a chance to break into the big time when he got an offer to perform with Liberace in Reno, Nevada. The other members of the trio were amazed when Billy said no. Perhaps he feared that the wider publicity might have led to his exposure and a public scandal. He was running into a lot of musicians and friends from his early days who knew his secret. Instead of the glamour of Liberace and more recording spots in Nevada, he chose to move to Spokane, Washington, and split his time between performing and working at a musicians' booking agency. It gave him the security of a day job and a regular paycheck plus the opportunity to carry on performing in the evenings.

After seven years, Billy walked out on Maryann and set up house with a vivacious red-haired stripper called Kitty Kelly. Her stage name was "The Irish Venus." They went through a civil marriage ceremony arranged by Billy, but there is no record of the marriage, and the marriage certificate was later found to be a forgery. Like Betty and Maryann, Kitty later said she never knew Tipton was a woman. In the 1960s, they adopted three children and fostered a fourth, all boys, who were also completely unaware of Tipton's true identity.

In the 1970s, Billy started suffering from arthritis, which made it increasingly difficult and painful for him to play the piano. As he cut back on performing, the family's financial situation worsened. Kitty had to work to help out. There were more and more arguments. Finally, in

1980, after eighteen years together, Kitty and Billy split up. The three boys still living with them by then moved to a trailer home with Billy.

In addition to arthritis, Billy was suffering from an ulcer and was often short of breath. In 1982, he took over the booking agency when his boss retired, but it' declined almost to bankruptcy under his management. He sold it to a businessman and went back to working on commission. As his health problems worsened, he steadfastly refused to see a doctor, presumably because he feared discovery. On January 21, 1989, his adopted son, William, helped him to the bathroom. Soon afterward, he lost consciousness and never came around. He was taken to the hospital and pronounced dead in the emergency room. Dorothy Lucille "Billy" Tipton had succumbed to a bleeding ulcer.

THE SURGEON'S SECRET

James Barry was a distinguished military surgeon who managed to conceal his real identity throughout his life. His lifelong secret only came to light when his body was being prepared for burial.

James Barry's story began when he arrived in Scotland in 1809 at the age of only about fourteen to study medicine at the University of Edinburgh. He graduated three years later and moved to London, where he trained as a surgeon at St. Thomas's and Guy's Hospitals. In 1813, he joined the army and worked in military hospitals in England before being posted all over the British Empire, from South Africa to Canada.

Soon after his arrival in South Africa in 1816, he was promoted to the position of physician to the governor's household. He formed a very close friendship with the Cape Colony's governor, Lord Charles Somerset. This led to accusations of homosexuality and a scandalous libel case. Barry disappeared for a year around 1819. He said he had been sent to Mauritius, but official records do not confirm this. So his disappearance remained a mystery for years.

In 1821, he was promoted to the position of colonial medical inspector in the Cape Colony. In this capacity, he toured the colony's hospitals and prisons. He was shocked by what he discovered. In Somerset Hospital, he found cats, dogs, and wild birds wandering about in filthy wards. Wherever he worked, he advocated good hygiene, sanitation, and diet. He also fought for proper medical care for prisoners and lepers.

In Cape Town in 1826, he performed the first successful Caesarean section by a British surgeon. While he was in South Africa, he acquired a servant who stayed with him for the next fifty years. He left South Africa in 1828 for a series of postings to Mauritius, Jamaica, St. Helena, Corfu, and Canada.

A Secret Revealed

In 1857, Barry was posted to Canada, but after so many years in the tropics, his health deteriorated in the cold Canadian weather. Two years later, he was so ill that he returned to England. By the time he retired in 1864, he was Inspector-General of Hospitals, the army's most senior medical officer. On July 25, 1865, less than a year after his retirement, he succumbed to dysentery.

People often commented on Barry's effeminate behavior and dandy-like appearance—dyed hair or wig, thigh boots, long scarlet coat, and sword, more typical of the earlier Regency period than Victorian England. An ambassador's daughter described him as having a squeaky voice and mincing manner. He was quick to take offense at comments like this and often challenged men to duels, although he is thought to have fought only one. Women were attracted to him and he flirted with them, but he never formed any lasting relationships.

He had left strict instructions that he was not to be changed out of the clothes he was wearing when he died and there was to be no postmortem examination of his body. However, when Sophia Bishop prepared his body for burial, she ignored his last wishes. She undressed him and discovered that he was a woman, but she didn't reveal her discovery until after Barry's burial. She also saw what she thought were stretch marks on Barry's stomach, so he may have had a baby. This raises the possibility that Barry's disappearance in 1819 may have been due to a pregnancy. The discovery was so shocking in Victorian England that it was kept quiet, and Barry's records were sealed for a century.

James Barry is thought to have been born Margaret Ann Bulkley some time around 1795 in Ireland. She was a niece of the famous Irish artist James Barry, who left her family some money when he died in 1806. They moved to London, where Margaret showed an interest in medicine and took lessons from Edward Fryer, the physician who had attended James Barry. It was Margaret Ann Bulkley who boarded a ship from London and James Barry, named after her famous uncle, who stepped ashore in Edinburgh. Her mother traveled with her and was aware of her false identity. She became Barry because it was the only way for a woman to study medicine or train as a surgeon in England at that time.

Ironically, the first woman to qualify as a physician and surgeon in England, Elizabeth Garrett Anderson, did so after overcoming great resistance in 1865, the year Barry died.

THE INFANTRYMEN WHO WEREN'T

Up to 750 women are thought to have served in the Union and Confederate armies during the Civil War. Here are a few of the most amazing stories of them.

In March 1913, attendants in an Illinois hospital undressed an elderly patient for a bath. They were about to make a startling discovery. The patient was a veteran of the Civil War called Albert Cashier. He had fought for the Union in General Ulysses S. Grant's Army of the Tennessee, in the thick of the fighting throughout the war, and his 95th Illinois Infantry Regiment suffered some of the heaviest casualties.

Cashier stood only five feet three inches tall and weighed 110 pounds. He was the unit's shortest soldier but also one of its bravest. And ironically, his fellow soldiers said he fought like a man.

After the war, Cashier returned home to Illinois. Over the next forty years, he worked as a church janitor, cemetery worker, shepherd, and lamplighter. He was hard-working but led a solitary life. He had a reputation for being rather eccentric. Local boys teased him by calling him "Drummer Boy," which angered him. He is said to have shouted back at them "I was no drummer. I was a fighting infantryman."

In 1911, a few months after being injured in a car accident, he was moved to the Soldiers and Sailors Home in Quincy, Illinois. While he was there, his mental state deteriorated and he was moved to the Watertown State Hospital for the Insane. It was here that the former soldier was undressed and discovered to be a woman. After this, she was forced, against her wishes, to wear a dress. When a soldier she'd served with visited her, she said, "Lots of boys enlisted under the wrong name. So did I. The country needed men, and I wanted excitement."

Albert Cashier's record was impressive. Between 1862 and 1865, he fought in about forty battles and skirmishes. He was at the siege of Vicksburg and the surrender of Mobile. During the Vicksburg campaign, he was often selected for foraging and skirmishing duties, because his commander said he was, "very dependable, was in vigorous good health, and was apparently fearless." Foraging parties went out into the surrounding countryside and raided local communities for the supplies the army needed. Skirmishing parties scoured the area for small straggling groups of enemy soldiers and fought them.

Cashier's secret probably explains why it took her so long to secure an army pension. She joined the Grand Army of the Republic, the largest Union veterans' organization, and applied for a pension in 1899. She didn't complete the process until 1907, probably because a medical examination was required. Somehow, she managed to get through the examination—or get around it—and was finally awarded a soldier's pension. The public first became aware of her story in 1913 when it was covered by the *Washington Sunday Star* newspaper. Soldiers of the 95th came forward and spoke about her bravery.

A Family at War

A husband and wife fighting shoulder to shoulder in the army was both officially impossible and unheard of in the 1860s. Nevertheless, it happened during the Civil War.

Frances Clalin was born in Illinois in the 1830s. She married Ohio-born farmer Elmer L. Clayton, and they had three children. When the Civil War broke out in 1861, men all over the country left home and took up arms to fight for their states. The Clayton family, happily farming in Minnesota, did something dramatically different. Frances and her husband, Elmer, *both* left home and enlisted in the army. They traveled to Missouri to join up, presumably because no one would recognize them there. As women weren't allowed to enlist, Frances became Jack Williams. Her tall stature and rather masculine looks helped her to carry it off. She was no demure shrinking violet. By all accounts, she smoked, drank, swore, and gambled like her fellow soldiers.

She served with artillery and cavalry regiments and fought in something like eighteen battles, being wounded three times. Tragedy struck at the Battle of Stones River, also known as the Battle of Murfreesboro. It was one of the bloodiest battles of the war.

Sadly, one of the 1,636 Union troops killed during the battle was Elmer Clayton. His wife, Frances (Jack Williams), had been standing just a few feet behind him when he fell dead. When commanded to move forward, she simply stepped over his body and carried on fighting.

There are two different stories about how she was revealed as a woman. She may have volunteered the fact that she was a woman after her husband's death and was then discharged from the army. According to another story, she was wounded at the Battle of Stones River and was found to be a woman during her treatment, swiftly followed by her discharge. On her way back to Minnesota, her train was attacked by Confederate troops who stole all her papers and money. She ended up in Quincy, Illinois, where friends and fellow soldiers raised money to support her.

Reluctant Soldiers

One of the strangest Civil War service stories involved two brothers, Sam and Keith Blalock. It was strange because the Blalocks supported the Union, but on March 20, 1862, they enlisted in the *Confederate* Army! They had no choice because of new conscription laws that required all men between the ages of eighteen and thirty-five to present themselves for military service. The Blalocks served with the 26th North Carolina Regiment. However, because of their Union sympathies, they intended to desert to the Union once they reached the front line. Unfortunately, they were sent south, a long way from the Union forces.

Unable to stomach service with the Confederacy, Keith found a novel way of engineering his discharge. He rolled naked in poison ivy! His skin erupted in boils. Fearing that he might be suffering from smallpox, the Confederate army discharged him immediately on medical grounds. Sam's request to accompany his brother on his journey home was refused. He then informed one of the officers, Colonel Zebulon Vance, that "he" was a woman. The officer summoned the surgeon, who confirmed it. In fact, Sam was Keith's wife, Sarah. She was immediately discharged from the army. In 1864, Keith crossed the mountains into Tennessee and enlisted in the 10th Michigan Cavalry. According to some accounts, his wife accompanied him on raids against farms owned by Confederate supporters. Despite their opposition to the Confederacy, they returned home to North Carolina after the war and lived there until their deaths in the early 1900s.

The Woman in Battle

In 1876, a book called *The Woman in Battle* was published in the United States. It told the story of a woman named Loreta Janeta Velázquez, who disguised herself as a man to serve with the Confederate States Army during the Civil War. It was written by Velázquez herself.

Velázquez was born in Havana, Cuba, in 1842 and was brought up by an aunt in New Orleans. She is said to have been inspired by the story of Joan of Arc and often dressed as a man. When she was only fourteen, she ran away with a Texas Army soldier called William and married him. Within four years, they had had three children, but all of them died as babies. When Texas seceded from the Union in 1861, William joined the Confederate Army. Velázquez wanted to go with him, but he refused to allow it. When he'd gone, she got herself a uniform and disguised herself as a man. A false mustache and beard completed her transformation into Lieutenant Harry T. Buford. She went to Arkansas and recruited her own battalion of 236 men to fight for the Confederacy. Then she took them to Florida, where her husband had been posted as a training officer.

Unfortunately, her husband died in a shooting accident, so she left her battalion behind and set off for the front on her own.

Eventually, tiring of life in uniform, she dressed as a woman again and went to Washington, DC, as a Confederate spy. While she was there, she claimed to have met the president, Abraham Lincoln. On her return to the South, she was assigned to the detective corps for a short time. Then, back in uniform again, she was posted to Tennessee, where she saw the closing stages of the siege of Fort Donelson in February 1862.

> Velázquez describes fighting at the First Battle of Manassas (Bull Run) and the Battle of Ball's Bluff in Virginia in 1861—both Confederate victories. She was thrilled by the danger and excitement of battle. She said, "There is a positive enjoyment in the deadly perils of the occasion that nothing can equal."

In April of the same year, she also fought at the Battle of Shiloh, where she was wounded by an artillery shell. The military doctor who treated her discovered that Lieutenant Buford wasn't the man he appeared to be, but she managed to escape to New Orleans. There, she met Captain Thomas DeCaulp, with whom she had fought at Shiloh. She presumably revealed to him that she was a woman, because they married. However, when he returned to his unit, he was captured and died. Soon afterward, she was employed as a spy again and then as a double agent. After the war, she traveled the world and tried her hand at gold prospecting.

Usually, the stories of women who took up arms disguised as men are corroborated by their fellow servicemen. But there is no such corroboration in this case. Even in her own time, several critics found her story unbelievable because of a large number of inaccuracies and mistakes. She explained this by saying that she wrote the book without any of her records, which had been lost. Today, historians are divided, and the jury is still out on whether Loreta Janeta Velázquez was the impostor she claimed to be, or a fraud.

THE SAPPER WITH A SECRET

When Private Denis Smith arrived at the front line in France during World War I, he was put to work with a mine-laying unit.

After only ten days as a mine-layer, Smith fell ill with exhaustion and fainting fits. Then he went to a sergeant and amazingly admitted that he was an impostor! "Denis Smith" was actually a nineteen-year-old Englishwoman called Dorothy Lawrence who wanted to be a war reporter. Lawrence, from Warwickshire, had been living in Paris when the war started. Every evening, she saw troops arriving at the city's railway stations on their way home on leave from the fighting. She wanted to see the war for herself, so she traveled to London and tried to get a commission from a newspaper as a war reporter. However, as editors couldn't get their own male reporters to the front, they certainly weren't going to send an inexperienced, untrained woman. She returned to Paris and decided to make her own way to the front. But she'd have to disguise herself first.

Lawrence managed to trick

Mine-laying work was hazardous. The soldiers, combat engineers called *sappers*, dug tunnels under enemy lines and placed mines inside them. When the mines were detonated, the trenches and underground shelters above them were blown apart. Troops who weren't killed by the blast could be buried alive in the collapsed earthworks. Mine-laying soldiers worked very close to enemy positions and were constantly under fire. In addition, they risked being entombed in muck if their tunnel roof fell in.

To look the part, Lawrence made friends with a couple of British soldiers in a Paris café and persuaded them to give her a spare uniform. To avoid suspicion, they smuggled it to her piece by piece as if it was laundry that she was washing for them. They didn't think she'd get anywhere near the front. Under the uniform, she bound her chest and padded her body with sacking and cotton to hide her feminine curves. She also cut off her waist-length hair and darkened her pale skin with diluted furniture polish!

a local official into giving her a pass for travel into the war zone. Then, equipped with forged identity papers, she boarded a train for Amiens. From there, she simply got on her bike and cycled to the front. As she got closer to the fighting, she passed abandoned trenches and military vehicles. In a town called Albert, still wearing civilian clothes, she took a British soldier, sapper Tom Dunn, into her confidence and asked him to help her. He hid her in a dugout, where she could change into her uniform. Unfortunately, when she stripped off, she discovered that the dugout was infested with blood-thirsty, hopping fleas. The hungry insects jumped all over her. She was soon covered with swollen bites. She ran from the dugout to an abandoned cottage nearby.

She didn't formally enlist in the army. She simply walked out of her hiding place one night and mingled with the other soldiers. Thus, she became Private Denis Smith of the first battalion, Leicestershire Regiment.

When she revealed her true identity ten days later, she was immediately arrested and transferred to the Third Army Headquarters, where she was interrogated as a suspected spy. She was also accused of being a "camp follower," or prostitute.

She was moved to the General Headquarters in Saint-Omer for more questioning, where she was housed in a convent. Army commanders were angry that their security had been breached, but in a very British way, they were also worried that Lawrence's experience might encourage more women to take on men's jobs, upsetting what was seen as

Traditionally, there were two kinds of camp followers who traveled with armies. One was composed of the wives and children of soldiers. The other was a group of people providing all sorts of services to the armies, including sexual services, and this is what Dorothy Lawrence was accused of—being a prostitute.

the natural order of things at that time. Lawrence was put onboard a ship bound for Folkestone on England's east coast, where she was interrogated yet again. She made a promise not to talk or write about her experiences, which she then broke. However, her work was censored by the War Office, so her full story didn't emerge until many years later.

In 1925, Lawrence accused her church guardian of raping her. Her story was not believed. She was declared insane and committed to Colney Hatch Lunatic Asylum in Barnet, London. She was never released, dying there nearly forty years later in 1964.

A SAILOR'S LIFE FOR ME

About two dozen women are known to have served with the British Royal Navy between 1650 and 1850. Two of the best-known are Hannah Snell and Mary Anne Talbot.

If only James Gray's shipmates had known who they were sleeping alongside, they might have treated him differently. He served for five years in the thick of battle with the Royal Navy before revealing his true identity to his fellow sailors.

In 1750, the crew of the British warship HMS *Eltham* returned to England from service off the coast of India. Its crew members made their way to London to collect the pay due to them. As they gathered in a London tavern, one of the marine soldiers who had served with them dropped a bombshell. James Gray announced to the battle-hardened fighting men, "Why, gentlemen, James Gray will cast off his skin like a snake and become a new creature. In a word, gentlemen, I am as much a woman as my mother ever was, and my real name is Hannah Snell." She joked with the man she had often slept next to,

"Had you known, Master Moody, what you had between the sheets, you would have come to closer quarters!"

Master Moody's response, on discovering that one of his fellow marines was a woman, was to propose marriage!

Hannah Snell was born in Worcester, England, on St. George's Day (April 23rd), 1723, one of nine children. She was orphaned in her late teens and moved to London to stay with her half-sister Susannah Gray in Wapping, a district of east London. There, at the age of twenty-one, she married a Dutch sailor called James Summs. He turned out to be a poor catch. One account accused him of keeping "criminal company with other women of the basest character" and stealing from Hannah when he needed money. Then, in 1745, he disappeared. By then, Hannah was pregnant. She gave birth to a daughter who sadly only lived to the age of seven months.

James Gray

Hannah was determined to find her missing husband. She thought he might have been pressed into military service, so she bound her breasts to hide them, dressed in men's clothing, and set off to find him.

Snell traveled to Coventry and joined the Sixth Regiment of Foot as James Gray—the name of her half-sister's husband. The Sixth Foot made a twenty-two-day march to Carlisle. There, a sergeant tried to pressure Gray into helping him rape a girl, but instead she warned the girl. The furious sergeant had her charged with neglect of duty.

This was the time of the Second Jacobite Rebellion, when the supporters of the exiled royal House of Stuart tried to remove King George II and replace him with "the Young Pretender," Bonnie Prince Charlie. There was a demand for troops to be sent north to take on the rebels in Scotland.

Her punishment was 600 lashes. She was tied to the gates of the barracks and whipped. After 500 lashes, officers stepped in and ended the punishment.

When she spotted that another recruit was a former neighbor who might reveal her true identity, she deserted and made for Portsmouth on England's south coast. There, she enlisted in Frazer's Regiment of Marines and was assigned to the warship HMS *Swallow*. The *Swallow* was dispatched to India, where it took part in the siege of the French-held port of Pondicherry. Gray was wounded in the fighting. She escaped discovery by treating her own wounds, including, according to one account, performing surgery to remove a musket ball from her groin. She remained in the hospital at Cuddalore for a year.

Good Golly, Miss Molly!

When she was discharged from the hospital, she served for a while as a seaman on the HMS *Tartar* while she waited for another ship. On October 13, 1749, she was transferred to HMS *Eltham* for the journey home to England. During the voyage, Gray's shipmates noticed that she didn't shave. She claimed it was because she was so young. However, her fellow sailors and marines joked that she must be a woman and took to calling her Molly Gray. During a stop in Lisbon, Portugal, she finally discovered what had happened to her husband. She found a sailor who had served on a Dutch vessel. He told her about a Dutch sailor by the name of Summs, who had stabbed a man in Genoa and had been executed for the crime. His body was said to have been sewn up in a sack with stones and tossed into the sea.

The *Eltham* arrived at Spithead on the south coast of England in May 1750. Snell returned to her sister's home in Wapping. Her life story was published in a book called *The Female Soldier: Or, The Surprising Adventures of Hannah Snell*. She earned a living by touring the country with a stage act based on her exploits. When her popularity began to fade, the Duke of Cumberland, Commander-in-Chief of the Army, granted her a pension of £30 a year. She married twice more. In the 1780s, she was committed to Bethlem Royal Hospital, also known as Bedlam, the first hospital to specialize in mental illness. She died there a few months later in 1792 at the age of sixty-nine.

The Accidental Sailor

While Hannah Snell made a conscious decision to join the navy, Mary Anne Talbot became a sailor by accident.

Mary Anne Talbot's short life was difficult from beginning to end. We know her story because she wrote it down herself, and it was published in 1804. Talbot was born in Lincoln's Inn Fields in London on February 2, 1778. Her mother died giving birth to her, so she was brought up by a series of guardians. She ended up in the care of a Mr. Sucker in Shropshire.

> Talbot served on land and sea during the Napoleonic Wars under the name of John Taylor, almost losing a leg when she was wounded in action, but surprisingly, none of it was her own choice.

Sucker passed her on to a Captain Essex Bowen of the 82nd Regiment of Foot, who promised to place her in the care of a female friend and see that she completed her education.

He took her to London in January 1792, but instead of placing her in school, he made it clear that he expected her to be his mistress. She had no choice but to comply. When Bowen was ordered to embark for Santo Domingo in the West Indies, he took Mary with him. He disguised her as a footboy, or servant, called John Taylor. On March 20, 1792, they set sail from Falmouth in the transport ship *Captain Bishop*. Conditions onboard were filthy and hard. The only food she had were the leftovers from Bowen's meals. She joined in with the work that had to be done onboard, including the risky business of going aloft in the rigging.

> Sucker seems to have cared little for Talbot. According to Mary's own account of her life, she was allowed out of her room only at mealtimes.

When the ship arrived in Port-au-Prince in June, Bowen immediately received orders to return to the Continent to join the Duke of York's troops. To keep Mary with him, Bowen gave her a position in the regiment as a drummer boy. When she objected, he threatened to sell her as a slave.

Sold into Service

While serving with the regiment in Europe, Mary witnessed savage hand-to-hand fighting. She was wounded herself—shot in the chest and slashed with a sword across the small of her back. She hid both wounds, fearing that her secret might be discovered. When Valenciennes in northern France fell, Mary was with the troops who entered the town. She witnessed the execution of a soldier who had deserted. She also learned that her master and tormentor, Captain Bowen, had been killed.

She was at her lowest ebb—alone and wounded in a strange country, and only fifteen years old. She changed out of her military uniform and made off across the country. When she reached the coast, she boarded a French lugger on September 17, 1793. She thought the ship was a mer-

chantman, but it was actually a privateer (a ship licensed by the government to attack enemy vessels). When they happened upon the British fleet under the command of Admiral Lord

> While Mary was going through Bowen's belongings, she found letters written by her former guardian, Mr. Sucker, to him and discovered that Sucker had sold her to him!

Howe, Mary refused to take part in an attack on her own countrymen despite being beaten by the ship's captain. The British fleet prevailed, and Mary was arrested under suspicion of being an English boy fighting for the French. She told Lord Howe about the death of the man she was traveling with and of boarding the French ship in an attempt to return home without realizing that it was a privateer. Fearing execution as a deserter, she said nothing about her previous military service.

Powder Monkey

Howe believed her and gave her a job as a powder monkey onboard HMS *Brunswick*, a seventy-four-gun warship.

The *Brunswick*'s commander, Captain John Harvey, noticed that "John Taylor" was different from the other young lads. He wondered if Taylor might be a runaway from a school somewhere. She told him her story but didn't reveal she was a girl. Harvey took pity on her and promoted her to be his cabin boy.

> Powder monkeys were young boys who carried bags of gunpowder from a warship's magazine to the gun crews. Mary worked at a gun on the quarterdeck.

After a vicious engagement with the French fleet on June 1, 1794, the *Brunswick* was all but wrecked. Mary had been struck in the left ankle by grapeshot and suffered a musket ball shot straight through her left thigh. She finally reached England on June 12 and was taken to Haslar Hospital in Gosport. It proved impossible to remove the grapeshot from her leg, which troubled her for the rest of her life.

When she was well enough to return to service, she joined the *Vesuvius* as a midshipman, the lowest rank of officer. While on patrol along the French coast, *Vesuvius* was attacked by a French privateer. Mary was taken prisoner and incarcerated in Dunkirk. She was later freed during a prisoner exchange.

Becoming Mary Again

Just after her return to London, she was seized by a press gang, a group charged with the task of taking men into naval service, by force if necessary.

To avoid being forced back into military service, she finally revealed that she was really a woman. In desperate need of money, she made a successful application to the Navy Pay Office for back pay owed to her for her navy service.

Her leg wound flared up again. The grapeshot worked itself out, and she is said to have kept it until it smelled so bad that she had to throw it on the fire! She spent four months in St. Bartholomew's Hospital having splinters of bone removed from her leg. She petitioned the Duke

> Destitute, Mary offered her services as a steward onboard the *Ariel*, a ship bound for America. On arrival in New York, she spent a fortnight with the captain and his family. She must have been completely convincing as a boy, because the captain's niece was so taken with her that she proposed marriage. Mary politely declined and returned to England on the *Ariel*, arriving on November 20, 1796.

The Royal Navy had trouble recruiting enough sailors in past centuries, especially during wartime, because the conditions onboard British warships were pretty grim. When sailors were needed, press gangs were empowered by law to seize suitable men between the ages of eighteen and forty-five. Press gangs operated in British ports between the seventeenth and early nineteenth centuries.

of York for relief and received five guineas. Her leg worsened, and she spent another seven months in St. George's Hospital.

Eventually she visited Mr. Sucker, the man who had sold her to Captain Bowen, but Sucker didn't recognize her. She asked if he knew a Miss Talbot. Sucker said he did, but she had died abroad in 1793. Mary revealed her real identity to him and demanded from him everything that had been stolen from her. After taking advice from a lawyer, she returned to Sucker's house, only to find that he had been found dead.

While Talbot was in the hospital, a man, possibly a young doctor, offered her half a crown a week for as long as she lived in return for her body when she died. Fearing for her safety, she left the hospital soon afterward, although she was not fully recovered.

From then on, she lived on the generosity of others. Her leg wounds worsened again, and she was unable to walk. Misfortune and money trouble dogged her for the rest of her life. She died on February 4, 1808, at the age of only thirty, having seen more, done more, traveled farther, and suffered more than most people of twice her age at that time.

At least, that would be the case *if* Mary Anne Talbot's story were true. Talbot may be more of a fantasist than a gender-bending sailor. While researching her for book *Female Tars*, author Suzanne Stark found no trace of Essex Bowen in the army lists for the 1790s, although his name does appear in navy lists for the period. She also discovered that the regiment Talbot said she served in didn't exist when Talbot was supposed to have joined it. And navy records show that the vessel Talbot claims to have traveled in to the West Indies was sailing from

India to England at that time. Whether Talbot merely exaggerated the truth or invented it all isn't known. The true story of her life went to the grave with her.

THE LIEUTENANT NUN

Alonso Díaz Ramírez de Guzmán was a fearless Spanish swordsman, serving with Spain's conquistadors in South America. But his nickname, La Monja Alférez (the Lieutenant Nun) holds a clue to his real identity.

On March 18, 1600, a fifteen-year-old girl called Catalina de Erauso had an almighty row with a nun at the convent in San Sebastian she had attended since the age of four. She ran away. She had the presence of mind to take a sewing kit, which she used to transform her convent uniform into a more masculine doublet. She also cut her hair short so that she could pass for a boy and look for work.

While she was working as a page for the king's secretary, she encountered her father, who had come to ask for help to find his missing daughter. He didn't recognize her. Then she made a daring, or foolish, visit to her old convent and bumped into her mother, who didn't recognize her either. This is when she seems to have decided to leave Spain altogether. She signed up as a cabin boy aboard a ship bound for Panama.

> In the sixteenth century, Spain was a global superpower with valuable colonies in the New World. Silver and gold shipped from the Americas bankrolled the Spanish Empire. The flow of treasure across the Atlantic to Spain was matched by the flow of soldiers, explorers, traders, and government officials in the opposite direction. Adventurous Spaniards headed for the New World to make their fortune or to escape the straitjacket of life in Catholic Spain. This is precisely what the Lieutenant Nun did.

The Dashing Swordsman

By the time she was nineteen years old, Catalina was working as a shopkeeper in Saña, Peru, and still living as a man. She seems to have been quick to take offense and reacted violently. She was often involved in sword fights, which she invariably won, and then she made for the nearest church to claim sanctuary and avoid arrest.

After several jobs, Catalina joined the army under the name Alonso Díaz Ramírez de Guzmán and was sent to Concepción, Chile. By an amazing coincidence, the governor's secretary there was her brother, Miguel. She was assigned to his office and worked there for three years. This posting was ended prematurely by Catalina's usual problem—a woman falling for her disguise. This time, though, the woman was her brother's mistress. Catalina lost her job. She returned to the army and was sent to Paicabí, where she was involved in one of Spain's bloodiest campaigns against the native Mapuche Indians.

> Some of Catalina's problems, fights, and arguments resulted from women falling for her, not realizing that the dashing young swordsman they desired was a woman.

Posted back to Concepción, she fell into old habits, getting into fights and running from the law. After one altercation, she hid in a Franciscan church for several months before she was able to escape. Then she agreed to act as a second in a duel fought by a fellow officer, Lieutenant Juan de Silva. The duel was fought on a dark, moonless night. When de Silva was injured, Catalina stepped in to protect him and ended up fighting his opponent's second. Of course, Catalina won. As the man fell to the ground, he shouted out. She thought she recognized his voice. It turned out to be her own brother! Unfortunately, he died.

She didn't change her ways, carrying on getting involved in fights. A disagreement over a card game resulted in a fight that ended with Catalina killing the man. For once, she didn't run for the nearest church. She thought she hadn't been seen, but she was wrong. She was arrested and sentenced to death by hanging. On the way to the gallows, at the last possible moment, she was pardoned.

I Confess

The experience doesn't seem to have discouraged her from fighting. In fact, it wasn't long before she was on the run after yet another killing.

In about 1620 in Cuzco, she got involved in an argument over a game of cards. She fought and killed the man, but she was badly wounded too. Believing she was dying, she confessed her sins to a priest. In fact, she survived and went on the run again.

Eventually, she was cornered by officers who had been ordered to kill her. A bishop, Agustín de Carvajal of Guamanga, Peru, stepped in and took her to his house, where she finally confessed that she was a woman. Two women called to examine her found that she was not only a woman but also a virgin. She was sent to a convent while the church investigated her story. It took three years before the church discovered that she had not taken her vows as a nun and she was allowed to leave the convent.

She returned to Spain in the early 1620s. The story of her extraordinary adventures in South America made her famous in her homeland. In 1625 in Madrid, she was presented to King Philip IV, who awarded her a military pension for her services to Spain. She was also granted an audience with Pope Urban VIII. When he heard her story, he gave her permission to continue dressing as a man. She wrote her life story between 1626 and 1630. She seemed to tire of life in Spain, because she returned to the New World, where she lived

The Mapuche Indian uprising was part of the Arauco War, which began in the 1530s and went on for almost 350 years, making it one of the longest wars in history. Catalina took part in the suppression of a native uprising in which thousands of Indians were killed. In one battle, her company flag was captured. She ran after it and got it back, for which she was promoted to the rank of lieutenant.

as a man for the rest of her life under the name Antonio de Erauso. She was last seen working as a mule-driver in Mexico, still with a sword and dagger hanging from her belt…just in case.

THE PETTICOAT CAVALRYMAN

The gender of an accomplished French spy was a matter of hot debate and even open betting in the eighteenth century. He or she lived forty-nine years as a man and thirty-three years as a woman, but which was he, or she?

In 1756, a French government official called Charles Geneviève Louis Auguste André Timothée d'Éon de Beaumont was sent to Russia on a secret mission by King Louis XV. Relations between France and Russia were poor, and France was keen to repair them. French diplomats couldn't get close to the Russian royal family, but d'Éon managed to reach the Empress Elizabeth by the simple ruse of disguising himself as a woman. If he had been discovered, he would have been executed.

Following his covert activities in Russia, he was given a commission in a cavalry regiment and saw action at the Battle of Villinghausen in 1761 during the Seven Years' War. At the end of the war, he was sent to London to take part in the peace negotiations. His work was recognized by an award of the Order of Saint-Louis, enabling him to call himself Chevalier d'Éon. He returned to London in 1763 as acting ambassador. At this point, d'Éon's story takes a surprising turn.

A "Secret" Discovered

In Paris, King Louis XV was alarmed to find that his mistress, the Marquise de Pompadour, had gone through his most personal and secret papers, including details of a secret network of spies called the *Secret du Roi* (the King's Secret). Unknown even to the French government, these spies worked to further the king's interests, which weren't necessarily the same as the government's, and they reported directly to the king. Chevalier d'Éon was one of the king's spies. Madame de Pompadour and her allies in the government focused on d'Éon and his activities.

Pompadour's allies ensured that one of their men, the Comte de Guerchy, was appointed ambassador to London. D'Éon had become accustomed to living the life of an ambassador and resented being demoted to a mere secretary when de Guerchy arrived. The two men argued constantly. D'Éon refused to hand over his diplomatic papers and ignored instructions to return to France.

Behind the scenes, no sooner was the peace treaty between France and England signed at the end of the Seven Years' War than the French king was planning an invasion of England, acting in direct opposition to French government policy, which was to avoid another war that France couldn't afford by developing more friendly relations with England. D'Éon was involved in the secret preparations for the invasion. If the king's secret plans had been discovered, it would likely have led to renewed war between the two countries and a total breakdown of trust between the French king and his government. The stakes could hardly have been higher.

D'Éon was a key figure in the intrigue, because he knew the king's secrets. Revealing them could destroy the monarchy. D'Éon carried on behaving as if he was the ambassador, running up huge bills and causing resentment and anger in London and Paris. Furious letters flew between the French king, government ministers, and diplomats. Publicly, the king recalled d'Éon to Paris, but privately he told his spy to stay in England and hide from view, disguised as a woman. Then d'Éon did an extraordinary thing. In 1764, fed up with his treatment by the French government, he published his diplomatic correspondence, although he didn't include his secret

> Despite the fact that d'Éon was a government representative of a country England had recently fought a war against, he was generally supported by the English public. This made it more difficult for the French to silence him or extradite him to France.

orders from the king. It caused a scandal in both countries.

Man or Woman?

Rumors about d'Éon's gender began circulating in 1770. Bets were laid on the matter. D'Éon responded by challenging the rumormongers to duels. The betting collapsed when the Lord Chief Justice ruled that matters like this could not be settled by a court of law.

In May 1774, Louis XV died and the *Secret du Roi* was wound up. In 1775, d'Éon signed an agreement known as "the Transaction" that enabled him to return to France. One of its conditions was that he should continue to dress as a woman. He returned to France in 1777 and went to live in Tonnerre, the city of his birth in 1728. In 1779, he was presented to King Louis XVI as a woman, but the court was not convinced by him. It was said that there was nothing feminine about d'Éon beyond petticoats and curls.

In 1785, he was back in London. The royal pension granted to him under the terms of the Transaction ended when the monarchy fell during the French Revolution in 1789. The king himself was executed in 1793. To raise money, d'Éon toured England giving fencing displays wearing a full-length gown. He was badly hurt in a fencing match in Southampton at the age of sixty-eight. He retired from public life and moved in with a widow, Mrs. Cole. He died, aged eighty-two, on May 21, 1810. When Mrs. Cole laid out his body, she was surprised to discover that he was a man. She had thought she was sharing her home with another woman.

THE BRICKIE IN THE TOP HAT

On October 24, 1859, a body was found in the River Irwell, standing upright in the water, still wearing a top hat! It was carried to a nearby public house, where it was identified as a local bricklayer called Harry Stokes. An inquest was opened, and the case seemed to be a straightforward suicide, when a member of the jury questioned Stokes's gender. It seemed ludicrous, but it had to be checked. The coroner sent someone to examine the body, which revealed that Harry was in fact Harriet!

The person known as Harry Stokes was born a girl in a village near Doncaster, England. The date of her birth is unknown, but it was probably around 1799. Her father was a bricklayer who put her to work almost as soon as she could stand. When she was only eight years old, she ran away from home. She ended up in the village of Whitby, where she looked for work. A bricklayer there mistook her for a young boy and took her on as an apprentice. She had become Harry Stokes.

Wedding Bells

About twenty years later, Harry married Betsy, a widow who kept a Manchester beerhouse where Harry was a regular customer. Predictably perhaps, there was a terrible argument between them on their wedding night. Betsy stormed out, claiming that her husband was not a man. Stokes accused her of being mad, and the two went their separate ways. Soon afterward, Stokes married another widow, Frances Collins. She was much older than her "husband." They stayed together for twenty-five years until Stokes's death. Collins made the highly improbable claim that she had no idea Stokes was a woman, even though they had shared a bed throughout their marriage. Neighbors were suspicious of Stokes, because they thought "he" had a peculiar build for a man.

On the evening of October 23, 1859, Stokes drank in the Swan public house in Pendlebury. The next morning, someone noticed a hat on the surface of the nearby river. On closer inspection, Stokes was found standing up in the water underneath it. Her age is unknown, but she is thought to have been about sixty years old at death. It seems that she had fallen on hard times, and it was likely the fear of poverty that may have driven her to suicide.

> Stokes worked all his life as a bricklayer and was well known as a most skillful builder of fire-grates and chimneys. During the Chartist riots of the 1840s, when workers pressed for political reform, Stokes served as a special constable and rose to the rank of captain of a company of men.

ONE-EYED CHARLEY

When one of the best-known stagecoach drivers in California's Wild West died, friends who'd known him and worked with him for years were astonished to find that he was not the person they thought he was!

In the 1840s, gold was found in Coloma, California, triggering the California Gold Rush (1848–55). The state quickly became a magnet for fortune hunters, its population of about 92,000 in 1850 swelling by almost 300,000 to about 380,000 people just a decade later. Amid all the new arrivals, there was a great demand for stagecoach drivers.

Charley Parkhurst weighed 175 pounds and stood just over five feet tall. Still, she accomplished some pretty big feats for such a short person.

A young man called Charley Parkhurst moved to California in 1851 and quickly gained a reputation as one of the best stagecoach drivers in the state.

Fearless Reputation

Driving a stagecoach was a hazardous occupation. The Wild West was a lawless place, especially outside the towns. Armed holdups were common. There could be rich pickings from coaches transporting wages or gold. After Parkhurst's first holdup, by an outlaw called Sugarfoot, he carried a .44 pistol for protection. The next time Sugarfoot held him up, Parkhurst shot him dead. Wells Fargo gave him a solid gold watch and chain to reward his bravery. He was handy with a whip too, gaining a reputation as a fearless driver that outlaws didn't want to tangle with. He drove stagecoaches in California and western Nevada for the California Stage Company, the Pioneer Line, and then the famous Wells Fargo company until the 1860s.

Stagecoach drivers faced other dangers. While Parkhurst was handling a horse in Redwood City, the animal kicked out and caught him in the face. He lost sight in his left eye and wore an eye patch from then

Nature could conspire against stagecoach drivers. Dirt tracks could be washed away or disappear in a landslide. Stagecoaches could be blown off roads in storms. There is one report of Parkhurst crossing a rain-swollen river just in time to see the bridge collapse behind him. Another report describes him being thrown off a coach but hanging onto the reins while being dragged along on his stomach and bringing the horses to a halt. Stories like these were often told, making Charley a hero among the drivers in the West. He held down this tough and hazardous job for almost thirty years.

on, earning the nickname "One-Eyed Charley." On another occasion, he rolled a stagecoach, suffering several broken ribs.

Eventually, Parkhurst retired from stagecoach driving in the late 1860s. There was less work for drivers by then, because the new railroads were taking a lot of their business.

To make ends meet, he ran a stagecoach station, where the coaches changed horses, and then worked in logging, cattle ranching, and chicken farming, finally moving to a cabin in Watsonville, California, in 1876. He was found dead in bed there on December 18, 1879, after suffering from cancer of the mouth and throat.

But when his neighbors prepared his body for burial, they were shocked to discover that the cigar-smoking, tobacco-chewing, cussing, gambling, gun-toting, whip-cracking former stagecoach driver they had known for twenty-five years was not the man they thought they knew. In fact, "he" was a woman!

Charlotte Darkey Parkhurst had been born in Lebanon, New Hampshire, in 1812. Very little is known about her childhood. There is even some doubt about her real name, which is given as Mary, Charlene, or Charlotte in various records. She appears to have spent some time in an orphanage and to have escaped from it disguised as a boy. She probably maintained the deception to find work, because a young girl on her own wouldn't have been able to get a job. One of her first jobs was as a stable boy at a livery stable in Worcester, Massachusetts, near Boston. There, she showed an aptitude for handling horses, so her employer, Ebenezer Balch, trained her to ride horses and drive coaches pulled by up to six horses. When Balch moved to Providence, Rhode Island, "Charley" went with him. Then the Gold Rush took her to California and a new life as a stagecoach driver.

> At the end of his working life, Parkhurst is quoted as saying, "I'm no better now than when I commenced. Pay's small and work's heavy. I'm getting old. Rheumatism in my bones—nobody to look out for old used-up stage drivers. I'll kick the bucket one of these days and that'll be the last of old Charley."

Californians took part in the presidential election of 1868. No one knows if Parkhurst voted, but as she had taken the trouble to register on the voters' list, she probably did. If she did vote, she would have been the first woman in California to cast a vote. It would be another fifty-two years before all American women were officially allowed to vote, following the 19th amendment to the U.S. Constitution in 1920.

Parkhurst's body held one more surprise for her neighbors. A doctor who examined her found that she had given birth. A trunk containing baby clothes was also found in her home. She was buried in the rather aptly named Pioneer Odd Fellows' Cemetery in Watsonville. Sadly, the fate of her baby went to the grave with her.

A THOUSAND MILES TO FREEDOM

In 1848, Mr. Johnson, a wealthy, young, white cotton planter in the American south, embarked on a thousand-mile journey north with his black servant. But in actuality, Mr. Johnson wasn't wealthy, white, or even a man! This is one of history's most inspiring stories of total deception for a very good reason.

William Craft, a cabinetmaker, and his wife, Ellen, a lady's maid, were slaves in Macon, Georgia, in the 1840s. They had been separated when they were sold to different masters. In 1848, they made the courageous decision to run away.

The Crafts hatched a daring plan. Ellen was a quadroon, the daughter of a mulatto slave and her white master, so she had pale skin. In fact, she was sometimes mistaken for a white woman. The couple decided to disguise Ellen as a white slave-owner. William would travel with her as her slave servant. As a woman would be unlikely to travel with a male slave, they decided they would arouse less suspicion if Ellen were disguised as a man.

They both managed to obtain some leave from work at Christmas, giving them a few extra days to get away before their absence would be noticed. William cut Ellen's hair short. One problem they foresaw was that Ellen would be expected to sign the register at any hotels they stayed in, but she couldn't write—it was illegal in Georgia at that time to teach slaves to read and write. They solved this by putting her arm in a sling as if it were injured so she would be unable to write. They also bandaged her face so that she looked as if she had a severe toothache and she wouldn't have to speak to anyone. With men's clothes, glasses, and a top hat that they had collected bit by bit, Ellen looked the part.

Mr. Johnson Catches a Train

After saying a prayer, they set off for the Macon railway station and bought tickets for the two-hundred-mile journey to Savannah. As companions of different races, they couldn't travel together, so William had to sit in one car while Ellen sat in another.

Their bid for freedom almost ended before it began. William was nearly spotted by the owner of the cabinetmaking shop where he worked, and Ellen found she was sitting next to a friend of her master. She pretended to be deaf when he spoke to her. Fortunately, neither of them was recognized. In Savannah, they caught a steamship for Charleston, South Carolina. A slave-trader on the ship offered to buy William, and Ellen was admonished by another passenger for being too polite to her slave. In the evening, she retired to her cabin, while William had to bunk down on some cotton bales on the open deck.

They hit their first serious problem in Charleston. When they tried to book their passage on a steamboat to Wilmington, North Carolina, the ticket-seller refused to give them tickets. Passengers traveling to

Most slaves rarely tried to escape, because they knew that runaways were hunted down with dogs and brought back to their owners, who meted out severe, violent punishment as a deterrent to others. Successful escapes were very rare indeed. The most ambitious runaways tried to get to the north and gain their freedom in states where slavery had been outlawed.

the north had to convince officials that slaves they were traveling with were indeed their property. The ticket-seller insisted that "Mr. Johnson" had to sign for his slave, but of course Ellen couldn't write. She asked the ticket-seller to enter their names in the register, but he refused. Then they had a stroke of luck. A fellow passenger from the ship they'd arrived on came by and vouched for them, and then the captain of the ship they wanted to board arrived and agreed to take responsibility for them.

In Wilmington, they took a train to Richmond, Virginia. There, a woman accused William of being her own runaway slave, Ned, and insisted that he come with her, but he managed to get away from her. From Virginia, they took a steamboat to Washington, DC, where they caught a train to Baltimore, Maryland. In Baltimore, the border guards were particularly alert to runaway slaves trying to cross the state line into neighboring Pennsylvania, a free state. The Crafts had to leave their train and report to officials. They thought they were about to be arrested, but the officials took pity on Ellen when they saw her sling and bandages and let them back onto the train seconds before it left.

The Best Christmas

They arrived in Philadelphia on Christmas Day—free at last. Ellen grasped her husband's hand, burst into tears, and said, "Thank God, William, we are safe." Abolitionists helped them and found them lodgings. Just three weeks later, they had both found work in Boston. William worked as a cabinetmaker, and Ellen was a seamstress.

However, their problems were not over. In 1850, Congress passed the Fugitive Slave Bill. This made it a crime for anyone in a free state to protect or aid runaway slaves. The Crafts would have the dubious honor of being the first runaway slaves to be hunted under this law. News of their arrival in Boston and speeches they'd made at antislavery meetings had been covered in newspapers that reached as far as Macon, Georgia, where their former masters read about them. Two slave hunters, Willis Hughes and John Knight, arrived in Boston to capture the Crafts and take them back to slavery in the south. Sympathetic Bostonians hid them until Hughes and Knight gave up and left. The Crafts no longer felt safe. They could be taken south by force at any moment. The risks increased when their former masters wrote to President Filmore asking for help. Filmore agreed that the Crafts should be returned to their owners and approved a military force to assist officers in arresting them. They had to leave Boston by a circuitous route because the ports were being watched for them. They threaded their way north to Canada. At Halifax, Nova Scotia, they boarded the *Cambria*, bound for Liverpool, England.

Five children and twenty years after their arrival in England, they returned to the United States with two of their children. Slavery had ended at the close of the Civil War three years earlier in 1865. Sadly, prejudices did not end with the abolition of slavery. Their first home, a cotton plantation in Savannah, Georgia, was attacked and burned down by the Ku Klux Klan in 1870. They leased another plantation outside Savannah and established a farm school there for freed slaves. In 1876, William was accused of stealing money donated to him for charitable purposes. He went to court to clear his name but lost. The farm school closed soon afterward, and the Crafts moved to Charleston to live with their daughter's family. Ellen died in 1891, followed by William in 1900. Their courage and determination in overcoming injustice in the face of appalling odds is still inspirational today.

After a stay in Bristol at the invitation of a friendly minister, the Crafts moved to London and toured Britain, giving speeches about slavery. They also educated themselves at Ockham School, an agricultural school in Surrey. Their story, *Running a Thousand Miles for Freedom: Or, The Escape of William and Ellen Craft from Slavery*, was published in 1860. William made several visits to Dahomey (Benin today) to teach Christianity and agriculture.

THE NEW DARWIN?

In the 1970s, an evolutionary theorist called Dr. Charlotte Bach announced that she had developed a new theory of evolution to replace Darwinism.

Instead of natural selection, Bach's theory was based on sexual deviation providing the impetus for evolution.

Mainstream academics showed no interest in the Hungarian-born academic's work, but she attracted a small following of committed supporters through her tireless promotion of her theory.

Then, in 1981, the robustly built, six-foot-tall academic became frail and ill. On June 17, a neighbor noticed that she hadn't taken her milk in for several days and called the police. Officers entered her home and found her body lying on her bed. Nearby, a medical dictionary was open at a page about liver cancer, which was indeed found to be the cause of her death. However, the postmortem examination of her body revealed something much more surprising. Dr. Charlotte Bach was a man. But since he clearly wasn't Charlotte Bach, who was he?

> Dr. Charlotte Bach spent years trying to convince anyone who would listen that Charles Darwin was wrong, but she was never awarded the Nobel Prize she thought she deserved.

Hungarian Origins

Dr. Bach's story began in Hungary on February 9, 1920. His real name was Karoly Hajdu, and he was a clever little boy who taught himself to read and write by the age of four. He seems to have led quite a solitary childhood, spending a lot of time reading books in the public library in Budapest.

He was called up for military service in 1941 but managed to get a student exemption. The next year, he created his first false identity, becoming the aristocratic Karoly Mihaly Balazs Agoston Hajdu, son of the Baron of Szadelo and Balkany. His aim was to mingle with the wealthy and separate them from their money, but he was drafted into the army before he could put his plan into action.

After the war, Hungary became a satellite of the Soviet Union. Hundreds of thousands of Hungarians were imprisoned. Karoly was jailed briefly by the communists, probably for black market activities, so he thought it best to leave the country while he could.

He traveled across Europe to Britain under the name Baron Carl Hajdu. He had taught him-self English, so he was put to

> Karoly had no passport, so he had to sneak across the border to Austria on foot in the dead of night!

work as an interpreter at the seaport of Harwich until 1950. At about this time, he started dressing in women's clothes occasionally. He took jobs in hotels along the south coast and briefly in London and the Cayman Islands.

By 1953, he was living in London, married to Phyllis Rodgers. They set up a business running an accommodation agency. Carl made frequent appearances in the local courts, charged with breaking various business regulations and laws. He made headlines in 1956. In that year, a large Hungarian resistance movement rebelled against Soviet control. After initial success, Soviet forces regrouped and retaliated, reimposing Soviet control of the country. While the borders were open, hundreds of thousands of people flooded out. Carl started raising money to help Hungary's freedom fighters and refugees. He gave interviews about the work of his grandly named UK Committee for the Assistance of Hungarian Freedom Fighters and made bold statements about arming the rebels. However, he soon had more pressing problems closer to home. Pursued for debts he couldn't pay, he was declared bankrupt in 1957. It was time to escape into a new identity.

Carl Becomes Charlotte

Now calling himself Michael Blaise Karoly, he took a hypnotherapy course and started working as a psychologist with an office in Mayfair, a swanky part of London. He also wrote articles about psychology and a book about hypnosis. When yet another of his moneymaking schemes was exposed by a newspaper, many of his clients left and his marriage collapsed. His hopes of saving his marriage were dashed when his wife fell ill and died. A few weeks later, his stepson died in a car accident.

As he mourned his losses, he started dressing in his late wife's clothes. He took scores of photographs of himself wearing them. His money troubles multiplied until he had to apply for National Assistance, a safety net introduced in 1948 to support Britain's poorest people. His mental state was such a concern that he was admitted to a hospital psychiatric ward. Soon after his release, he was in court again, charged with obtaining credit under false pretenses and working as a psychologist under an assumed name while he was bankrupt. This time, he was sent to prison. On his release, creditors continued to chase him for payment of past debts, leading to a second term of imprisonment. After this, he started dressing as Charlotte in public, and Dr. Charlotte Bach was born.

In 1970, Carl Hajdu ceased to exist—he changed his name officially to Charlotte Hajdu. While he lived as Charlotte Bach, he created yet another alter ego—a dominatrix called Daphne Lyell-Manson, who charged men for her expert services.

Dr. Charlotte Bach sought fame and wealth by trying in vain to interest academics, newspapers, and broadcasters in her evolution theories, but she had few supporters. A few others listened to her out of curiosity, but they found her theories incomprehensible. She still held out the hope of winning a Nobel Prize when she finally succumbed to that liver cancer in 1981.

FRAUD ALERT: MILITARY MAIDENS

As we've seen, women served secretly in every branch of the armed services. They fought as infantrymen in the thick of the action on battlefields, cavalry soldiers on horseback, artillery officers, and sailors in warships.

- Vilhelm Edstedt enlisted in the Swedish Army in 1713 and served for thirteen years. In 1716, Edstedt married Maria Lönnman, who was unaware that her new husband was actually a woman, real name Ulrika Eleonora Stålhammar. In 1728, Stålhammar, whose sister disapproved of her conduct, sent a letter of confession to the Swedish government. Posing as a person of the opposite sex and marrying someone of the same sex were crimes, and Stålhammar was put on trial. She was sentenced to one month in prison.

- In the 1740s, Ann Mills disguised herself as a man to serve onboard the British naval frigate, HMS *Maidstone*. During a battle, she is said to have been involved in hand-to-hand combat with a Frenchman, whose head she cut off!

- After the American Declaration of Independence in 1776 and the outbreak of the Revolutionary War, there were urgent calls for volunteers to fight the British. The offer of a bounty to each new recruit led a Massachusetts woman, Deborah Sampson, to wonder about joining the army. She made a suit of men's clothes to disguise herself and enlisted as Robert Shurtliff. When she was wounded in 1782, she let a doctor treat her head wounds but hid gunshot wounds to her thigh, fearing that her gender might be discovered. Later, when her secret was finally revealed, she received an honorable discharge from the army.

■ At the beginning of 1807, the French army under Napoleon Bonaparte had conquered most of western Europe. The combined armies of Prussia, Russia, Saxony, Sweden, and Britain formed a coalition to stop the French onslaught. The Russian army needed all the young men it could get. One applicant, Alexander Sokolov, joined an Uhlan (lancer) regiment. In fact, Sokolov was a woman named Nadezhda Durova, the daughter of a military family from Kiev. In her early twenties, she abandoned her husband and son and transformed herself into Alexander Sokolov to join the army. She left as a captain in 1816, having seen action in several battles.

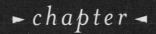

► *chapter* ◄

3

FALSE HEIRS

For thousands of years, the traditional way to pass power from one head of state to another was by hereditary succession—the son replaced the father. It was vital, therefore, for kings and emperors to produce an heir and, if possible, a spare—just in case. But there were plenty of times when a succession was unclear or could be challenged, and false heirs quickly jumped on these opportunities to step in and try to seize power.

The lure of inheriting kingdoms, empires, and noble titles has prompted scores of people to claim to be princes, princesses, or aristocrats. Many of them had a genuine claim of sorts, but some were opportunistic impostors. While they might be ridiculed or pitied today, in past times they were playing a very high-stakes game. They risked everything. Many of them came to a very unpleasant end when they were exposed as liars. These pretenders were often assisted by the vagrant sexual behavior of the aristocracy, namely the tendency of noblemen to take mistresses. These liaisons provided a rich vein for impostors, who could claim to be the product of illicit relationships. While they might not inherit a title or the throne from the wrong side of the blanket, they could cause serious embarrassment to well-connected families unless

In England, execution often meant being hanged, drawn, and quartered in front of hundreds or thousands of people who gathered to watch. It was a particularly vicious way to go. First, the victim (always male—women were not hanged, drawn, and quartered to preserve their modesty) was hanged, but rather than the quick dispatch of the neck-breaking long drop, he faced slow strangulation. As he slipped into unconsciousness, kicking and struggling, he was cut down. If necessary, he was revived to ensure his undivided attention for what came next. His stomach was slashed open. His bowels were pulled out and burned on a fire in front of him. He was castrated too. Remarkably, some victims were still alive at this point. At least two, Dr. John Story in 1571 and Major-General Thomas Harrison in 1660, fought with their executioner while being disemboweled. Death finally came with the removal of the heart and/or decapitation. The body was then cut into quarters. The head was often displayed on a spike on London Bridge as a warning to people entering the city. This unimaginably savage method of execution continued in England until well into the nineteenth century.

they were "looked after." Royal families offered the richest pickings. Pretenders repeatedly tried to unseat monarchs in turbulent times. It rarely ended well. To deter royal pretenders, the losers faced the most brutal form of execution.

From India to Greece to South America and Serbia, people have invented connections to royalty throughout the ages. The days of the great royal pretenders are more or less over. DNA profiling can now establish familial relations beyond doubt. In addition to exposing frauds, DNA tests have shattered the illusions of several families who genuinely believed they were descendants of royalty. But as we'll see in this chapter, the stories of these royal ruses live on, luckily for us.

A PRINCE AMONG MEN

Cremation is usually terminal. In other words, it's impossible to survive. But some people, including law courts in India and Britain, believe an Indian prince managed it!

In the early 1900s, India was part of the British Empire. Some parts of the country were governed directly by British officials. Others were ruled by Indian princes under British control.

Ramendra Narayan Roy was one of three princes, or kumars, who jointly owned the Bhawal Estate in Bengal (Bangladesh today). Ramendra was the second, or middle, of the three kumars. Bhawal was one of the biggest, oldest, and most prosperous estates in Eastern Bengal. Ramendra enjoyed life to the fullest, and, as a result, by 1906 he was suffering from syphilis. On May 8, 1909, while he was in Darjeeling for treatment, he was overwhelmed by a sudden illness and died. He was cremated there the next day, and his relatives returned home.

In September 1910, the eldest kumar died. A few month's later, the third kumar was judged unfit to manage the estate. As a result, the estate was taken over by the government's Court of Wards. The third kumar died in 1913.

From time to time over the years, rumors reached Bhawal that the second kumar had not been cremated and was still alive. Then in 1921, the family heard that a sannyasin, or holy man, had appeared in the city of Dhaka and had been recognized as the second kumar. The kumar's nephew went to Dhaka to see him. He thought the man resembled his uncle, but he couldn't be sure if it was really him. The man was brought to meet the kumar's relatives. He arrived in style, on an elephant. After talking to him, some of the relatives and tenants of the estate were convinced that he was Ramendra, the second kumar of Bhawal. When he was questioned, he was able to remember the name of Ramendra's wet nurse, something that was not widely known. However, Ramendra's widow, Bibhabati, refused to accept him as her husband.

The British authorities questioned all the interested parties and came to the conclusion that the kumar had been cremated and so the claimant must be an impostor. Despite this, there was widespread support for the man. Wild accusations flew between his supporters and opponents as each tried to discredit the other. One man was shot dead when disorder broke out during a demonstration in support of the returned kumar.

Call the Lawyers

In 1930, the claimant went to court to establish that he was the second kumar. It was another three years before the case began. A central question was how he could have survived cremation without so much as a singed eyebrow. He accused his brother-in-law of poisoning him and hurriedly taking his body to a nearby funeral ground for a cremation, which was in fact never carried out.

In court, the witnesses for both sides batted facts and accusations back and forth. There was no shortage of expert witnesses, but they couldn't agree on anything. A handwriting expert who examined the second kumar's signature and the plaintiff's signature concluded that they were both written by the same person. However, another expert hired by the defense testified that they were *not*. A photographer and an artist appearing for the plaintiff said that photographs of the second kumar and the plaintiff showed the same person, but defense experts were equally certain that the photographs showed *different* people. Medical experts for each side argued over whether marks on the plaintiff's body matched those on the second kumar's body. Inconsistencies in the testimonies of the doctors who saw the second kumar in his last few days cast doubt on the nature and severity of his illness. Experts in mental illness disagreed about whether the plaintiff could really have forgotten his early life for eleven years.

It took more than a year to hear over a thousand witnesses, but this

According to one account, the second kumar's cremation didn't go ahead, because the people hired to perform the cremation abandoned the body before the pyre was lit when a sudden rainstorm began and they ran for shelter. When they returned, the body had disappeared. A group of Naga sannyasis (holy men) had been passing by and saw the man lying on the ground. They picked him up and took him away to nurse him back to health. They were overjoyed to have found such a miraculous thing—a dead man who had returned to life. When he recovered, he had lost his memory. After a few years, he said he started remembering his former life.

was merely the case for the plaintiff. Then the case for the defense began, taking another year. The defense produced nearly four hundred witnesses who were convinced that the holy man was an impostor. The second rani, the kumar's widow, gave evidence that she had sat up all night beside her dead husband's body, so there was no doubt in her mind—her husband was dead and the holy man was an impostor. The third rani, widow of the third kumar, also insisted that the plaintiff was an impostor. However, the first rani thought he *was* the second kumar.

> The evidence presented in the first case was brought to Calcutta for the appeal, all 11,327 pages of it in twenty-six heavyweight volumes! This case took 164 working days, finishing on August 14, 1939!

The court finally adjourned on May 20, 1936. The judge took three months to consider the merits of the case and write his judgment. The case was so sensitive that he locked up his paperwork each night and slept with the key under his pillow.

When he finally announced his decision, he found in favor of the plaintiff...and then retired! The plaintiff was awarded the second kumar's one-third share of the family's estate.

Call the Lawyers...Again!

Despite the court's judgment, the British authorities refused to release any funds to the claimant and immediately appealed. The appeal was heard in Calcutta's High Court. Three judges began hearing the case on November 14, 1938. The appellants picked the trial judge's verdict apart line by line, and the respondents defended the trial judge.

Then one of the judges left for Britain and couldn't return to India because World War II had broken out. After another year passed and it became clear he was not going to be able to get back to India for the foreseeable future, the other judges decided that they couldn't delay the proceedings any longer. So the judge trapped in Britain sent his judgment in writing. The first two judges were split. It was time to open the sealed written judgment sent from Britain. The final judge found against

Although three courts had decided that the holy man with amnesia was the second kumar of Bhawal, his wife Bibhabati steadfastly refused to accept him. The Court of Wards had been holding back money due to the kumar until the legal process was completed. When the claimant was confirmed as the second kumar but then died, the Court of Wards informed Bibhabati that she was now entitled to the considerable sum of money that had been withheld. Interestingly, however, she contended that taking this money would mean that she accepted the court's decision that the claimant was indeed her husband, which she had always denied. So she refused to accept the money.

the appellants, and so the appeal against the lower court's decision was dismissed—the claimant was confirmed as the second kumar.

The kumar's widow refused to give up. She made a further appeal to the Privy Council in London. Delayed by the war, this appeal was dismissed on July 30, 1946. The news reached Calcutta the next day. The legal process on two continents had finally been exhausted, and the claimant had won at every stage.

Over the next few days, people arrived at the kumar's residence to congratulate him. They were stunned to be told that he was dead. On the day when he learned of his success, he had suffered a stroke and died two days later. Some of his opponents claimed it was divine retribution. Spookily, before the Privy Council appeal, astrologers had told the kumar's widow that she would lose the appeal but the winner would never enjoy his success.

The claimant might have been the second kumar, or he might have been a clever impostor. According to one account, he was the illegitimate son of the second kumar's father, which would account for his resemblance to family members and knowledge of the family. But without the battery of identity and relationship tests available today, no one can be certain who he really was.

THE LOST DAUPHIN

The French king, Louis XVI, and his queen, Marie Antoinette, were sent to the guillotine in 1793. The fate of their young son, the Dauphin, was not so certain. Did he die? Did he survive? The confusion created fertile ground for impostors.

When their parents were executed in 1793, the eight-year-old Prince Louis-Charles and his older sister, Princess Marie Thérèse, were held at the imposing medieval Temple prison in Paris.

Marie Thérèse was sent into exile in 1796, but by then Louis-Charles had disappeared. The official story is that he died on June 8, 1795. The boy's body was autopsied by Dr. Phillipe Jean Pelletan, who found the cause of death to be tuberculosis. Everyone who had seen the body was sworn to

The massive rat-infested tower at the Temple prison was a former Knights Templar stronghold built in the thirteenth century.

secrecy or imprisoned in order to stop news of his death leaking out. The boy's body was said to have been buried in an unmarked grave at the Sainte Marguerite cemetery. Inevitably, there were rumors that he had been murdered by revolutionaries, and because he was the focus of royalist hopes, there were also rumors that his supporters had managed to get him out of the vermin-ridden prison alive.

When the French monarchy was restored in 1814, it wasn't long before people started lining up to claim the throne as the missing Louis-Charles, King Louis XVII. There were more than a hundred of them.

The most persuasive claimant was a German clockmaker called Karl Wilhelm Naundorff. Naundorff came to Paris in 1833 and met several members of the old royal court, who believed he was genuine even though he spoke French badly and with a strong German accent. He also managed to convince the Dauphin's nurse, Agathe de Rambaud, who probably knew the Dauphin better than anyone. However, the Dauphin's sister, Marie Thérèse, refused to accept him.

Naundorff claimed that he, the Dauphin, had been replaced in prison by a boy who died soon afterward. Naundorff, who had been

One of the more famous names linked with the lost Dauphin story was that of the naturalist James Audubon. Audubon himself never claimed to be the Dauphin, but it was noted that he was the same age as Louis-Charles would have been if he had survived, and he was adopted after Louis-Charles is said to have escaped from prison. However, Audubon was later shown to have been born in Saint-Domingue (Haiti today).

hidden elsewhere in the prison, said he was smuggled out in the dead boy's coffin. However, he was captured and held in several different prisons until he finally escaped again. To further his claim, he sued Princess Marie Thérèse for the return of his property. The king's response was to have him arrested and deported to England.

There, he invented a device he called the Bourbon Bomb. In May 1841, a fire broke out in his workshop. While he was trying to save his bomb, it exploded and he was badly burned. Less than a year later, the workshop was destroyed by another fire. People living nearby wanted to be rid of the accident-prone foreigner. The Bourbon Bomb turned out to be a financial disaster, and Naundorff ended up in a debtors' prison. The Dutch Ministry of War came to his rescue. They bought his invention. When he left prison, he moved to the Netherlands, where he was appointed Director of Pyrotechnics for the Dutch military. He fell ill and died there on August 10, 1845, amid rumors that he had been poisoned. He was buried as Louis XVII, King of France. Some of his descendants adopted the surname "de Bourbon," Bourbon being the European royal house that Louis belonged to.

When DNA analysis became available, it settled the matter once and for all…or did it?

The Heart of the Matter

In 1950, Naundorff's grave was opened and a bone was removed for analysis. DNA from this bone did not match DNA from Marie Antoinette. So Naundorff was not the lost Dauphin, but another question remained to be answered—was the boy who died in the Temple prison the real Dauphin, or could one of the other claimants have been genuine after all? Remarkably, part of the dead boy's body still existed, so it was available for DNA analysis.

When Philippe Jean Pelletan autopsied the boy's body, he stole the heart.

He pickled it in alcohol and hid it in his library, where it was later stolen by one of his students, the only person he had shown it to. He traced the student, who had just died, and managed to get the heart back from the man's widow. He tried to return it to the restored monarchy, but Louis XVIII declined to accept it, doubting it was genuine. Pelletan tried again when Charles X succeeded Louis. The Archbishop of Paris finally accepted it in 1828. Eventually, after making its way through a revolution and to Spain and back, the heart was returned to France in 1975 and kept in the royal crypt at Saint-Denis Basilica near Paris.

It was normal practice at that time for the heart of a member of the royal family to be removed before burial, but it was not normal practice for the doctor to keep it!

In 1999, samples were taken from it and sent to two different laboratories in Belgium and Germany along with samples of hair from Marie Antoinette, her sisters, and living descendants. The DNA between the various samples matched. So the boy who died in the Temple prison *was* the lost Dauphin and the rightful King Louis XVII of France, right? Well, not necessarily. The DNA match showed that the owner of the heart and the owners of the hair were related. It didn't establish that Marie Antoinette and the owner of the heart were mother and son or identify the heart's owner as the lost Dauphin. Also, between the autopsy and the DNA tests, the heart traveled far and often, so ultimately its authenticity can't be proved.

Conspiracy theorists continued to speculate on the fate of the boy who would be king. However, it is now generally accepted that Louis XVII died in the Temple prison in 1795 just as history records and that Karl Wilhelm Naundorff was simply one of many impostors who tried in vain to claim his throne.

KINGMAKERS' PUPPETS

Upon the death of Richard III, the last king of the House of York, the English throne was seized by Henry VII, the first Tudor monarch. Henry faced several challenges to his reign, some by very talented royal impostors.

When Henry VII won the throne in battle in 1485, England's two competing royal houses—Lancaster and York—had been fighting over the crown for thirty years. Henry was a descendant, through his mother's family, of a branch of the House of Lancaster. He tried to settle the rivalry between the two houses by marrying Elizabeth of York. The Tudor rose he chose as his badge combined the emblems of the two houses—the red rose of Lancaster and the white rose of York. However, Henry faced a series of Yorkist plots to remove him. He neutralized the threat from one possible rival, Edward Earl of Warwick (1475–99), by imprisoning him in the Tower of London.

Simon the Puppet-Master

When an Oxford priest named Richard Simon heard rumors that the Earl of Warwick had died in the Tower, he saw an opportunity to be a kingmaker. He was already tutoring a boy named Lambert Simnel with the intention of passing him off as Richard Duke of York, one of the two princes in the Tower.

The princes, heirs to the throne, had not been seen alive since the summer of 1483 and were thought to have been murdered by the

The princes in the Tower were the two sons of the Yorkist king, Edward IV. When Edward IV died in 1483, his eldest son was proclaimed King Edward V. As he was only thirteen years old, his uncle, the Duke of Gloucester, was appointed as his protector. However, Gloucester had his eye on the throne for himself. He had the boy placed in the Tower of London, where he was joined by his younger brother, the Duke of York. The boys were then declared illegitimate, and Gloucester seized the crown as King Richard III. Richard reined until 1485, when he was killed at the Battle of Bosworth Field and the crown passed to Henry VII.

Duke of Gloucester's henchmen. With their fate unknown, a convincing impostor could stake his claim to the kingdom. This was the role Richard Simon planned for Lambert Simnel.

Simnel didn't have a drop of royal blood in his veins. He was the son of an Oxford tradesman. Simon chose him as the key actor in his plot because of his resemblance to the princes in the Tower, but when he heard that the Earl of Warwick may have died in the Tower as well, he changed his plans. Simnel was quickly retrained to become Warwick and was thoroughly schooled in Warwick's life and family.

Simon started a rumor that Warwick had escaped from the Tower. He presented Simnel as Warwick and took him to Ireland, where there was still considerable support for the House of York. The Earl of Kildare, Lord Deputy of Ireland (the king's representative in Ireland), was a Yorkist sympathizer who was happy to accept Simnel's claim and use him as a pretext for overthrowing Henry VII and restoring the House of York to the English throne.

On May 24, 1487, Simnel was crowned Edward VI in Dublin. Kildare then raised an army and prepared to invade England. Meanwhile, the Earl of Lincoln traveled to Burgundy to appeal for help from Margaret of York, Dowager Duchess of Burgundy. Margaret agreed to send two thousand soldiers to supplement Kildare's forces. When King Henry learned what was happening, he had the real Earl of Warwick brought from the Tower and paraded him in public to discourage the English lords and barons from supporting the impostor. While the English nobility accepted that Warwick was still in London under the king's control, the Irish persisted in their belief that Simnel was Warwick. They also held the mistaken belief that there was a groundswell of popular support in England for the restoration of the House of York to the throne.

Let Battle Commence

Simnel's troops landed in England on June 5, 1487. Most of the English support they were expecting did not materialize. The invaders continued and met King Henry's army eleven days later at the Battle of

Richard Simon's life was spared only because he was a priest. He was confined to a monastery for the rest of his life.

Stoke Field in Nottinghamshire. A rebel army of 8,000 faced the King's army totaling 12,000, many of whom were more experienced and better equipped than the invaders. Simnel's army was defeated in just three hours, ending his bogus claim to the throne. He fared better than many of his supporters, who were either killed on the battlefield in the thousands or imprisoned and had their estates confiscated by the king.

Although Simnel was clearly guilty of treason, he was a young lad only about twelve years old, and Henry could see that he was a mere puppet in the hands of manipulators. He pardoned Simnel and gave him a job in the royal kitchen as a turnspit, a worker who turned meat roasting over a fire. Later, he was promoted to the position of King's falconer. The precise date of his death is unknown, but he is thought to have died between 1525 and 1534.

The Flanders Fraud

Just four years after Henry VII saw off the challenge from the impostor Lambert Simnel, a more dangerous plot involving another false heir began to unfold. This time the impostor would not be as fortunate as Simnel.

Perkin Warbeck was born in the city of Tournai in Flanders in about 1474. His father was the city's comptroller, a government official who supervised public expenditure. When he was about ten years old, his mother took him to Antwerp to learn Dutch. He had several jobs there, eventually working for a silk merchant with whom he traveled to Ireland in 1491. When Yorkist supporters saw the elegant young man dressed in fine silk, they believed (or wanted to believe) that he was the Earl of Warwick, the same man who Lambert Simnel had impersonated. Warbeck insisted that he wasn't Warwick, but he was then identified as Richard Duke of York, the younger of the two princes imprisoned in the Tower of London by King Richard III. He was presented to Irish noblemen in the hope of gaining their support.

However, most of them were reluctant to get involved in another rebellion so soon after their defeat in the Simnel campaign.

News that Richard Duke of York might have survived and may be free again spread across Europe. In the summer of 1492, Warbeck was invited to France by King Charles VIII. Charles welcomed him as a royal prince. Unfortunately for Warbeck, relations between France and England improved. In November 1492, Charles signed a peace treaty with England at Étaples to head off the threat of an English invasion. As a result, the French agreed to expel Warbeck. He moved to Flanders, where he met Margaret of York, Dowager Duchess of Burgundy, the real Duke of York's aunt. It is possible that she had already been involved in his imposture for some time, pulling the strings behind the scenes.

Henry was so angered by Margaret's support for Warbeck that he imposed an embargo on trade with Flanders. Margaret confirmed Warbeck's identity as the Duke of York and introduced him to important people, notably the most powerful ruler in Europe, Maximilian I, the Holy Roman Emperor. Maximilian backed him wholeheartedly, and preparations for an invasion of England began.

> When Lambert Simnel's claim to the crown of England failed, King Henry might have thought that the Yorkist threat was over and done with. However, Margaret of York, Dowager Duchess of Burgundy, simply sought a more convincing impostor who might succeed where Simnel had failed. She would find a suitable candidate in a youth named Perkin Warbeck.

Invasion

Henry's spies were already monitoring Warbeck's activities. When they discovered that there were Warbeck conspirators and Yorkist sympathizers within the king's own court, Henry had them executed.

Warbeck's invasion went ahead in 1495, but it was a pitiful affair. Only fourteen small ships could be mustered. Many of the invaders were killed on the beach at Deal in Kent. It was such a rout that Warbeck stayed onboard his ship and immediately sailed for Ireland.

With little support remaining there, he moved on to Scotland, where he received a warm welcome from the Scottish king, James IV. James even arranged for him to marry his cousin, Lady Catherine Gordon.

In September 1496, King James and Warbeck mounted an invasion of Northumberland in northeast England. It was no more successful than Warbeck's first attempt at an invasion. They ventured only four miles or so into England and retreated back to Scotland when English troops approached. James soon tired of the young pretender and sent him on his way. After a brief visit to Ireland, he landed in Cornwall in September 1497, hoping to make use of a Cornish revolt against higher taxes. Ironically, one of the reasons for the tax rise was to fund the campaign against Scotland prompted by Warbeck's activities there.

King Richard IV

With the support of up to 8,000 Cornishmen, Warbeck was proclaimed King Richard IV on Bodmin Moor. His army of supporters marched on Exeter, but they failed to take the city. Soon afterward, with the king's men approaching, Warbeck fled to Beaulieu Abbey in Hampshire, where he later surrendered. Henry executed the leaders of the Cornish revolt and imprisoned Warbeck, who readily agreed to sign a confession.

On November 23, 1499, the twenty-five-year-old Perkin Warbeck was taken from the Tower of London to Tyburn, where he publicly denied that he was the son of Edward IV or of any royal blood. Minutes later, a noose was tightened around his neck. He was hanged and then beheaded.

THE FALSE DMITRYS

The early seventeenth century in Russia was a time of civil unrest, famine, and invasion. More than a dozen impostors claimed to be heirs to the throne of Ivan the Terrible, Tsar of All the Russias. The most notable were three men known as the false Dmitrys.

Ivan IV was the first Russian leader to take the title tsar. He ruled from 1533 to 1584 and earned the nickname Ivan the Terrible because he was prone to outbursts of extreme rage and violence. During one outburst, he attacked his oldest son and heir, Ivan Ivanovich, so violently that the young man died. When Ivan the Terrible himself died, power passed to his younger son, Feodor. Tsar Feodor I was a sickly and simple-minded man who had little interest in politics. He failed to produce a male heir. In 1598, he was succeeded by the man who had been the power behind Feodor's throne, Boris Godunov.

Godunov's reign marked the beginning of a turbulent period of Russian history known as the Time of Troubles. One-third of the population died in a famine when harvests failed. There was great unrest and discontent throughout the country, which Godunov failed to control. The time was ripe for the appearance of an alternative leader. Right on time, a man named Dmitry popped up, claiming to be Dmitry Ivanovich, the youngest son of Ivan the Terrible.

The First False Dmitry

The first false Dmitry appeared in the early 1600s in Poland. As news of his claim began to spread, he attracted the backing of several Polish noblemen. His support grew further when he converted to Catholicism. He managed to gather an army big enough to march on Moscow. When he crossed into Russia, anti-Godunov border towns supported him. The Don Cossacks and boyars fell in behind him too. The revolution was gaining momentum.

Meanwhile, Godunov died and was succeeded by his son, Feodor II. But Feodor would rule for less than two months before Dmitry's army reached

The real Dmitry Ivanovich had died in 1591 under suspicious circumstances. He was stabbed, but no one knows who wielded the knife. He might have been killed by Boris Godunov to remove the last obstacle standing between him and the throne. The mystery surrounding Dmitry's death enabled rumormongers to claim that he wasn't dead at all but was in hiding, waiting for the right moment to return and claim the throne.

The first false Dmitry is thought to have been a young monk named Grigory Otrepyev.

Moscow and imprisoned him. On June 20, 1605, Dmitry entered the city and was crowned tsar a month later.

Tsar Dmitry made himself unpopular by breaking several traditions. As a Catholic, he failed to form the close relationship between the tsar and the Russian Orthodox Church that had become the norm. When he married, his wife did not convert to Orthodox Christianity, as had been the custom. There were rumors that he planned to convert Russia to Catholicism. This earned him powerful enemies in the church and aristocracy, and his support drained away, especially when he ran out of money to keep powerful landowners happy.

Prince Vasily Shuisky led a rebellion against him. On May 17, 1606, the rebels stormed the Kremlin. Dmitry escaped through a window but fell awkwardly and broke his leg. He was shot dead where he lay. His body was displayed publicly for several days and then cremated. According to one account, his ashes were blasted out of a cannon pointing at the place he had come from—Poland. Vasily Shuisky succeeded him as Tsar Vasily IV.

False Dmitry II

Almost exactly a year after the first false Dmitry was killed, another one surfaced. The second false Dmitry appeared in the town of Starodub in Russia's far west. At first, he claimed to be a boyar nobleman. The townspeople were suspicious of him and interrogated him. Under torture, he changed his story and claimed instead to be Dmitry Ivanovich, heir to Ivan the Terrible's throne. As his claim was revealed under torture, he was believed. Poles and Lithuanians who had supported the first false Dmitry rallied to him and gave him money and soldiers. His small army headed for Moscow and met with early successes. He even defeated the tsar's army at the Battle of Bolkhov in 1608. By the time he reached Tushino, near Moscow, his army of 7,500 soldiers had grown into a formidable 100,000-strong military force. His sprawling encampment there earned him the nick-name "the rebel of Tushino."

This false Dmitry looked unstoppable, but when the Polish King Sigismund III invaded Russia, Dmitry's Polish troops left to join the Polish invasion forces. At the same time, a large combined Russian-Swedish army arrived to defend Moscow. Dmitry was forced to flee, disguised as a peasant. He fled to Kostroma in central Russia. From there, he mounted a second unsuccessful attack on Moscow. His attempt to claim the Russian throne ended on December 11, 1610, when he was shot in the head by Prince Peter Urosov, a member of his own personal guard. Dmitry had humiliated Urosov a few weeks earlier by having him publicly flogged.

> The second false Dmitry's real identity was never established. He was a well-educated man, fluent in both Russian and Polish, perhaps a priest's son.

False Dmitry III

Only three months later, in March 1611, a third false Dmitry surfaced. Very little is known about him. He walked into the town of Ivangorod, near the Estonian border, claiming to be the Tsarevich Dmitry Ivanovich. Thought to have been a deacon named Sidorka, he attracted some support but was quickly seized by the authorities in Moscow and executed.

Two years later, the Time of Troubles came to an end with the establishment of the Romanov dynasty. The Romanovs would rule Russia for more than three hundred years, from 1613 until 1917, when Bolshevik revolutionaries removed Tsar Nicholas II from power and executed him with his family, ending the reign of the tsars once and for all.

THE PRINCESS PAINTER

In 1817, the Prince Regent of England received a letter from Olivia Serres. She claimed to be the daughter of the Duke of Cumberland, who happened to be the king's brother. She also claimed to have been created Duchess of Lancaster and was therefore entitled to income from the Duchy of Lancaster.

Serres's claim to be Princess Olive of Cumberland, as she called herself, was based on being the product of the Duke of Cumberland's dalliance with a Mrs. Olive Payne. If the gossip of the day is true, they did indeed have a relationship. There were even rumors that the Duke and Miss Wilmot (who later became Mrs. Payne) had secretly married in 1767. Serres's claim was strengthened by a reported resemblance between her and the duke. However, the royal family rejected her.

She renewed her claim in the 1820s. A newspaper called *The British Luminary* took up her case, and a genealogist, Henry Nugent Bell, is said to have investigated her and supported her. But her story had changed. She now claimed that a Dr. James Wilmot (more on him later) had secretly married Princess Poniatowski, a sister of King Stanislaus I of Poland, and that their daughter had been placed in the care of Dr. Wilmot's sister, Mrs. Payne. When the girl reached her eighteenth birthday, she caught the eye of both the Duke of Cumberland and the Earl of Warwick. The Duke won the day and married her in 1767. Olivia claimed to be the only child of this marriage. She said that when she was only ten days old, she was substituted for the stillborn daughter of Dr. Wilmot's brother, Robert, who then brought her up as his own daughter.

> The Duchy of Lancaster was established in the thirteenth century to provide an income for the sovereign. Today, it covers about 46,000 acres of town and countryside in England and Wales, with a value of around half a billion U.S. dollars.

Immune from the Law

Olivia had continual money problems and was repeatedly sent to debtors' prison, where the conditions were decidedly grim. When she was arrested for debt in 1821, she insisted that she was immune from arrest and trial for a civil matter like debt because she was the Duke of Cumberland's daughter. The court disagreed and ruled against her.

Records show that Olivia Wilmot was born on April 3, 1772, in Warwick, but she spent much of her childhood in the care of her unmarried uncle, Dr. James Wilmot, rector of Barton-on-Heath. When she was seventeen, she took painting lessons from an artist named John Thomas Serres. They clearly got on well together, because on September 17, 1791, they were married by Dr. Wilmot. However, the marriage was not as happy as the courtship, because they separated in 1804. Olivia went on to give art lessons herself and exhibited her paintings at the Royal Academy. In 1806, she had her first brush with royalty when she was appointed landscape painter to the Prince of Wales. This enabled her to glimpse the staggering wealth and luxury enjoyed by members of the royal family. This and the rumored affair between her aunt and the king's brother very likely sowed the seeds of her claim. She may even have believed it.

In 1823, a Member of Parliament, Sir Gerard Noel, asked questions in Parliament about Olivia's claim. The Home Secretary, Sir Robert Peel, responded by denouncing the claim as baseless. Her husband, who had kept out of the public controversy, left a statement in his will after his death in 1825 denying that there was any truth in her claim. Meanwhile, the royal family had obtained Olivia's birth certificate. This revealed that her father was Robert Wilmot, a house painter from Coventry. He made a statement confirming that he was her father. Mrs. Payne, the woman she claimed as her mother, was actually her aunt.

A Family Tradition

When she died on November 21, 1834, Olivia's daughter, Lavinia, carried on the family tradition by claiming to be Princess Lavinia of Cumberland and the Duchess of Lancaster. Sir Gerard Noel, the MP who had helped her mother, formed a committee to assist her. It filed a claim against King George IV's executor, the Duke of Wellington, for a legacy she claimed had been left to her by George III. However, the claim failed. She tried again in 1866, but the signatures on some of the documents she produced in evidence were judged to be forgeries. The royal family was finally free of Olivia and her daughter.

THE TROUBLE WITH ANNA

When a woman who became known as Anna Anderson claimed that she was the daughter of Russia's last tsar, arguments about her true identity raged for decades. Was she the Grand Duchess Anastasia or an impostor?

The story of Anna Anderson begins with events in Russia in 1917. Tsar Nicholas II ruled a Russian empire of 130 million subjects. He was an absolute ruler who wielded total power. The times were changing, but unfortunately Tsar Nicholas was not. Growing numbers of people wanted a say in their government. Nicholas responded by forming a secret police network to spy on the ringleaders.

As conditions in Russia worsened during World War I, workers and political activists demanded change, but Nicholas refused. His wife, Alexandra, was increasingly unpopular too because of her German origins. Strikes and rallies followed. Revolutionary talk was rife. On March 11, 1917, Nicholas ordered the army to put down rioting in Petrograd (St. Petersburg today). However, many of the troops refused to open fire on the people and mutinied. When Nicholas arrived in the city a few days later, his ministers and army chiefs advised him

Nicholas and his wife, Alexandra, had five children—Olga, Tatiana, Maria, Anastasia, and Alexei. Unfortunately, Alexei inherited the curse of Queen Victoria's family, hemophilia, and had to be protected from the slightest injury at all times. The family's search for a cure famously led them to admit the eccentric holy man, Rasputin, into their inner circle.

to abdicate, which he did the following day. The tsar and his family were then placed under house arrest. They were held in a number of houses, eventually finding themselves in the Ipatiev House in Yekaterinburg. It was ominously known as the "House of Special Purpose."

While civil war raged across the country, the Bolsheviks, who were holding the royal family, feared that approaching anticommunist troops might free the family and restore the tsar to power. Their solution was barbaric. On the night of July 16, 1918, the family was awakened and told to get dressed. They were informed that they were going to be photographed. Just after midnight, the door of the basement opened, but instead of a photographer, a squad of soldiers entered the room. The royal family was told that they were to be executed, and then the soldiers opened fire. The girls survived the gunfire and were bayoneted to death. They were found to have several pounds of gemstones hidden in their clothing, which had protected them like bulletproof vests.

A Lone Survivor?

In the following years, there were persistent rumors that at least one of the family had escaped the carnage. The name that kept coming up was Anastasia. Three years after the tsar and his family disappeared and 820 miles to the southwest, a woman jumped from a bridge into the Landwehr Canal in Berlin. When she was rescued from her apparent suicide attempt, she refused to say who she was. She was taken to an asylum in Dalldorf. The staff thought they could detect a Russian accent when she spoke.

Two years later, in 1922, another of the patients announced that the mysterious woman was the Grand Duchess Tatiana, one of the tsar's daughters. The news that Tatiana might be alive got out, and Russian émigrés were soon visiting the hospital to see her. Most of them accepted her as Tatiana until a former lady-in-waiting to the royal family saw her and declared that she was too short to be Tatiana.

The patient herself denied she was Tatiana but then claimed to be another of the tsar's daughters, Anastasia. She claimed that a Bolshevik soldier had found her alive after the rest of her family had been executed and he had helped her to escape. Her body did indeed bear terrible scars that could have been evidence of a failed execution. Once again, Russian émigrés readily accepted her and curried favor with her. If the old order was ever restored in Russia, Anastasia's friends and benefactors might expect a place at court. But could a patient in a German asylum really be a Russian Grand Duchess?

She called herself Anna Tschaikovsky, but her acolytes insisted on calling her Anastasia. There was no shortage of people willing to house her and feed her. However, a succession of people who had known

Anastasia visited her and failed to recognize her. While her identity was investigated, she was supported by Anastasia's great uncle, Prince Valdemar of Denmark. To allow her to travel, she was issued with a certificate of identity in the name of Anastasia Tschaikovsky.

The empress's brother, Ernest Louis, Grand Duke of Hesse, was determined to prove that Anna was an impostor. He hired a private detective to investigate her. In due course, the detective, Martin Kopf, reported back that her real name was Franziska Schanzkowska—not a Russian Grand Duchess but a Polish factory worker. She had been injured in an accident with a grenade in the munitions factory where she worked. This accident explained her scars. Early in 1920, she disappeared from her lodgings in Berlin and hadn't been seen since then. Her story dovetailed precisely with the appearance of the mysterious woman claiming to be Anastasia.

When Prince Valdemar's family persuaded him to withdraw his support, Anna was given a home at Castle Seeon in Bavaria by Duke George of Leuchtenberg, another distant relative of the Romanovs. She had garnered a seemingly inexhaustible number of supporters.

Franziska's brother traveled to Wasserburg, near Castle Seeon, and met Anna. He is said to have recognized her as his sister, but in an affidavit, he agreed only that she bore a strong resemblance to his sister. She didn't appear to recognize him. Later, he was accused of knowing that Anna was his sister but failed to confirm her identity so that she might have the chance of a better life.

Going West

By this time, the question of Anna Tschaikovsky's identity had spread further afield. In 1928, Xenia Leeds, a Russian princess married to a wealthy American industrialist, paid for Anna to travel to the United States. On the way, she passed through Paris, where she met the tsar's cousin, Grand Duke Andrei Vladimirovich of Russia, who thought she was indeed Anastasia. When she arrived in New York City on the liner *Berengeria*, she was welcomed by Gleb Botkin, the son of the Romanovs' family doctor. The doctor had been executed with the family. Gleb Botkin confidently asserted that Anna was undoubtedly the Grand Duchess Anastasia and addressed her as "Your Highness."

Anna left her accommodation with the Leeds family and moved to the Garden City Hotel in Hempstead, New York, with support from the Russian composer Sergei Rachmaninoff. To throw reporters off her scent, she was registered as Mrs. Anderson. She was now Anna Anderson.

When the tsar's mother, the Dowager Empress Marie, died in October 1928, a dozen close relatives of the tsar met and signed a declaration known as the Copenhagen Statement, branding Anna Anderson as an impostor. Anna's supporters accused the family of trying to cheat her out of her inheritance.

In 1928, it was ten years since the tsar and his family had disappeared. The tsar could legally be declared dead, and any of his estate that remained outside the Soviet Union could be released to his relatives. The tsar was rumored to have moved a fortune abroad. A lawyer, Edward Fallows, set up a company to raise money from investors who bought shares in any part of the tsar's estate that was secured. However, apart from a small amount of money discovered in Germany, no fortune was located.

In 1929, Anna was on the move again. Now she stayed with a wealthy spinster, Annie Burr Jennings, on Park Avenue in New York City. She enjoyed the attention of New York society for eighteen months, but then her behavior began to deteriorate. She suffered from fits of great anger, killing her pet parakeet and running around on the roof naked. In July 1930, a judge committed her to a mental hospital. She had to be taken there by force. A year later, she was released and returned to Germany. On her arrival, she was taken to a psychiatric unit near Hanover. There, she was found to be sane, but as Annie Burr Jennings had already paid for her room for six months, she stayed there. Aristocrats were still ready and willing to support her, so she had no shortage of offers of accommodation when she left the unit. Lawyers continued to prosper from the case. Anna's lawyers tried to stop the tsar's estate from being released to proven relatives, while the relatives' lawyers contested Anna's identity.

In 1938, Anna met her Polish relatives again. They were absolutely certain that she was Franziska Schanzkowska. However, Germany's Nazi government let it be known that if she were an impostor, she would be imprisoned. Not surprisingly, the family refused to give evidence against her. Supporters continued to help her, and she moved from place to place. Meanwhile, friends, relatives, and acquaintances of the Romanovs continued to be split on the issue of Anna's identity. While she was living in a small village in the Black Forest, a friend of the tsarina visited her and accepted her as Anastasia. But when one of Anastasia's tutors saw her, he was adamant that she was not Anastasia.

> Anna Anderson's story and the question of who she really was inspired a string of books, plays, and movies. A French play called *Anastasia* opened in 1954. It was made into a film starring Ingrid Bergman, who won an Oscar for the role.

Staying Stateside

In 1968, Anna was rushed to the hospital after being found semiconscious. Her home was in a terrible state. While she was in the hospital, the house was cleaned up and her dog and sixty cats were removed and destroyed. She was so angry when she found out that she accepted an invitation from her long-standing supporter, Gleb Botkin, to return to the United States under a six-month visa. However, just as her visa was about to expire, she married a friend of Botkin's, history professor John Eacott Manahan.

In 1979, Anna was taken to the hospital with an intestinal problem. She was found to have a tumor, which was removed. She was unaware at the time that a discovery in Russia that same year was opening the last chapter of the Anna Anderson story. News would not reach the wider world for another ten years, but Anna would be dead by then. She died from pneumonia on February 12, 1984.

The DNA Decider

In the 1960s, surviving members of the 1918 execution squad had been traced and questioned. They described the bodies of the Russian royal family being put in a shallow pit. However, the commander thought they might be found, so they were pulled out of the water-logged ground, and an attempt was made to burn them, but they were too wet. They were driven away on the back of a truck to another burial site, but the burial activity was spotted by someone, so the bodies were loaded on the truck again and taken away. When the truck got stuck in soft ground, the bodies were offloaded and buried for the last time. Railroad ties were piled on top to hide them.

> The last of many legal cases concerning Anna's identity ended in 1970. The remaining part of the Romanov estate was released to the Duchess of Mecklenberg.

Later, two amateur investigators, geologist Alexander Avdonin and ex-policeman Geli Ryabov, were looking into the Romanov mystery. They discovered official documents that contained clues, and in 1979, they located a pit containing the remains of nine bodies. The bodies had been burned before burial. Initially, the men agreed not to reveal what they had found, but it was too big a secret to keep. Ryabov released news of the discovery in 1989.

DNA was taken from the skeletons. First, they were tested to find out the sex of the bodies. The tests revealed that there were four males and five females. The next question was—were they related to each other? The DNA tests showed that there was a father, mother, and three daughters. The others were unrelated. Who were they? Were they the Russian royal family, and was Anastasia among them? The DNA was compared to a sample provided by Prince Philip, Duke of Edinburgh, in Britain. His maternal grandmother was the tsarina's sister. This and other tests involving DNA taken from the body of Grand Duke George, the tsar's brother, confirmed that the remains belonged to the tsar, tsarina, and three of their daughters. The unrelated remains were likely those of servants known to have been executed with the family.

The last tsar of Russia, his wife, and his three daughters were reburied in 1998 in the crypt of St. Petersburg's Peter and Paul Cathedral, where Russian emperors have been buried since Peter the Great. But one of the daughters was still missing. Could it be Anastasia? The answer came in 2007 with the discovery of the remains of two more individuals. They were the lost son, Alexei, and the last daughter. There was now proof that none of the tsar's family had survived the execution in the Ipatiev House.

At least four other women made claims to be Anastasia between the 1920s and the 1990s. More than a dozen people claimed to be other members of the Romanov royal family.

The final proof that Anna Anderson was an impostor came with tests on the part of her intestine that was removed during her tumor surgery in 1979. DNA from the sample did not match that of Prince Philip or any of the Russian royal family's remains or other relatives of the family. However, it did match DNA provided by Karl Maucher, a member of the Schanzkowska family. Anna was indeed a humble Polish factory worker, Franziska Schanzkowska, not the Grand Duchess Anastasia.

FRAUD ALERT: CUNNING CLAIMANTS

In 1910, *Dracula* author Bram Stoker published a book called *Famous Impostors*, which exposed a variety of false heirs, bogus claimants, and hoaxers. It included the tale of Arthur Orton, also known as the Tichborne Claimant. The false heirs discovered since then could have filled several volumes, so we will recap some of the most interesting here.

- On April 20, 1854, a sailing ship called the *Bella* left Rio de Janeiro for Jamaica. It was never seen again. One of its passengers was Roger Charles Tichborne. His father, Sir James Francis Doughty Tichborne, was the tenth Tichborne baronet. When Sir James died, followed by his son, Alfred, the missing Roger became heir to the Tichborne fortune IF he was still alive. In Australia, a man named Thomas Castro claimed to be the missing heir, saying that he had been rescued by a passing ship. He arrived in England on Christmas Day 1866 to secure his inheritance. Lady Tichborne, Roger's mother, accepted Castro as her son, but the rest of the family did not. Investigations revealed that his real name was Arthur Orton. His claim failed in court, and he was sent to prison for perjury. He died penniless in London in 1898.

- In 1959, the CIA started receiving anonymous letters containing Polish and Soviet intelligence secrets. The CIA called their mysterious pen pal Sniper. MI5 (British military intelligence) gave him the code name Lavinia. He provided alarming information about high-level security leaks from the West to Poland and Russia. His information led to the discovery of the Portland Spy Ring, a network of Soviet spies that had infiltrated the Royal Navy's Underwater Weapons Establishment. Sniper/Lavinia was later revealed to be a Polish intelligence officer named Michael Goleniewski (1922–93). In the early 1960s, he claimed to be the missing son of the last tsar of Russia, Nicholas II, and started calling himself Alexei Romanov. He was one of several men who claimed to be Tsarevich Alexei, but they were all proved to be impostors.

■ Eugenio Lascorz (1886–1952) decided that his name was a Spanish corruption of the name Lascaris, one of the ruling families of the Byzantine Empire. In 1923, he changed his name to Eugenio Lascaris Comneno. Comneno, or Komneno, was another Byzantine ruling family. By 1943, he was calling himself Prince Eugene Lascaris Comnenus Paleologus, Duke of Athens, but despite his best efforts, his claims never received official recognition.

■ A Latvian man named Harry Domela (1905–78) rather liked the idea of being a titled nobleman. Shortly after World War I, a few German aristocrats thought they could see a resemblance between Domela, who was calling himself Prince Lieven of Latvia, and the grandson of the deposed Kaiser. Rumors began circulating that he was the heir to the German throne traveling undercover. When the rumors reached the authorities, they arrested him, but when he was put on trial in 1927, he argued that his imposture was harmless, and he was acquitted.

■ Alexis Brimeyer (1946–95) was addicted to royal titles. Born in Costermansville (Bukavu, Democratic Republic of Congo today), he started collecting royal titles at the age of only ten. Through his various invented titles and names, he claimed connections with Italian, Spanish, Russian, and Serbian royal families. His claims continued until his death but attracted little support.

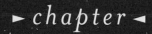

► *chapter* ◄

4

FUGITIVES FROM JUSTICE

Some impostors have used a false identity to escape the consequences of their crimes and start a new life. Some of them managed to elude capture while living openly, simply by carrying ID cards with false names on them. Legendary Boston crime boss, James "Whitey" Bulger was a wanted man on the run for sixteen years before he was finally caught in 2011. The eighty-one-year-old, who was wanted for nineteen murders, drugs offenses, money laundering, and extortion, carried a wallet full of fake cards. He could change his identity in the blink of an eye simply by producing a different card.

One of the most famous fugitives in the world, Dr. Crippen, adopted a false identity to escape from Britain after his wife's mysterious disappearance. Another, John List, was on the run with a false identity for eighteen years after slaughtering his family. Yet another, British politician John

Bulger was finally caught after an FBI publicity campaign that targeted women. His companion, Catherine Greig, was known to be a frequent visitor to beauty salons and dentist's offices, had undergone plastic surgery, and loved dogs. A tip-off about her led agents to a house in Santa Monica where the couple was living.

Stonehouse, fled from his financial problems by starting a new life with a new name. Crippen, List, and Stonehouse were caught, but the real identity of a fugitive named Dan Cooper has never been discovered. He held a commercial airliner for ransom and made off into the night with the money, never to be seen again. Here, we'll explore the bizarre stories behind these men and their deeds and disguises.

CHASING DR. CRIPPEN

On July 20, 1910, the SS *Montrose* steamed out of Antwerp, Belgium, on its way to Canada. She had 373 souls onboard—107 crew and 266 passengers. Her commander, Captain Henry George Kendall, noticed that two of his passengers seemed to be acting oddly. The sharp-eyed captain had spotted suspects on the run from one of the most notorious British murder cases.

One of the most notorious murderers in British history fled the country under a false identity while police investigated the disappearance of his wife. His arrest made history, because he was the first convicted murderer to be caught with the help of a new-fangled invention called radio.

The two passengers were traveling under the names of John Robinson and his sixteen-year-old son, Edmund. However, they weren't behaving like a father and son, and the boy was built more like a girl. Kendall knew that the police in Britain were searching for an American doctor, Hawley Harvey Crippen, following the discovery of human remains in his cellar. Robinson didn't have Crippen's luxuriant mustache and he was growing a beard, but Kendall strongly suspected that Robinson was Crippen. Fortunately, the *Montrose* was equipped with one of the new Marconi ship-to-shore radio telegraphs. Kendall sent a message saying he thought the father and son were actually Crippen and his mistress, Ethel Le Neve.

The hunt for Crippen had begun after a grisly discovery at his home. On July 13, Chief Inspector Walter Dew and a team of police officers were searching the house in Hilldrop Crescent, north London. When they lifted the brick floor of the cellar, they found decomposing human remains covered with lime. They thought they had found Crippen's missing wife, but where was Crippen?

Hawley Harvey Crippen was born in Coldwater, Michigan, in 1862. His first wife, Charlotte, died of a stroke in 1892. He married his second wife while he was practicing as a doctor in New York. Her birth name was Kunigunde Mackamotski. At some point, before Crippen met her, she changed her name to Corrine "Cora" Turner. As a professional singer, she was known by yet another name—Belle Elmore. In 1897, Dr. Crippen and his wife moved to England. Managing Cora's career took up so much of his time that he was sacked by a company he sold patent medicines for. He then went to work for Drouet's Institute for the Deaf, where, in about 1903, he met a young typist named Ethel Le Neve.

Crippen and Cora moved to 39 Hilldrop Crescent in 1905. They had to take in lodgers to make ends meet, and Cora had an affair with one of them. By 1908, Crippen was having an affair with Ethel Le Neve.

The Disappearance

Cora Crippen suddenly disappeared after a party at the Hilldrop Crescent house on January 31, 1910. She was never seen alive again. Crippen told friends that she had returned to the United States, where she had died. Friends of Cora's were alarmed and puzzled by her disappearance. They couldn't find out anything about her death. Their alarm increased when Le Neve moved into the Hilldrop Crescent house and was seen wearing Cora's jewels and furs. They reported their concerns to the police.

Chief Inspector Dew visited Hilldrop Crescent, questioned Crippen, and searched the house. Crippen told the officer that he had lied about Cora's disappearance to avoid embarrassment. He said the truth was that Cora had left him for someone else.

Dew had been satisfied with Crippen's account, but Crippen was so spooked that he went on the run. His disappearance aroused further police interest. Dew returned to Hilldrop Crescent and made a more thorough search of the house, which ended with the discovery of the human remains in the cellar.

The remains were the flesh of a human torso. No head, limbs, or skeleton were ever found. When the flesh was examined and tests were carried out, traces of the drug scopolamine (also known as hyoscine) were found. The remains were identified as belonging to Cora by the presence of a scar on the abdomen, similar to a scar that Cora was known to have had.

The police began a nationwide search for the doctor and his secretary, Ethel Le Neve, who was also missing. Every newspaper carried their photographs with lurid descriptions of the gruesome discovery at Hilldrop Crescent.

The Transatlantic Chase

When the police learned of the radio message from the *Montrose*, Chief Inspector Dew set off across the Atlantic in a faster ship, the White Star Line's SS *Laurentic*. As the *Montrose* entered the St. Lawrence River, Dew boarded it disguised as a river pilot. When he greeted "John Robinson," Crippen recognized him as the police officer who had questioned him three weeks earlier. Dew arrested Crippen and Le Neve and brought them back to Britain on the SS *Megantic*.

If Crippen had sailed for the United States instead of Canada, he would have been beyond the reach of the British police. However, in 1910, Canada was still part of the British Empire and thus subject to British law, enabling Dew to make his arrest.

Crippen and Le Neve were tried separately at the Old Bailey in London in October 1910. Crippen was tried first, accused of poisoning his wife with the scopolamine that was found in her remains. The poisons book of a New Oxford Street, London, chemist recorded a purchase of scopolamine on January 19, nearly two weeks before Cora Crippen's disappearance. The record is accompanied by the signature of H. H. Crippen. Although the remains in the cellar were not recognizable, it was argued that the scarred skin strongly suggested that the remains were those of Cora Crippen. Dr. Crippen's affair with Le Neve and his behavior, fleeing to Canada, also suggested his guilt.

The defense argued that Cora had gone to the United States with another man and that the remains in the cellar had been placed there by a previous owner of the house before the Crippens moved to Hilldrop Crescent in 1905. It was also argued that the "scar" on the remains was just a fold in the skin and therefore the remains were not Cora Crippen's. The prosecution produced a fragment of a pajama jacket that was found with the remains. It matched pajama trousers belonging to Dr. Crippen that were found in the house. The fragment bore a manufacturer's label, saying "Jones Brothers." Someone from Jones Brothers gave evidence that the pajamas dated from 1908 or later, after the Crippens moved into Hilldrop Crescent, and so the remains could not have been placed under the cellar floor before the Crippens moved in.

Guilty

The jury was sent out on October 22. They took just twenty-seven minutes to return a verdict of guilty. The judge donned the black cap and sentenced Crippen to death. Three days later, Ethel Le Neve's trial began. She faced the lesser charge of being an accessory after the fact and was quickly acquitted. Crippen appealed his conviction.

> Friends of Crippen petitioned the Home Secretary, Winston Churchill, for clemency, but Churchill rejected the petition.

While he waited in prison to learn his fate, he wrote several letters to Ethel Le Neve. He said he was optimistic that his appeal would succeed.

Crippen then wrote a farewell letter, which was published in *Lloyd's Weekly News*. It stressed Ethel Le Neve's innocence. He did not admit to any crime relating to Cora, merely saying that they had drifted apart.

At 9:00 a.m. on November 23, 1910, at Pentonville Prison,

executioner John Ellis and his assistant secured Crippen's ankles and wrists with leather straps, pulled a hood over his head, and placed a noose around his neck. Seconds later, he was dead. He was buried within the prison grounds.

In the years following the case, doubts about Crippen's guilt surfaced. If he disposed of his wife's head and limbs so successfully that they were never found, why would he keep the rest of her body in his home where the police could find it? In 2007, a comparison between DNA from the flesh thought to be Cora's and DNA taken from Cora Crippen's descendants failed to find a match, suggesting that the remains were not Cora's. A further DNA test found that the flesh belonged to a man. In addition, the microscope slide of the "scar" from the remains was found to contain hair follicles, which would not be found in a genuine scar.

Others have argued that these discoveries don't necessarily exonerate Crippen. It is possible that Cora's descendants were not actually her blood relations—stranger things have happened within families. The DNA test that found the remains to be male has been disputed, but the team who carried out the test insists that the result is correct.

If the remains belonged to a woman who was not Cora Crippen, then who was she? It has been suggested that Dr. Crippen, always short of money, may have been performing illegal abortions and the remains in the cellar belonged to a patient who had died during one of these procedures. If this is the case, then Crippen was still guilty of homicide. Whether or not the scar really was a scar doesn't prove or disprove that the remains were Cora's.

Whoever the remains belonged to, there is still the matter of how and why Cora Crippen disappeared and whether she vanished voluntarily. If she was still alive, would she really have let her husband go to the gallows? The Criminal Cases Review Commission looked at the Crippen case in 2009, but none of these doubts or questions persuaded it to send the case to the appeal court, and so Dr. Crippen's guilty verdict still stands.

DAN THE SKYJACK MAN

Theft is a common motive for imposture, but few impostors go as far as hijacking a commercial jet and demanding a ransom. A man known as Dan Cooper chose this extraordinary method to steal a fortune. But who was he?

On November 24, 1971, a man who called himself Dan Cooper arrived at Portland International Airport in Oregon. He was in his forties, smartly dressed in a dark suit, and he carried a black attaché case. He looked like a businessman about to embark on a routine trip and aroused no suspicions. He bought a one-way ticket to Seattle, Washington, and boarded the 2:50 p.m. Northwest Orient Airlines flight along with thirty-six other passengers. In 1971, airline security was minimal in some places, especially within the United States. Baggage was not routinely scanned by x-ray machines, and passengers were not searched.

"I Have a Bomb"

Just after the plane took off, Cooper passed a note to Florence Schaffner, one of the flight attendants. She assumed it was a businessman giving her his phone number, so she dropped it in her pocket without looking at it. Cooper leaned across to her and said, "Miss, you'd better look at that note. I have a bomb." Schaffner unfolded the note, which said, "I have a bomb in my briefcase. I will use it if necessary. I want you to sit next to me. You are being hijacked." Cooper opened his case enough for her to see red sticks or cylinders connected to a battery, but she couldn't tell if it was a real bomb. Then he told her what he wanted—$200,000 in unmarked $20 bills, two back parachutes, two chest parachutes, and a fuel truck ready to refuel the plane when it landed. Schaffner then went to the cockpit and told the crew what had happened. They relayed the news to air traffic control, who informed the authorities.

The aircraft was instructed to circle Puget Sound for two hours while preparations on the ground were made.

The FBI collected the money from banks. They photographed every one of the ten thousand banknotes. They offered Cooper military parachutes, but he demanded civilian chutes with manually operated ripcords. The plane was finally given permission to land, and it touched down at Seattle-Tacoma Airport at 5:45 p.m. Cooper instructed the crew to taxi to a remote, brightly lit part of the airport and turn off the cabin lights to foil snipers. The airline's operations manager, Al Lee, delivered the money and parachutes to the aircraft. While the plane was being refueled, Cooper let all the passengers and two of the flight attendants, including Schaffner, leave. Refueling took longer than expected because of a problem with a vapor lock in the fuel lines. A second fuel tanker was brought up to the aircraft and then a third.

Meanwhile, Cooper briefed the crew on what was to happen next. They were to head southeast toward Mexico City at a height of no more than 10,000 feet. Cooper warned the crew that he had an altimeter, so he would know if they tried to fly higher. He also insisted that the flaps must be set to fifteen degrees and the airspeed must not exceed 150 knots, or about 175 miles per hour. The landing gear was not to be raised after takeoff, the cabin was to remain unpressurized, and the plane's rear stairs were to be left down during the flight. The airline said it would be unsafe to take off with the rear staircase down, so Cooper agreed to lower it after takeoff. The crew told Cooper they could not reach Mexico City without refueling, so he agreed that they could land at Reno, Nevada, for fuel.

> Cooper appeared to be familiar with the ground below. As he chatted to Schaffner, he mentioned that he recognized Tacoma as they flew over it and he knew that McChord Air Force Base was a twenty-minute drive from the airport. He remained calm and polite throughout the time they circled the airport.

The Endgame

The plane took off at 7:40 p.m. It was followed by two Convair F-106 Delta Dart fighters from McChord Air Force Base. Cooper told flight attendant Tina Mucklow to go to the cockpit and close the door behind her. As she left the cabin, she saw Cooper tying something around his waist. Twenty minutes after takeoff, a warning light came on in the cockpit, showing that the rear staircase had been lowered. Then the crew noticed a change in air pressure, indicating that the rear door had been opened. A few minutes later, the plane's tail lurched upward, requiring the crew to take action to stabilize the aircraft.

When they landed at Reno at 10:15 p.m., the plane was searched. There was no sign of Cooper, his bomb, or the money. He must have stood on the lowered rear staircase and jumped into the darkness, wearing ordinary street clothes and two parachutes, with his case and a bag of money the size of a toddler tied to him. The air temperature at the plane's altitude would have been below zero. He would have landed on mountainous ground among 150-foot-tall Douglas fir trees. It would have been a challenging jump even for an experienced parachutist jumping in daylight.

Cooper appeared to have chosen the flight specifically because of the plane used—a Boeing 727-100—and he'd done his homework on it. The position of the engines, high in the tail, and the availability of a rear exit under the tail, well below the engines, meant that Cooper could jump from the plane without risking being incinerated by engine exhaust. He was also aware of the flap setting necessary for flying at 150 knots, and he knew that the plane could fly at this speed without stalling. He chose the altitude so that the plane could fly unpressurized, making it possible to open the rear door without causing explosive depressurization. He also appeared to know how long it should take to refuel the plane, because he could tell that refueling was taking too long when the vapor lock problem occurred. And he knew more about the operation of the plane's rear staircase than the crew did. When flight attendant Tina Mucklow said she didn't think the staircase could be lowered when the plane was in the air, he insisted to her that it could.

The Search for Cooper

The police and FBI began the search for Cooper. They spoke to everyone who had seen him and used their descriptions to create sketches of him. They lifted sixty-six unknown fingerprints from the plane.

Agents and officers tried to find where Cooper had landed. They knew precisely when the plane's back door was opened and when Cooper jumped out, causing the tail to rise. The unknown factor was how long he was in free-fall before opening his chute. The pilots following the plane saw no one exit from it. The plane was flown along the same course again, and a two-hundred-pound weight was pushed out of the rear door to check that the upward motion of the plane's tail did indeed mark Cooper's departure. It did. His landing area was thought to be southeast of Ariel, Washington, near Lake Merwin. The ground was searched on foot and from helicopters. During the search, a skeleton was found, but it wasn't Cooper's. It was the remains of a teenage girl who had gone missing several weeks earlier. No trace of Cooper was found.

Just in case Cooper had been stupid enough to use his real name, the FBI questioned an Oregon man named D. B. Cooper. He was quickly cleared, but his name became confused with that of the real culprit, who has been known as D. B. Cooper ever since.

A later analysis of the flight found that both the plane's course and the wind direction used in the original analysis were incorrect. When the new landing zone was calculated, a new search began in the area of the Washougal River valley, but once again nothing was found. By the end of the year, the FBI had released the serial numbers of the banknotes to banks, casinos, racetracks, law enforcement agencies, and businesses that dealt with large cash transactions. Early the following year, the numbers were made public. The airline, the *Journal* newspaper in Portland, and the *Post-Intelligencer* in Seattle all offered rewards for the recovery of any of the money, but none was found.

In 1978, a notice with instructions for lowering the rear stairs of a Boeing 727 was found north of Lake Merwin. Then in February 1980, an eight-year-old boy named Brian Ingram found three packs of the stolen money amounting to $5,800 buried in the sandy shore of the Columbia River, twenty miles southwest of Ariel.

If Cooper had landed near the Washougal River, which merges with the Columbia River, the money could have been washed down to the place where it was discovered. Analysis of the sand the money was buried in indicated that the money could not have been washed up there before 1974, begging the question—where had it been between the hijacking in 1971 and being washed up and buried some time from 1974 onward? And why were only three packs of the money found? Just three months after the money was discovered, the nearby Mount St. Helens blew its top in a violent volcanic eruption that carpeted the ground with a thick layer of ash, perhaps obliterating further evidence. Since then, no more of the money has been found.

The riverbank was searched in 1981, and a human skull was found, but it wasn't Cooper; it turned out to be a woman's skull. In 1988, part of a parachute was found in the Columbia River, but inquiries found that it could not have been the parachute that Cooper used. In 2008, children found another parachute six miles south of Lake Merwin, but it was dated to the 1940s.

Forensic Analysis

The hijacking and the evidence have been analyzed and reanalyzed several times as new forensic techniques became available. When DNA analysis was developed, the clip-on tie left behind on the plane by Cooper was investigated and a partial DNA profile was obtained. The tie was also studied by electron microscope to try to identify pollen grains on it that might give away its origins. When GPS and satellite maps became available, river currents were studied to find out where the money that was found might have come from.

At first, Cooper was thought to be an expert parachutist, perhaps an ex-paratrooper, but the FBI later revised their view on this. They decided he was more likely to be inexperienced, because he turned down military chutes, chose the inferior of the two main chutes he was given, and paired it with an unusable dummy reserve chute, which he was supplied with by accident. The chute was marked with an X to indicate that it was a training chute, and it was sewn shut. Cooper clearly didn't check it or didn't understand the significance of the X. He also jumped from the plane into a 200-mile-per-hour wind in subzero temperatures wearing ordinary clothes and no helmet. Some FBI agents think he probably did not survive the jump. He may have landed in the Columbia River, where his parachute and the weight of the money-bag may have dragged him down below the surface. It is possible that the bag holding the money decomposed until several packs of the cash were washed out and deposited on the riverbank, where they were subsequently found. Alternatively, the money may have fallen out of the bag during the parachute jump.

Cooper's fate remains a mystery. If he died during his parachute jump, it is odd that not one friend or relative has reported him missing and no remains have been found. If he survived, it is equally odd that none of the money he risked his life to steal has been spent anywhere. His crime is the only unsolved commercial aircraft hijacking. And still, no one knows who Dan Cooper really was, but the source of his false name may have been found. Dan Cooper was the name of a French comic book hero, a Royal Canadian Air Force test pilot. The Dan Cooper comic books were never translated into English, so the FBI think the hijacker may have lived in Europe at some point, perhaps stationed there while serving in the Air Force. They think he may have been a loader on cargo aircraft, which would have given him a working knowledge of the aviation industry and parachutes—cargo loaders wear parachutes but are not

The FBI investigated more than one thousand suspects, but nearly all of them have been ruled out. Some of them have even claimed to be Cooper. However, some were ruled out by a DNA test, which didn't match the DNA recovered from Cooper's tie. Others didn't match the physical description of Cooper, especially his height. Yet others could not have been on the plane at the appointed time because of evidence that they were elsewhere. A new suspect was identified as recently as July 2011.

expert parachutists. And he must have been a loner with no friends or family to miss him when he disappeared. But who was he? The FBI is still waiting to hear from someone with the vital piece of evidence that will wind up this case.

Even though the case wasn't solved, it had a lasting effect on air travel. As a result of the Cooper hijacking and several copycat attempts, a device called a Cooper Vane was added to the Boeing 727-100 to stop the rear stairs from being lowered during flight. Some airlines went further and sealed the door so that it couldn't be used at all. Cockpit doors were fitted with peepholes so that the crew could see what was happening in the passenger cabin when the cockpit door was closed. The Federal Aviation Administration also required passengers and hand baggage to be screened. Dan Cooper's legacy will continue to affect our travel for a long time to come.

THE BREEZE KNOLL MURDERS

On June 1, 1989, the family and friends of mild-mannered Virginia accountant Robert Clark were astonished when he was arrested for murder. They were even more amazed when they discovered which murders he was charged with.

On December 7, 1971, police officers entered Breeze Knoll, the home of John List in Westfield, New Jersey. Neighbors hadn't seen anyone coming or going from the house for several weeks, and List's daughter, Patricia, had been missing her drama classes. Inside, they found the bodies of List's wife Helen, daughter Patricia, sons John and Frederick, and mother Alma. All of them had been shot. Eerily, organ music was playing through the house on an intercom system.

Four of the bodies were laid out on sleeping bags in the ballroom under a stained glass skylight. The body of List's mother was found in her attic apartment. All of them had been shot once in the head apart from List's fifteen-year-old son John, who had been shot at least ten times.

It quickly became clear that the murders were not an impulsive, spur-of-the-moment act. They had been planned meticulously. List had told everyone that the family was going away on a trip to North Carolina and then canceled his paper and milk deliveries, thus delaying discovery of the crime and giving him more time to disappear. He also tore his face out of every photograph in the house to make it harder for the police to identify him. And he turned on the house lights so the house would look occupied at night.

When officers investigated List's background, they found that he had lost his job and was deeply in debt. He owed $11,000 on his mortgage. He left a letter at the crime scene, addressed to his pastor at a Lutheran church where he taught Sunday school, explaining that there was too much evil in the world and so he had sent his family to heaven to save their souls.

List was the prime suspect for the murders, but where was he? His car, a Chevrolet Impala, was found at Kennedy Airport, but police found no record of anyone matching his description taking a flight. Nearly a year after his disappearance, Breeze Knoll was mysteriously destroyed in an arson attack. Despite a nationwide hunt and hundreds of sightings followed up by the FBI and police, List could not be found.

America's Most Wanted

In 1989, prosecutors took the case to the Fox television program *America's Most Wanted* to see if they could help. The program's producers consulted Frank Bender, a forensic sculptor, and Richard Walter, a criminal psychologist. Bender was asked to produce an image of List as he might look in 1989. Working from photographs of List in his forties and photographs of his parents, Bender created a lifelike bust of an older John List. On May 21, 1989, it was shown to a television audience estimated at 22 million. One viewer thought it bore a resemblance to Robert Clark, who had been one of her neighbors in Denver, Colorado. Police traced Clark to Virginia. When FBI agents went to his home, they found that he had remarried. After talking to his wife, Delores, they went to the office where he was working as an accountant and arrested him. He strenuously denied being John List, but his fingerprints proved otherwise. He was extradited to New Jersey, where he finally admitted that he was indeed John List.

Interviews with List revealed that he was so ashamed when he lost his job that he hid the fact from his family. He carried on going out each morning as if to work but spent the day at the local bus station. Without any income, he resorted to stealing money from his mother's bank accounts. At the same time, he was dealing with another problem that was doubly shaming to him. His wife was suffering from syphilis, and she had known she was suffering from it when she married him in 1951. She had contracted the disease from her first husband, a soldier who had been killed in action during World War II. She had been treated for it, but the treatment was unsuccessful. She hid her medical condition from List for eighteen years. After a series of health problems, including blackouts, signs of dementia, and failing sight, she finally revealed her condition to doctors in the late 1960s. Medical tests revealed that she was suffering from brain damage caused by tertiary syphilis, the final stage of the disease.

Unbearable Shame

To someone with John List's austere religious and moral upbringing, a sexually transmitted disease, especially syphilis, in the family would have been very shaming and difficult to deal with. In addition, he was worried about the welfare of his children, growing up at a time when drug-taking and recreational sex were becoming more commonplace. Rather than deal with his problems and face the shame and ridicule the family would probably suffer, List opted to push the nuclear button and destroy his family.

Once List started putting his plan into operation, he couldn't stop. He killed his wife first. Then he went upstairs and killed his mother. When his children came home, he killed them too, one by one. While the bodies lay undiscovered for a month, List laid a false trail for the police by leaving his car at the airport and then escaping to a new

In List's twisted logic, he was doing the right thing, a good thing, by killing his family and ensuring that their souls would go to heaven. He claimed that he didn't kill himself because he believed that suicide was wrong and it would have prevented him from entry to heaven and being reunited with his family.

life as Robert Clark in Denver, Colorado. Later, he moved to Richmond, Virginia.

On April 12, 1990, he was convicted of five murders, and on May 1, he was sentenced to five consecutive life terms. He appealed on the grounds that he was suffering from post-traumatic stress caused by his military service in World War II and Korea, but the appeal was unsuccessful. List died from complications of pneumonia on March 21, 2008, aged eighty-two.

THE COPYCAT JACKAL

British politician John Stonehouse tried to escape his financial problems by starting a new life with a false identity, but an observant bank worker on the other side of the world ruined his plans.

In 1974, police officers in Melbourne, Australia, closed in on a suspect they had been watching. He was using the names Joe Markham and Clive Muldoon, but they weren't entirely sure who he really was. One possibility was Lord Lucan, who had disappeared several weeks earlier in London after the murder of his children's nanny and the attempted murder of his wife. Another possibility was John Stonehouse, a former British government minister who had disappeared in the United States soon after Lucan. Lucan was known to have a scar on his right leg, so the arrested man was told to drop his trousers to settle the question of his identity. It was Stonehouse.

Missing, Presumed Drowned

John Stonehouse had been a rising star of British politics. He was Postmaster General in Prime Minister Harold Wilson's Labor government in the 1960s. When Labor lost the 1970 general election,

Stonehouse was not invited to join the shadow cabinet. It was later revealed that he had been suspected of spying for Czechoslovakia, but there was not enough evidence to bring charges against him. With his political ambitions thwarted, he embarked on a business career.

Stonehouse set up a series of companies, but within a few years, they were in trouble. By then, the married Stonehouse had also begun an affair with his secretary, Sheila Buckley. Facing failure and prosecution, he decided to run away. He stole the identities of two deceased constituents, Joseph Markham and Clive Muldoon. He is said to have gotten the idea from the story of *The Day of the Jackal* by Frederick Forsyth. Then he faked his death on November 20, 1974, by leaving a pile of his clothes on Miami Beach to create the impression that he had gone swimming and drowned.

While the House of Commons held a minute's silence as a mark of respect for their fellow Member of Parliament, he was very much alive. He had fled to Hawaii and then to Australia. He thought the use of two different fake names would give him a better chance of evading detection, but ironically it actually hastened his arrest. He deposited money at the Bank of New Zealand under the name of Muldoon. Unfortunately for him, the bank teller he dealt with became suspicious when he saw "Muldoon" also going into the Bank of New South Wales. Inquiries revealed that he had used the name Markham there. After a trip to Copenhagen, he returned to Australia, where the police placed him under surveillance. He was arrested on Christmas Eve 1974 and deported to Britain the following June after failed attempts to find asylum in Sweden and Mauritius.

Stonehouse stood trial on twenty-one charges of fraud, theft, forgery, conspiracy to defraud, causing a false police investigation, and wasting police time. He conducted his own defense during the sixty-eight-day trial at the Old Bailey. He was found guilty on eighteen of the charges and sentenced to seven years' imprisonment. Sheila Buckley was also tried, found guilty, and sentenced to two years. Stonehouse's wife divorced him in 1978.

Stonehouse suffered three heart attacks while he was in prison and underwent open heart surgery. He was released early, in August 1979, because of his poor health. After his release, he worked for charities and wrote several books, including an autobiography called *Death of an Idealist*. He married his former secretary and mistress, Sheila Buckley, in 1981. In 1988, he collapsed during a television show. He appeared to be making a recovery but suffered his fourth heart attack and died on April 14, 1988.

A MURDERER IN OUR MIDST

The man known to his Canadian friends as polite and hard-working hid a terrible secret from them. His true identity and past were revealed only after a brutal murder that shocked the community.

In 2000, the population of Chilliwack in British Columbia, Canada, increased by one. The new arrival was a friendly American named Reno Trevor Hogg. Known as Trevor, he fitted in quickly and made friends, although a few people were suspicious of him and didn't trust him. They noticed that he avoided answering questions about his past. He worked at the Sto:lo Nation, an organization that serves native Canadian Indian communities. He met Susan Reinhardt through the Sto:lo Nation, and they had a relationship, which led to the birth of a baby boy.

However, the relationship foundered and Reinhardt left for Saskatoon, Saskatchewan, with their son. Hogg followed her, determined to get access to his son. Friends had advised him not to do that, but to go through the courts. Apparently, he didn't listen to their wise counsel.

In the early hours of July 15, 2006, Susan Reinhardt was killed in her bed by a shotgun blast. David Ristow, who was lying beside her, was wounded but survived. Three children sleeping in the house at the time were unhurt. The killer appeared to have entered the property through a patio door left open for Ristow's cats. The police suspected Hogg, but they couldn't find him. He was finally tracked down and arrested on January 8, 2010, in North Battleford, a small city northwest of Saskatoon.

The murder of Susan Reinhardt had been shocking enough, but when the full truth about Hogg was revealed to the friends and work-mates he'd lived among in Chilliwack for years, they were doubly shocked. Unknown to them, he was already a convicted murderer when he arrived in Chilliwack. And he wasn't Reno Trevor Hogg. His real name was George Mitchell Allgood. A former navy cook, Allgood had been sentenced to thirty years in prison for the brutal murder of an elderly man in Baltimore, Maryland, in 1983. The man, in his seventies, had been tied up and beaten to death with a shovel. It isn't known how Allgood entered Canada after his release from prison in the United States.

When he appeared in court in 2012 charged with Reinhardt's murder and Ristow's attempted murder, he denied the charges, but the preliminary hearing established that he had a case to answer, and he was sent for trial, scheduled for the fall of 2013. If found guilty, he could expect to spend many more years in prison.

FRAUD ALERT: FELONIOUS FLIERS

Bogus pilots risk passengers' lives when they trick their way into airliner cockpits by using false documentation. And even with all the certificates, licenses, medical checks, and security precautions that go with civil aviation today, a few fake fliers still manage to get through. Let's look at some of the most bizarre and intriguing ones here.

■ In 2007, a Chinese "pilot" was arrested at the end of a flight from Beijing to Guizhou after the plane's other pilot became suspicious of his lack of knowledge. The fake flier had bought his uniform on the Internet and downloaded fake documents!

■ In March 2010, police officers removed a Swedish pilot from the cockpit of a Boeing 737 that was about to leave Amsterdam's Schiphol Airport for Turkey with 101 passengers onboard. Turns out he had been flying airliners for thirteen years on a forged license and had logged 10,000 hours in the air!

■ In 2012, Italian police arrested an impostor who posed as an airline pilot and flew in the cockpit on at least one flight, although he didn't take the controls. He was discovered after another pilot became suspicious of this captain, who was unusually young, only thirty-two. When police officers searched his home, they found fake uniforms and identity documents.

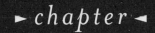

► chapter ◄

5

FRAUDS AND FREEBOOTERS

Patricia Highsmith's Ripley novels tell the story of cash-strapped Tom Ripley, who murders Dickie Greenleaf, the wealthy son of a wealthier businessman, and steals his identity and lifestyle. Ripley believes that it's better to be a fake somebody than a real nobody. The pursuit of wealth is a powerful motive for imposture in the real world too.

Fortunately, few real frauds and freebooters are as brutal as *The Talented Mr. Ripley*. Their aim is to persuade their victim to hand over money or property willingly. And the vehicle for the scam is often a bogus business deal or a dodgy investment. Pick the right victim and make the deal attractive enough, and their greed will do the rest. You can even get people to invest in a totally fictitious country or buy the Eiffel Tower if you're persuasive enough!

It seems that if you can play the part of a famous person (or a famous person's son) convincingly, people queue up to hand over money and give you a roof over your head, cars, and all sorts of other goodies. The key to success is to pick an alter ego that potential victims have heard of, but not so famous that everyone knows what he or she looks like. David Hampton convinced his victims that he was Sidney Poitier's son. Christophe Rocancourt played the part of a French relative of the Rockefeller family. The fact that Sidney Poitier didn't have a son and the Rockefellers didn't have a French relative was no barrier to success, because most of the victims failed to make the most basic checks on the impostor.

For Lewis Morgan, the perfect alter ego was Randy Meisner. If you're saying "Randy who?" you're not alone. Randy Meisner was a bass player with the 1970s rock band The Eagles. Morgan started off posing as another Eagles member, lead singer Don Henley, but he was arrested in Las Vegas in 1988. By then, Henley was enjoying a successful solo career and was becoming too recognizable to be impersonated. Morgan jumped bail and switched his attention to the less well-known Randy Meisner. And the scams kept working for nearly ten years. One woman was left with a bill of nearly $3,000 after picking up his expenses for two weeks. Morgan also conned guitar-makers out of guitars, which he then sold or pawned for thousands of dollars. He was finally arrested in 1998 and spent sixteen months in jail. He has been spotted repeating his Randy Meisner scam from time to time, but smartphones are making it more difficult for anyone posing as a real person. Anyone who runs into Morgan can have a photo of the real Randy Meisner on his or her phone in seconds.

The impostors I have selected for this chapter include a man who sold the Eiffel Tower and conned Al Capone, a woman who led the life of a real Moll Flanders, fraudsters who exploited the fame of others for their own benefit, and even one who invented a country so that he could enrich himself. Let's dig in.

THE MAN WHO SOLD THE EIFFEL TOWER...

Victor Lustig impersonated a French government official so convincingly that he managed to sell the Eiffel Tower...twice!

In 1925, the Eiffel Tower was rather shabby, rusty, and badly in need of repairs. The famous Paris landmark had been expected to last only twenty years when it was built in 1889, so it was *long* overdue for an overhaul. When small-time criminal Victor Lustig read about the sorry state of the tower, he saw an opportunity to make money…a lot of money! He invited France's biggest scrap metal dealers to a meeting in the Hotel de Crillon in Paris. Lustig impersonated the deputy director of the Ministry of Posts and Telegraphs, the government department responsible for the Eiffel Tower. He told the dealers that the government had decided not to repair the tower because of the cost, and so it was to be demolished.

The prospect of getting their hands on 7,000 tons of iron thrilled the scrap dealers. Lustig told them that the government wanted to act quickly, so he needed their tenders for the work within a week—and the deal was top secret. The dealers thought the highest bidder would win, but in fact Lustig had already chosen his "victim"—an ambitious businessman and scrap dealer named André Poisson. Poisson was invited back for a second meeting. Lustig told him his bid of 250,000 francs had been successful but that a sizable bribe would guarantee he got the job. This seems to have convinced Poisson that he was dealing with a genuine government official! He took the hint and paid a bribe of $70,000. In return, he got a worthless bill of sale saying that he was now the owner of the Eiffel Tower.

It seems unthinkable today that the French might tear down the Eiffel Tower, but it was perfectly believable in the 1920s. There were many Parisians who hadn't wanted the tower in the first place. The huge iron structure was widely seen as a blot on the cityscape, an unwanted hangover from the Paris Exposition it was built for. The government had planned to move it elsewhere, but the cost proved to be prohibitive. Over the years, it fell into disrepair, and Parisians wanted rid of it.

Lustig immediately left the country and went into hiding in Austria. He expected to be a wanted man, but nothing happened! Poisson had been so humiliated when he realized he'd been conned that he hadn't reported it to the police! Incredibly, when Lustig realized that he wasn't being hunted, he went back to Paris and pulled the same stunt again with another scrap dealer! However, this dealer did go to the police. Lustig escaped arrest by fleeing to the United States.

A Life of Crime

Lustig was a lifelong gambler and con artist. Born in Bohemia (in the Czech Republic today) on January 4, 1890, young Victor was a bright child, but he had a habit of getting into trouble. While he was a student at the University of Paris, he spent a lot of time playing cards and billiards instead of studying. He was a talented linguist, fluent in English, French, German, Italian, and Czech. He traveled around Europe as a petty criminal under a series of false identities. He is said to have been arrested forty-five times all over Europe under twenty-two different aliases!

He often claimed to be a count in order to fleece wealthy passengers on cruise ships and ocean liners. The outbreak of World War I in 1914 put an end to this profitable scam. His solution was to move his criminal activities to the United States. He is one of very few people to have conned the notorious gangster Al Capone and gotten away with his life. He persuaded Capone to invest $50,000 in a scheme that promised to double his money in sixty days. The scheme didn't exist. Lustig simply went back to Capone two months later, told him the deal hadn't worked out, and returned all the money. Capone was so impressed by Lustig's "honesty" that he paid him a handsome reward. Capone had no idea he'd been conned!

In Missouri, Lustig bought a ranch and paid for it with Liberty Bonds. He also exchanged bonds worth another $10,000 for cash. He managed to make off with both the bonds and the cash, but he was tracked down in Kansas City and arrested. However, the experienced con artist managed to talk his way out of being charged. Once he was free, he did his usual disappearing trick and left the country. On his return to France, he carried out his Eiffel Tower scam. When his second victim went to the police, Lustig fled to the United States again.

In the States, he used an infamous con called the Romanian Box. He would show his victim a mahogany box, which he said was a money duplicating machine. He demonstrated it to the victim by feeding a banknote and a plain sheet of paper into it and then operating its levers and knobs. In due course, the original banknote would emerge from the machine together with a perfect copy. Lustig then sold the box to the victim for a large sum of money, usually around $10,000, although one "customer" paid $46,000. Of course, the box couldn't duplicate anything. Both of the banknotes used in the demo were genuine.

Betrayal

By the 1930s, Lustig was so notorious that a special Secret Service team was set up to deal with him. Their lucky break came with a tip-off that took them to New York. They arrested Lustig as he walked along Broadway on March 10, 1935. In his coat pocket, they found a key that led them to a locker in Times Square subway station. There, they found a set of printing plates and tens of thousands of dollars in counterfeit notes.

Lustig is thought to have produced several million dollars in all. It was the sheer amount of fake money appearing all over the country that attracted the attention of the Secret Service in the first place.

The plates had been made for Lustig by a Nebraskan chemist named Tom Shaw. The tip-off that led to the arrest had come from Lustig's own mistress, Billy May. She betrayed him when she discovered that he was cheating on her with Shaw's partner, Marie.

Lustig was taken to the Federal House of Detention in New York City, but he managed to escape! He was recaptured in Pittsburgh after twenty-seven days on the run. He stood trial in 1935 and was found guilty. The judge handed down a sentence of fifteen years plus another five years for his escape. He was taken to the notorious Alcatraz prison in San Francisco Bay. Twelve years later, he fell ill and was moved to the Medical Center for Federal Prisoners in Springfield, Missouri, where he died of pneumonia on March 11, 1947.

LEAVING BUFFALO

The bright lights of the big city attract young people like moths to a flame. Some of them thrive; others crash and burn. In the 1980s, a young man from Buffalo made his way to New York City in search of excitement.

David Hampton was desperate to get out of Buffalo. The routine of everyday life for most people—attending classes at college, getting a job, and paying for a roof over his head—weren't for him. He expected other people to pay his way and provide for his needs. In 1983, he was hanging around Columbia University, persuading students to let him stay in their dormitories. One night, he visited the famous Studio 54 nightclub in Manhattan, but he was turned away at the door. He came back claiming to be the son of Oscar-winning actor Sidney Poitier. It worked. He was ushered inside with a friend who claimed to be Gregory Peck's son. Later, he described it as a "magic moment."

A few days later, he was still jobless, penniless, and hungry, so he used the same trick again. He went to a restaurant and asked for a table for two—himself and his father, Sidney Poitier, who would be arriving a little later. Of course, Poitier didn't appear, but Hampton still got a free meal. Then he started using the same ruse to find somewhere to stay. While actor Gary Sinise was staying in Melanie Griffith's apartment, he let "David Poitier" sleep on his couch after Hampton gave him a hard-luck story about missing a flight. He also spun a yarn to Connecticut College students that he was casting a film that was to be directed by his father. Hopeful students let him sleep in their dorm.

While Hampton was staying at the college, he acquired an address book containing the names and addresses of influential New Yorkers.

The address book's owner said it was stolen, but Hampton vehemently denied this. He claimed he had been given the book so that he could add his own details and simply forgot to return it.

Its contents were a goldmine for an impostor and scammer like Hampton. When he introduced himself to the movers and shakers he found in the book, some of them were more than happy to help out Sidney Poitier's son by putting him up in their swanky homes. In some cases, he also accepted money and clothes from them. While he was staying at the home of Osborn Elliott, a former editor of *Newsweek* and dean of Columbia University's Graduate School of Journalism, Hampton smuggled a friend into the house during the night. When the man was found in bed with Hampton the next morning, Elliott threw him out.

Hampton was exposed when two of the families he had conned compared notes about recent events. When he realized that he had been found out, he phoned the Elliotts to apologize. Inger Elliott kept him talking while her husband called the police. Officers closed in and arrested him near a pay phone on the Avenue of the Americas in New York. When they checked him out, they found he was wanted for a string of other offenses including petty larceny, grand larceny, resisting arrest, failure to pay for service, illegal entry, and burglary. He agreed to plead guilty to a lesser charge of attempted burglary and received a suspended sentence. He later revealed his attitude toward his victims when he said, "I was the best thing that ever happened to them."

> The extraordinary thing is that none of Hampton's victims bothered to check whether Sidney Poitier actually had a son—he didn't!

Return to the Limelight

He went back to Buffalo for a while, but his wanderlust soon returned. This time he tried his luck on the West Coast. He worked as a housepainter in California for a time. Then he received some surprising news. Playwright John Guare had written a play called *Six Degrees of Separation* that had been inspired by reports of Hampton's story. Hampton returned to New York and hired a celebrity lawyer to sue Guare for $100 million compensation for the unauthorized use of events in his life. He had his day in court but lost. He was later charged with harassing Mr. Guare, but he was acquitted when the case came to court.

Six Degrees of Separation was a huge success. It went on to win the

New York Drama Critics' Circle Award, the Lawrence Olivier Award for Best New Play, and an Obie (Off-Broadway Theater Award). It was also a Pulitzer Prize finalist and received four Tony Award nominations. It was adapted for the big screen, earning Golden Globe and Academy Award nominations for leading actress Stockard Channing.

Hampton announced that he was pursuing an acting career, but old habits die hard. He was reported to have told students at New York University that he, not Guare, had written *Six Degrees of Separation*. The students got fed up with him when he started calling them at all hours looking for a place to stay. He was in trouble again soon afterward when he was arrested for refusing to pay for a taxi. When he failed to turn up for his court appearance, he claimed he had been in the hospital following a road accident. He produced ambulance records to back up his claim, but they were found to have been falsified, leading to a further charge and nineteen months in prison. Even while he was confined to a cell, he couldn't resist trying to scam his previous victims yet again. He called them and told them he was writing his life story, and if they sent him money, he would write about them favorably.

One of his last victims was a man who went out with him one evening in 2001. Hampton was going by the name David Hampton-Montilio. His date for the night went home $1,400 poorer but was later quoted as saying, "It was one of the best dates I ever went on."

David Hampton died on July 18, 2003, at the age of only thirty-nine from AIDS-related complications at Beth Israel Hospital in Manhattan.

THE FRENCH ROCKEFELLER

The Hamptons on Long Island are home to some of the most expensive residences in the United States. In 2000, a young man with a famous name arrived. He was a Rockefeller, a name synonymous with prodigious wealth.

Christopher Rockefeller readily gave advice on investment opportunities, and people willingly handed over large sums of money to him to invest on their behalf. They figured if anyone knew where the best investments were to be found, it would be a Rockefeller.

An artist named Ginés Serrán-Pagán had doubts about Rockefeller. He noted that Rockefeller made his frequent visits to Serrán-Pagán's studio in a Mazda and wondered if a member of the fabulously wealthy Rockefeller family would really be driving a Mazda. He arranged a dinner to investigate the mystery man. Rockefeller gave away very little during the evening, but there was uproar when one of the guests produced a camera and took his photograph. Rockefeller's "aide" rushed around the table to shield his employer and then offered thousands of dollars for the film in the camera. After the dinner, Rockefeller asked Serrán-Pagán for his bank account details so that he could wire money to pay for some of Serrán-Pagán's paintings. Serrán-Pagán, fearing that his bank account might be emptied by "Rockefeller," declined the offer.

Another Hamptonite, Kevin McCrary, had noticed the Mazda too and thought it an odd choice for a supposedly wealthy man. When he checked out the Rockefeller family on the Web—the only person who appears to have thought of doing this—he found that there was indeed a Christopher Rockefeller, but he had died in 1790! Rockefeller had also swindled one of McCrary's friends out of $14,000, and he was keen to get it back. McCrary traced him to the Mill-Garth Country Inn in the nearby town of Amagansett. When the police checked with the Mill-Garth, they found that Rockefeller had left that very day without paying his $8,000 bill. Detectives spotted him leaving a gym in East Hampton and arrested him. When they searched him, they found he was carrying a passport in the name of Fabien Ortuno.

The police fingerprinted him and checked for other offenses in New York. There were none. But they didn't look for outstanding offenses anywhere else. Bail was set at $45,000. He paid up and disappeared again. It was only when the story of the bogus Rockefeller was picked up by the press and made headlines that more offenses in Los Angeles came to light.

The Man of Many Names

George Mueller, chief investigator of the Los Angeles District Attorney's office, already knew the truth about Rockefeller—he was a con man who'd assumed at least a dozen names in the past. He'd been a race-car driver, a boxer, and a venture capitalist. He was Christopher De Laurentiis, the nephew of Dino De Laurentiis, when he wanted to con people in the movie business. He was Christopher de la Renta, the nephew of Oscar de la Renta, when he wanted to con people in the fashion business. At other times he was also known as Prince Galatzine Christo, Fabien Ortuno, Christopher Lloyd, and Christopher Reyes. Reyes was the maiden name of his Playboy model wife, Pia Reyes. But his real name was Christophe Rocancourt.

> Masquerading as so many versions of Christopher, there is no doubt this impostor was attached to the truth. It could prove to be his downfall.

Mueller first became aware of Rocancourt in 1997 as a result of complaints from people he'd swindled. A businesswoman invested $200,000 in a fashion boutique he was planning to open. He offered another woman a $4.2 million loan she needed for a business deal in return for a stake in the business and an up-front "commission" of $100,000. She paid. A film extra gave him $15,000 to invest on the promise of big returns. A French pop singer is thought to have lost $250,000 to him. When Rocancourt finally disappeared from Los Angeles, he left the Regent Beverly Wilshire Hotel with unpaid bills amounting to thousands of dollars.

Wherever he went, he was accompanied by a bodyguard named Benny, but the two men eventually fell out. While Benny was staying in an apartment provided by Rocancourt, he discovered pistols, rifles, and hand grenades hidden there and decided it was time to get well away from Rocancourt. He went to the police and told them everything he knew about the cons and the weapons. He also claimed that Rocancourt had bribed officials to obtain illegal passports. The passport case was easier to prosecute than scams involving businesspeople who were reluctant to appear in court, so that's what investigators went after.

Based on what Benny said, Mueller obtained a search warrant for Rocancourt's hotel suite in May 1997, but Rocancourt vanished just before he could execute the warrant. In the abandoned suite, Mueller found guns, money, plans for moneymaking schemes, and illegal passports. Rocancourt had fled to Asia, where he spent a month enjoying the best hotels in Hong Kong, Jakarta, Macao, and Bangkok. Then, even though he knew he was being investigated, he returned to Los Angeles. On the way, he parted the owner of a photocopying shop in Rome from $35,000. In Hollywood, he befriended actor Mickey Rourke and even moved in with him over the winter of 1997–8. Although still married to Pia, his constant companion at this time was another Playboy model and actress, Rhonda Rydell.

Shots Fired

In March 1998, while Rocancourt was partying at a Hollywood nightclub, a man confronted him and threatened to kill him. Clubbers stepped between the two to prevent a fight. The next day, Rocancourt ran into a sheriff's office and claimed he'd been shot at by the same man who had threatened him the night before. Rocancourt's Hummer, which was once owned by the late Princess Diana's partner, Dodi Fayed, was found abandoned at a road intersection. When police examined the vehicle, they found bullet holes, but all of them had been made by a gun fired from inside it. The gun was identified as a Glock pistol Rocancourt didn't have a license for. Then when the police ran a routine check on him, they found he was wanted for passport fraud too. His problems mounted when Rydell and Pia both arrived at the sheriff's office and Rydell discovered that Pia was his wife.

He posted bail and was released, but investigators hired by the French pop singer he'd scammed were on his trail now too. They followed him everywhere and watched his movements, but he managed to lose them and jump bail. He'd moved on to his next hunting ground—the Hamptons—and he had become Christopher Rockefeller.

After his exploits in the Hamptons, he popped up in Vancouver,

Canada, in April 2001. He tricked an elderly couple out of more than $100,000 in a real estate scam. It's said that the Mounties always get their man, and they got Rocancourt. They arrested him for fraud, along with his wife. She claimed to know nothing about any of his criminal activities. He pleaded guilty to scamming the Canadian couple and was sentenced to time already served (fourteen months) plus one day, ordered to return to the victims the money and property found on him when he was arrested ($16,000 cash, a Rolex watch, and a laptop computer), and ordered to pay $112,000 to his victims in restitution. He also agreed to return to the United States, where he pleaded guilty to the gun charges, bribing officials to obtain illegal passports, and fraud charges in the Hamptons. He was sentenced to five years in prison, fined $9 million, and ordered to pay back $1.2 million to his victims. While he was in prison, he wrote his autobiography.

In an interview, he claimed to have made $40 million from his various schemes. He dislikes the term "con man" and, bizarrely, claims that he never steals. He seems to think of himself as no more than a persuasive actor to whom people willingly give money.

As part of a plea deal, he agreed to leave the country at the end of his sentence. In 2006, he returned to France, where he made his living from books, interviews, photographs, and even a clothing line. He also anchored a series of television programs in France. He left his wife and had a relationship with a former Miss France, Sonia Rolland. They had a daughter, but he left her too.

In 2008, he turned up at the Cannes Film Festival with fashion model Naomi Campbell to publicize his debut as an actor with Campbell in a film called *Bad Love*. His role? An impostor who has an affair with a movie star played by Campbell. The director, Catherine Breillat, accused Rocancourt of swindling her out of about 700,000 euros while she was ill. He was subsequently dropped from the film. She wrote a book about her encounter with Rocancourt, called *Abus de Faiblesse* (*An Abuse of Weakness*), which has been adapted as a film of the same name.

What's next for Rocancourt? He knows that his face is probably too well known for a return to his old ways. But after attending a ceremony where he rubbed shoulders with guests that included former French President Nicolas Sarkozy, he hinted that he might try politics next!

A REAL MOLL FLANDERS

Daniel Defoe's 1721 novel, *Moll Flanders*, tells the story of a woman who pretends to be a wealthy widow to attract wealthy men. But as usual, real life is even more extreme. Decades earlier, a very determined fraudster had "done a Moll" many times over. But unlike Defoe's heroine, she paid a terrible price for it.

Mary Carleton arrived in this world in 1642, born Mary Moders in Canterbury, Kent, in the southeast of England. Little is known about her early life until she married an apprentice shoemaker, Thomas Stedman. She bore him two children, but they both died in infancy. She was unhappy living in poverty with Stedman, so she left him and moved to the port city of Dover in the hope of a better life. There, she married a more promising prospect, a surgeon, but she was still married to Stedman. This led to her first appearance in court for bigamy. Stedman was so poor that he couldn't afford to travel to Maidstone for the trial, so the case was dismissed for lack of evidence.

Soon after her release, she traveled to Cologne, France, where she worked in a brothel, paying particular attention to wealthy clients. One especially persistent suitor gave her expensive jewelry and large sums of money to tempt her into marriage. She milked him for all she could get and finally agreed to marry him. However, just before the ceremony, she packed her bags with everything worth stealing and returned to London.

She was now passing herself off as a German noblewoman, the daughter of Lord Henry von Wolway. And she married for a third time. When her third husband, John Carleton, learned of her other two marriages from an anonymous tip-off, he had her arrested and taken to the infamous Newgate Prison in London. She was tried for polygamy at the Old Bailey, the criminal court that still stands on the same site today. Once again, she managed to escape conviction when neither Stedman nor her second husband could be persuaded to appear in court and give evidence against her.

Mary Carleton was quite inventive as a con artist. She fabricated, or had someone else fabricate, letters from her nonexistent rich family and "carelessly" left them where her landlady would find them. When the landlady read them, they appeared to confirm Carleton's status and wealth. The landlady's greed got the better of her, and she encouraged a relationship between Carleton and her nephew. Carleton let it be known that her brother had died and she had inherited his estate, but her father was determined she should marry a man she detested. Her lover took her into his home to protect her, but—you guessed it—when she got into his home, she soon disappeared with all his money and valuables.

Next, she took to the stage, acting in a play called *The German Princess* about her own scandalous life. Her performances won her new admirers. The famous diarist, Samuel Pepys, was said to be a fan. Another fan offered to cover all of her living expenses if she would move in with him. It was too good an offer to refuse. Predictably, once she had access to the poor sap's money and valuables, she left him.

Exile and Return

Carleton's criminal activities were almost brought to an end when she was arrested for stealing a silver tankard from an inn in Covent Garden, London. This time, she was found guilty and sentenced to death, but the sentence was later commuted to transportation to Jamaica. Even this didn't stop her! Within two years, she was back in England and up to her old tricks again. In her usual role as a rich heiress, she snared an apothecary, married him, and relieved him of all his worldly goods. She is said to have stolen 300 pounds from him, a fortune in the seventeenth century. She fled to a boarding house, where she hatched a plot with the maid. Carleton took the landlady and the only other lodger, a watchmaker, to see a play. While they were out, the maid smashed every lock in the house and stole everything of value. Carleton gave her guests the slip and met the maid to divide the proceeds of their criminal enterprise.

She was arrested for the last time through sheer bad luck. When a brewer in Southwark, south London, was robbed, he asked a keeper (jailer) at the Marshalsea, a prison on the south bank of the River Thames, for help. They thought they knew who the culprit might be, so they went looking for him in nearby boarding houses. While they were searching one house, they became suspicious of a woman they found there. It was Carleton. They took her away with them. The law required them to put her before a court, so a month later, in January 1673, she was in the dock at the Old Bailey again, charged with returning from transportation without permission. This was a very serious offense, akin to breaking out of jail. She admitted the charge and was found guilty. Fearing that she would be sentenced to death, she "pleaded her belly," claiming to be in the late stages of pregnancy.

Matrons were called to examine Carleton, but they reported that no pregnancy could be detected. As she feared, she was indeed sentenced to death. While she was waiting for the sentence to be carried out, shackled in Newgate Prison, she received a steady stream of curious visitors keen to see the notorious polygamist.

On January 22, 1673, her shackles were removed for the last time. She pinned a picture of John Carleton to her sleeve. She was led out of the prison to a cart that bore her through the streets to Tyburn, where a crowd had gathered to watch her die. She told them she had been a vain woman and prayed to God to forgive her. Then the record in the Newgate Calendar, an official record of executions, simply reports that "she was turned off." An hour later, her body was cut down and placed in a cheap coffin, which was buried in the nearby St. Martin's churchyard.

"Pleading the belly" was a common way for women to avoid the death penalty in those days. In principle, their appointment with an executioner was merely postponed until the first hanging date after the child's delivery, but in practice women who pleaded their belly stood a good chance of being pardoned or transported instead.

IAN GRAHAM

THE CAZIQUE OF POYAIS

In the early 1800s, Britons were tempted by the opportunity to start a new life in South America. It came at a price, of course, and hundreds of people were prepared to pay to get their hands on a new life of wealth. But who exactly was the mysterious "Cazique" offering them the chance of a lifetime?

In 1820, a man calling himself the Cazique of Poyais arrived in London. The Cazique told everyone about his country, a land called Poyais on the Bay of Honduras. The government and civil service were based in the country's capital, St.

A *cazique* was a chief or tribal leader in the Americas.

Joseph. It was a young country, and now settlers were needed to farm the land, build new towns, and develop the country's gold and silver mines. British merchants were keen to invest in this new unknown country and trade with it.

On October 23, 1822, the Cazique offered 2,000 bonds for sale at £100 each. They all sold, raising £200,000, which was a lot of money in 1822. For people who couldn't afford £100, he offered parcels of land for a few shillings an acre. Some people sank their life savings into Poyais. The Cazique also printed his own currency and urged investors and settlers to exchange their own money for it. By 1823, he was a multimillionaire.

Two ships, the *Honduras Packet* and the *Kennersley Castle*, were chartered to take more than two hundred settlers to their new life in Poyais. When they arrived, eager to visit the grand buildings in the capital and inspect their land, they found a wasteland. They searched in vain for a port to land at. When they came ashore, all they found was a handful of derelict shacks left over from an earlier attempt to colonize the land, surrounded by wild snake-infested jungle. There were no gold and silver mines, no capital city, and no fertile land to farm. In short, there was no such place as Poyais. Although the settlers were eventually rescued and taken to British Honduras, many of them died from tropical diseases and the hardship of a long sea voyage. Only fifty got back to Britain alive. They brought the story of Poyais back with them. Newspapers published the whole sorry saga. The Poyaisan bonds became worthless overnight. All the settlers and investors lost their money.

The Cazique of Poyais was actually a Scottish soldier, Gregor MacGregor. He had fought in Portugal during the Peninsular War. In 1810, he left the army and returned to Scotland. Soon afterward, he was living in London and calling himself *Sir* Gregor MacGregor. When his wife died, he sold up and sailed for South America, where he joined the Venezuelan army with the rank of colonel. He saw action almost immediately and was promoted to brigadier-general. When the army's commander was captured by royalist forces, he fled to Curaçao, now with a new wife, and then to New Granada (Colombia today), where he joined liberation forces. Local soldiers and officials were not impressed with him. He gained a reputation as a bluffer and braggart. When the coastal city of Cartagena de Indias was besieged in 1815, MacGregor helped to organize a mass escape by sea to Jamaica. The next year, he was serving under Simon Bolívar, taking part in an invasion of Venezuela.

When he was exposed as an impostor and fraudster in Britain, he fled to Paris, where he tried the same scam again. When the French authorities started receiving requests for passports to travel to a country that didn't exist, they seized the ship being prepared to take French settlers to Poyais. MacGregor went into hiding, but he was eventually found and arrested. He was put on trial, but amazingly he was acquitted. He

In 1817, MacGregor engineered a clever military victory. He led a small force to take Amelia Island, off the coast of Florida, but he had spread rumors that a 1,000-strong force was on the way. When his attack began, the small Spanish garrison fled, thinking they were facing overwhelming odds. MacGregor took control of the island, formed a government, and had a new constitution written. This seems to have been when he formed his plan to create the fictional land of Poyais. He claimed that he had been given the land on the Mosquito Coast by a local chief, King George Frederic Augustus I of the Mosquito Shore and Nation.

returned to London in 1826 and tried the same scam again and again until 1837. When his second wife died, he returned to Venezuela, where he received a military pension until his death in 1845.

THE CAPTAIN FROM KÖPENICK

On October 16, 1906, a Prussian army officer arrived in a town near Berlin with a group of soldiers. He took over the town hall, raided the treasury, and then…disappeared! Everyone wondered what on earth had happened and who the Prussian officer was.

Ten days after the incident, a career criminal named Friedrich Wilhelm Voigt was arrested. His downfall was his distinctive appearance—broken nose, bandy legs, and thick gray mustache with a shaved chin.

Voigt was born in Tilsit in East Prussia (Sovetsk in Russia today) on February 13, 1849. His criminal activities began in his early teens, when he was accused of stealing from his classmates at school and then arrested for vagrancy. As a result, he was expelled from school. But his first spell in prison hadn't deterred him from a life of crime. Between the ages of fifteen and forty-two, he received prison sentences totaling more than twenty-five years for a series of thefts and forgery offenses. He was finally released from prison in February 1906. He moved from place to place, picking up whatever work he could, and eventually found a steady job as a shoemaker in a factory in the northern port of Wismar.

It was essential for him to have a passport to prove his identity and qualify for the residence permit he needed in order to keep his job. The rule was no passport, no job, no home. Voigt, intending to go straight and stay out of trouble, registered with the city officials, paid his taxes, and applied to his home city, Tilsit, for a passport. However, before he could get it, the authorities expelled him from the state because he was considered undesirable with his criminal record. He was forced out of his job and had to leave Wismar. He drifted from job to job, finally ending up living with his sister in Rixdorf on the outskirts of Berlin.

When the authorities there found out about him, he was ordered out of Berlin too. He secretly stayed in the city, working illegally. He was the lowest of the low in society. And then he hatched a new plan.

He bought parts of an army officer's uniform from secondhand clothes shops until he had a complete uniform. Then, wearing the uniform, he stopped a group of soldiers on their way back to barracks and another group at a firing range. He must have played his part well, because they accepted his authority without question. He explained that he hadn't had time to arrange transport, so he took them to Köpenick by train. When they reached the town hall, he ordered the soldiers to fix bayonets and guard the building's exits. When the local police arrived to find out what was going on, he ordered them to clear the square outside. He also closed down the post office so that no one could telephone or telegraph the outside world about what was happening. Then he had the town's mayor and treasurer arrested on suspicion of false accounting. He "confiscated" 3,557 marks of the town's funds and signed for them in the name of his last prison governor. He then sent the mayor and treasurer to a guardhouse in Berlin in two carriages he commandeered. He left the soldiers in control of the town hall and vanished.

The authorities quickly realized what had happened, but they had no idea who was responsible. Everyone who had seen the mysterious "captain" was questioned. It quickly became apparent that he was an impostor. He was too old to be an army captain, and small details of the uniform were not correct. A reward was offered for his capture, and posters with his description were plastered all over the town. Someone Voigt had shared a prison cell with suspected him and told the police. His former employer gave the police a photograph of him. When witnesses saw it, they recognized him as the "captain." He was arrested a few days later.

Voigt stood trial and was found guilty. He was sentenced to four years in prison. However, public opinion was with him. While he was in prison awaiting trial, he received gifts of flowers, chocolate, and money

The Kaiser was said to have found the whole episode amusing, so much so that he pardoned Voigt after two years. Voigt had spent more than twenty-nine of his fifty-nine years in prison.

from supporters. People liked the fact that he had fooled the stuffy and authoritarian officials.

When Voigt was released, he quickly became a celebrity. He made recordings, gave speeches, acted onstage, and sold autographs. He traveled to other countries to make appearances. In 1909, his autobiography was published. In it, he said his reason for raiding the town hall in Köpenick was to get the passport he needed. However, if that was indeed the reason, he picked his target badly, because Köpenick town hall didn't issue passports.

He moved to Luxembourg, where he finally got his passport in 1910. He lost all his money during World War I and died in poverty in 1922.

Interestingly, when the lease on Voigt's grave ran out in 1942, it was paid for by an anonymous donor until 1974, and a German circus cared for the grave.

His body was due to be exhumed in 1974, but there was such an outcry that the city of Luxembourg finally allowed his body to stay in the grave indefinitely.

Voigt's exploit is remembered today by a statue of the "captain" on the steps of Köpenick town hall. A play and several films have been made about the affair too.

FRAUD ALERT: TRUST ME, I'M A DOCTOR!

Bogus doctors are a continual problem for health authorities and regulators. The lure of the white coat and the gratitude of trusting patients are too much of a temptation for some people. Despite the best efforts of medical authorities, bogus doctors keep getting through. As we saw earlier, in the 1950s, the serial impostor Ferdinand Demara managed to pass himself off as a navy surgeon and even carried out surgery on wounded soldiers with no more than a medical textbook to guide him.

Fortunately, not all bogus doctors end up treating patients. Many of them invent medical qualifications and experience to secure jobs in management. A study at Bath University, England, in the 1990s identified more than one hundred bogus doctors in Britain.

- About two-thirds of them used their fraudulent qualifications for reasons other than practicing medicine.
- Of the others, some were exposed when they made medical mistakes, and others were revealed by investigations unrelated to medicine—immigration checks, for example.

If you thought bogus doctors must be a thing of the past, you'd be wrong. In just one month in 2012, eight fake doctors were arrested in Mumbai, India. Here are the strange cases of a few others:

- In Sydney, Australia, in 2008, Vitomir Zepinic was found guilty of six counts of falsely claiming to be a doctor. Undeterred, the next year he was working as a senior lecturer in psychiatry at a prestigious teaching hospital in London, England—Barts and the London School of Medicine and Dentistry. It was five months before the hospital found out about his conviction and suspended him. In 2010, he gave evidence in a war crimes trial in The Hague, still claiming to be a doctor.

- In 2010, Alice Springs Hospital in Australia discovered that one of its doctors had no medical qualifications. Balaji Varatharaju, who is thought to have treated more than four hundred patients, had studied medicine at the University of Adelaide but didn't finish his degree. He was jailed for fourteen months.

- In South Africa in 2012, a twenty-seven-year-old former sex worker managed to convince two hospitals in Durban that he was a cardiologist and cancer specialist. He took large sums of money from businesses in return for the promise of contracts with the hospitals. He worked for several months before he was found out. He had created his medical alter ego by buying a stethoscope and doctor's uniform and downloading the documents he needed from the Web. He claimed he'd impersonated a doctor to earn money to pay for expensive medications that he needed. However, a Durban court didn't believe him. He was sentenced to six years in prison, suspended for three years.

- In December 2012, a bogus doctor in Britain was ordered by a court to repay more than a quarter of a million pounds he earned while working for the National Health Service. Conrad de Souza's fraud was discovered when he was caught falsifying a DNA test to avoid having to pay maintenance costs for his lover's child. Checks into his past and credentials revealed that he had attended medical school in the 1980s but didn't graduate. It didn't stop him from claiming to be a qualified doctor and working in a clinical guidance role, although not treating patients, for ten years. He did it by stealing the qualifications and doctor's registration number of a genuine doctor with a very similar name. He was sentenced to two years in prison and later ordered to pay back money he had obtained fraudulently.

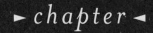

►chapter◄

6

IMITATION INDIANS

The American Indian is an attractive figure to many people—the proud native in tune with nature, the product of a long line of indigenous people with customs that stretch back into prehistory. Most people were satisfied to admire Native Americans, but a few individuals went further. They changed their identity to masquerade as Indians.

In some cases, people adopted a fake Indian identity to find work in the movie industry and television at a time when westerns were popular in the cinema and on the small screen too. They rubbed shoulders with genuine Indians who worked as actors, with the constant risk of exposure as fakes. The Native American was also a popular character in another form of entertainment—professional wrestling. Indian wrestlers would enter the arena in full feathered war bonnets and "go on the warpath," whooping a tribal chant if their opponents riled them. Audiences loved the spectacle. Wrestlers including Tatanka and Billy Two Rivers were genuine Indians, but others were not. One of the best known make-believe Indian wrestlers was Chief Jay Strongbow, who died in 2012 at the age of eighty-three. He was billed as a full-blooded Indian from Pawhuska, Oklahoma, but in fact he was Italian-American

Joe Scarpa from Philadelphia. During a forty-year career in the ring, he won several championship titles.

Attitudes toward Native Americans have changed over the years. The Native American is rightly treated with more respect today than in past times. However, fake Indians still pop up from time to time. Assuming a false Indian heritage associates an impostor with both the tragedy of Native American history and the respect accorded to Native Americans today. It can also give an impostor's work a higher profile, make it more attractive commercially, or imbue it with a greater sense of authenticity than it might otherwise warrant. These cultural impostors cause great offense to Native Americans because they misrepresent genuine native people and their descendants, tribes, history, and culture. And this matters, because most people will live their whole lives without ever meeting a genuine Native American. Their scant knowledge of Native American culture and history comes from the few voices that project the image of the Native American to the general public. And if that image is false, we all get a raw deal, Native American and audience alike.

LONG LANCE

Chief Buffalo Child Long Lance was the son of a Blackfoot Indian chief. At least, that's what he told everyone. His origins turned out to be rather different, but was he an impostor?

In the early hours of March 20, 1932, Anita Baldwin was alarmed to hear the loud report of a gunshot somewhere inside her palatial Californian mansion, Anoakia. She woke her watchman, Sergeant Joseph Hannah, who searched the house. In the library, he found the dead body of Chief Buffalo Child Long Lance. He had shot himself in the head. The pistol was still in his hand. It was a dramatic end to an eventful life.

Long Lance had become a celebrity after the publication of his autobiography in 1928. In it, he wrote about his birth in Montana in the closing years of the nineteenth century. His stirring firsthand account of

Tribes have strict rules about who can claim to be members, and they keep detailed records, or tribal rolls, to prove entitlement to membership, so attempting to be a fake Native American is a very difficult stunt to pull off!

a Plains Indian received almost universal praise, and the publicity made Long Lance famous. He became a favorite guest at high-society parties, where the men in tuxedos and women in elegant gowns couldn't get enough of his Indian stories. He was a star on the lecture circuit too. He was paid as much for one speaking engagement as most Americans earned in a month. Women were attracted to him in a big way. He danced with Rudolf Valentino's widow, Natacha Rambova. He dated actresses and singers and became acquainted with European royalty.

Long Lance began to use his public profile to speak out about the plight of Native Americans. Many of them endured hunger, poor health, and wretched living conditions. Long Lance was one of the first prominent figures to call for law reform and a reorganization of the Indian Bureau to improve the lot of the North American Indian.

A Question of Identity

When Long Lance wrote his next book, the publisher sent a copy of the manuscript to the Bureau of Indian Affairs to get their response. Their reply was a bombshell. The Bureau said the book was a work of fiction. They had investigated Long Lance and found that his claim to be a full-blooded Indian chief was false. They said he had been given the honorary title of chief and named Buffalo Child at a school reunion on the Blood Reserve in Canada in 1922. Beyond this, they didn't know who he was or where he came from.

Meanwhile, Long Lance had been hired to play the part of an Indian in a film, *The Silent Enemy*, being made in Canada. It was a worrying time for him. He faced exposure as an impostor by any of the genuine Indians working on the film, and news of the Indian Bureau's investigation had reached him. The pressure made him uncharacteristically short-tempered. In an extraordinary coincidence, he had a run-in with one of the local Canadian Ojibwa Indians, who turned out to be the daughter of Grey Owl, who was himself later exposed as a fake. One of the other actors, Yellow Robe, a genuine Sioux chief, became increasingly suspicious of Long Lance. He noticed mistakes in Long Lance's sign language and native dances, and his genial, outgoing personality seemed to have more in common with the white man than a Plains Indian. When filming finished, Long Lance returned to New York. He had survived making the film without being exposed, and he'd heard no more about the Indian Bureau's investigation. He thought he was in the clear.

In 1929, he was invited to join the Explorers Club in New York. It was a great honor—he was the first Native American member—but it also brought him to the attention of club members who were experts in American culture and history. One of them was Dr. Clark Wissler, an anthropologist who specialized in Native American culture. When Wissler read Long Lance's autobiography, he knew immediately from small inconsistencies that its author was a fake.

Finding Sylvester

Long Lance was finally challenged directly about his identity at the beginning of 1930. A lawyer acting for the company that made *The Silent Enemy* had learned of Yellow Robe's suspicions. Long Lance's identity and heritage mattered to the film company because he featured prominently in the film's publicity campaign, which described him as a full-blooded Indian. When Long Lance went to see the lawyer, he was greeted with, "Hello Sylvester."

The lawyer's inquiries had revealed that Long Lance's real name was Sylvester Long, but Long Lance claimed he had no idea who Sylvester Long was and insisted that he *was* Indian. He said he had worked in Wild West shows and circuses as a boy until he was injured in an accident. He was taken in by a Cherokee family, who nursed him back to health and sent him to school. However, when a former teacher at the school was contacted, he said he knew of no Cherokee connection. He said Long Lance's real name was Sylvester Long and he was African American, born

Long Lance was given an honorary title because he had spent time on the Blood Reserve as a journalist the previous year researching a newspaper article about the Indians. He'd told them he was a Cherokee from Oklahoma. To show their gratitude for the article he wrote, they invited him back to speak at the school reunion and made him an honorary chief.

in North Carolina. His father was a school janitor.

The revelation was explosive at a time when racial segregation was the norm in the United States. When rumors about Long Lance's identity began to circulate, the possibility that he might be African American was poison in race-obsessed times.

Many of his former society friends abandoned him. One of the few people who stood by him was Yellow Robe, the Sioux chief who had helped to expose him. When Yellow Robe was too ill to do publicity work for *The Silent Enemy*, he named Long Lance as his replacement. Despite their concerns, the filmmakers sent him on the publicity tour anyway. He mixed with the biggest film stars of the day in Hollywood.

While he was away, the filmmakers' lawyer sent an investigator to North Carolina to look into Sylvester Long's past. He found Long's parents. They told him they were Cherokee. Further inquiries revealed that Long had white, Cherokee, and Croatan ancestors. The Croatan Indians were known to have intermarried with African Americans. However, the investigator reported back that Sylvester Long's heritage was white and Indian. The filmmakers and their lawyer didn't care which tribe he belonged to or why he might have lied about his origins, as long as he was Indian. Long Lance was off the hook.

Real Life

It was now clear that his early life was not as he had described it in his autobiography. He claimed to have been born to a Blackfoot chief in a teepee in Montana. In fact, Sylvester Clark Long was born in Winston-Salem, North Carolina. Because of their mixed race background, the Longs were classified as "colored." Sylvester left school at thirteen and worked for several circuses and Wild West shows. He mixed with the

Indian performers and was often mistaken for an Indian himself. He picked up just enough bits and pieces of Cherokee language and customs to secure a place at the Carlisle Indian School in Pennsylvania in 1909. He saw it as his chance to get out of North Carolina and the second-class life mapped out for him there.

He started writing about Indian issues for the school newspaper and magazine. He soaked up every bit of Indian history and culture he could from his fellow students and began to incorporate some of the details into his own life story.

After an unsuccessful time at college and a brief military career with the Canadian Army in Europe during World War I, Long Lance was discharged in 1919 and headed back to Canada, settling in Alberta. He took a job as a reporter on Calgary's *Herald* newspaper. In an article introducing himself to the paper's readers, he spun a very fanciful yarn about his past. He changed his birthplace to Oklahoma, promoted himself to captain, and said he had attended West Point and served in Italy during the war. He also said he had won the Croix de Guerre, a French military decoration awarded for heroism. None of it was true, but no one checked. Long's press pass opened doors to all parts of Calgary society.

Indian Writings

Most of his work was in Calgary, but in May 1921, he was sent east to research a story about the Blackfoot Indian Reserve. His editor liked the article so much

> At one event, Long Lance took part in a traditional tribal dance with an Indian actor named Iron Eyes Cody, who was himself later exposed as a fake.

that he sent Long to write about other tribes, including the Sarcee and Blood Indians. All the time, he was learning more and more about the Indian way of life. He was particularly impressed with the Blood Indians, who were more independent than the others and didn't rely on government support. It was his article about the Bloods that resulted in his invitation to return, when he was given his Blackfoot name, Buffalo Child.

Soon he was calling himself Chief Buffalo Child Long Lance. He was

Long had made a great success of his work as a reporter, but in 1922, he was fired after a practical joke backfired badly. Bored with covering endless tedious meetings at City Hall, he tried to spice things up by throwing a fake bomb in among terrified officials! As a result, he left Calgary for Vancouver, where he worked as a freelance reporter writing about Canada's Indian tribes.

becoming increasingly aware of the difficulties and injustices faced by the Indians. They had few rights, and those they had were often abused.

At this time, he decided that a major change in identity was called for. As a "civilized" Cherokee, the wider public wasn't interested in him. But if he became a Blood Indian, born on the Plains, he would have a more exotic and interesting story to tell. The Bloods were a Blackfoot tribe. Long Lance was more "marketable" as a Blood or a Blackfoot. The Canadian Pacific railroad company employed him to represent them, and in 1925, he went on a very successful speaking tour of the United States. His appearances drew large crowds.

One of his stories, published in *Cosmopolitan* in 1927, caused a sensation. In it, he claimed that Custer's Last Stand never happened. He said Custer had committed suicide at the end of the battle. Although historians, frontiersmen, and Custer's widow ridiculed the story, the publicity didn't seem to do Long Lance any harm. In fact, no matter how much fiction he included in his articles and talks, he never seemed to be found out.

Return to Europe

In 1930, following the success of his autobiography and his well-received debut as a movie actor, he headed for Long Island, where

It was *Cosmopolitan*'s book publishing division that suggested Long Lance should write a book about his life as a Plains Indian. It became the autobiography *Long Lance*, which propelled him to celebrity and stardom.

he learned to fly. And he loved it. He was soon flying stunts and parachuting. Then, out of the blue, he received an unexpected job offer. While he was in Hollywood, he had met Anita Baldwin, the daughter of wealthy businessman and race-horse breeder Lucky Baldwin. She was fascinated by Indian history and culture. Long Lance clearly made an impression on her, because she kept in touch with him. Now, she was offering him the job of her secretary-bodyguard on a trip she was planning to make to Europe in 1931. He accepted.

In the early 1930s, parts of Europe were in economic melt-down. Long Lance witnessed the terrible situation in Germany and wondered how it would all end. While he was in Europe, he seems to have started behaving rather bizarrely. His employer, Anita Baldwin, later claimed that he had tried to commit suicide. He was also drinking heavily and threatened to kill another of Baldwin's traveling companions.

Unlike Long Lance's first visit to Europe as a soldier during World War I, this time he needed a passport. He lied on his application, giving his birthplace as Sweetgrass, Montana, and an incorrect birth date of December 1, 1896. He also invented a fictitious father named Pitah, who he claimed had died in Sweetgrass in 1900, whereas his real father, Joe, was still alive. Despite all the false information, the application went through unchallenged, and Long Lance received his passport.

After his return to the United States, he seemed to be back on an even keel, but during a stay in California, he started drinking again. He had been visiting Anita Baldwin, who had placed her extensive library at his disposal for research, but she became increasingly disturbed by his behavior. When he arrived on the evening of March 19, 1932, he had been drinking and, unbeknownst to Baldwin, he was carrying a gun. He was unusually quiet, so Baldwin left him in the library and went to bed. Then she heard the gunshot.

It's tempting to think that impostors must be either mad or bad, but Long Lance was neither. He was a man who merely found a way of surviving and prospering in a world that would otherwise have excluded him, while also bringing the plight of North American Indians to a wider audience.

IAN GRAHAM

HE WHO FLIES BY NIGHT

In 1937, the future Queen Elizabeth II was entranced by a special visitor to Buckingham Palace. The eleven-year-old princess listened intently to the Canadian Indian, resplendent in buckskins. However, after his death, his true origins turned out to be a lot closer to Buckingham Palace than the Canadian wilderness.

The man was known as Grey Owl. He was coming to the end of his second tour of Britain, giving lectures about his log cabin life in the Canadian wilderness. He was tired after delivering more than one hundred talks in three months. He faced another grueling tour when he returned to North America. Soon after he was finally able to retreat to his remote home, he fell ill with pneumonia. In the hospital, he drifted into a coma and never regained consciousness. He died on April 13, 1938. Within hours of his death, the truth about Grey Owl began to emerge.

He claimed to be the son of an Apache mother and a Scottish father, born soon after his parents returned to the United States after taking part in Buffalo Bill's Wild West Show that toured England in 1887. He started working as a wilderness guide in Western Canada while still in his teens and then became a fur trapper in Ontario. He made a good living as a trapper until 1926. It was such a poor year that he went hunting the following spring, something he wouldn't normally have done because it risked killing newborn animals. His worst fears were realized when he found that one of his traps was missing and beaver kittens were hiding nearby. If the mother had died in the missing trap, the kittens stood little chance of survival. After a roasting from his partner, a Mohawk-Iroquois woman named Anahareo (also known as Pony), he adopted the beavers, christened McGinnis and McGinty. Rearing them put paid to his appetite for trapping.

He moved to a remote lake, where he could raise a colony of beavers well away from trappers. He also started writing about the beavers to pass the time. He sent some of his work to a most unlikely magazine— *Country Life*—a British magazine for landowners and other well-to-do country folk. It was an odd choice, but they loved his writing and started publishing his work in 1929.

When he returned to the beaver colony from one trip, he was horrified to be presented with a well-meaning gift from an old friend who wanted to help with his money problems. It was the skins of his beavers! McGinnis and McGinty had been spared, but they too disappeared soon afterward. He acquired a new beaver, christened Jelly Roll, and started again.

From Trapper to Conservationist

Grey Owl's writings had aroused interest closer to home. He was invited to give lectures in Canada. He found the experience of standing in front of an audience terrifying, but his appearances were a great success.

The National Parks Service in Canada began to realize that Grey Owl was a valuable asset who could help them develop tourism. They produced a film about his beaver colony called *The Beaver People*. They also helped him to set up a beaver sanctuary at Lake Ajawaan in Prince Albert National Park in Saskatchewan. He continued writing too. By 1932, he and Anahareo had a daughter, Shirley Dawn.

When Anahareo left to go gold prospecting, Grey Owl agreed to a lecture tour in Europe. It was a great success, but it exhausted him. On his return, there was little time to relax. He wrote another book, *Tales of an Empty Cabin*, which turned out to be his last book, and made another film. Then in 1937, he agreed to another tour of Britain that ended with his personal appearance before the King, Queen, and two princesses at Buckingham Palace.

Exposing the Past

Just after his death, newspaper stories began to question his origins. A local paper, the *North Bay Nugget*, knew about his real past and had been sitting on the story for at least two years. Once the *Nugget* published its story, the news spread quickly. Grey Owl's real name was Archibald Stansfield Belaney. He was born near Hastings,

England, on September 18, 1888. Neither of his parents had any Native American blood. They emigrated from England, moving to the United States and leaving Archie behind in the care of his grandmother and her daughters, Archie's aunts Carry and Ada. He was fascinated by the Wild West and Native Americans from his childhood. He played as an Indian in nearby woods. In 1906, at the age of only seventeen, he left for Canada to study agriculture in Toronto, but he soon moved to Northern Ontario to work as a fur trapper and wilderness guide.

There, he met an Ojibwa woman named Angele Egwuna. They were married on August 23, 1910. Archie and Angele had a daughter, but he abandoned them. This is when he invented a bogus Apache parentage and claimed to have emigrated from the United States to join the Ojibwa tribe.

During World War I, he enlisted in the army and was posted to France. In 1916, he was wounded twice and affected by mustard gas. He was sent back to Canada in 1917 and discharged from the army with a pension as a result of his wounds. He had a difficult time when he returned to his remote home, but he was helped by the Ojibwa Indians, who took him in and cared for him. He learned the ways of the tribe and was eventually officially adopted by it. The tribe gave him the Ojibwa name Wa-sha-quon-asin (He Who Flies by Night, or Grey Owl).

Although Grey Owl turned out to be an impostor, he had a genuine concern for nature and wildlife conservation decades before the modern environmental movement began. His lectures, books, and films entertained and influenced countless people. In 1999, Richard Attenborough made a film called *Grey Owl* about his life, starring the former James Bond actor Pierce Brosnan. The

Huge numbers of people came to hear the Canadian Indian talk about life in the wilderness and the importance of preserving wild places. His writing and lectures were now bringing in a regular income that enabled him to put trapping behind him for good. He wrote his first book, *The Men of the Last Frontier*, published in 1931.

teenage Attenborough and his brother, David, had attended one of Grey Owl's lectures in 1936 and were deeply affected by it. David Attenborough went on to become a world-famous naturalist.

THE CRYING INDIAN

One of the best-known American Indians made a valuable contribution to awareness of Indian issues, but his origins may have been closer to the Mediterranean than the Cherokee-Cree tribal heritage he claimed.

On Earth Day (an annual day of education about environmental issues) in 1971, a television commercial in the United States turned a little-known actor into a nationally recognized figure. Known as the "Crying Indian" ad, the one-minute film made by the Keep America Beautiful campaign shows a Native American paddling his canoe along an increasingly polluted river. He passes industrial chimneys belching smoke and then pulls his canoe up onto a filthy riverbank. As he stands by a highway, a heap of litter thrown out of a passing car lands at his feet. He turns to the camera as a tear rolls down his cheek and the voice-over says, "People start pollution, people can stop it."

The star of the commercial was an actor named Iron Eyes Cody. He appeared as a Native American in more than one hundred films and television productions from the 1920s to the 1980s. He claimed to be of Cherokee-Cree descent. However, in 1996, a newspaper article alleged that Iron Eyes Cody was actually…an Italian-American.

Records show that he was born Espera de Corti on April 3, 1904, in Kaplan, Louisiana, the son of Italian immigrants from Sicily. When he was five years old, his father left home to escape a falling-out with a local crime gang and moved to Texas. His mother remarried. When Espera, known as Oscar, was a teenager, he and his two brothers moved to Texas to live with their father, who by then had changed his name to Corti. The boys took the Corti name too. When their father died in 1924 at the age of only forty-five, they moved to Hollywood and changed their name again to Cody.

All three brothers found work in the movie industry. Oscar, who had dressed up as an Indian since childhood, became Iron Eyes Cody to play small parts in westerns. One part led to another and turned into a career as a movie Indian. He started living as Iron Eyes Cody offstage as well as in front of the cameras. His success was rewarded with a star on the Hollywood Boulevard Walk of Fame.

Cody's devotion to Indian affairs was more than buckskin deep. He was a supporter and advocate of Indian interests and issues. The Hollywood American Indian Community recognized his contributions to the representation of Indian life while acknowledging that he wasn't a genuine Native American. He married an Indian woman and adopted two Indian boys. He always denied the allegation that he wasn't an authentic Indian. Iron Eyes Cody died on January 4, 1999, at the age of ninety-four.

THE HERBAL CHIEF

Chief Two Moon Meridas cut quite a dash in his feathered and horned headdress, but was he a real Indian?

In the early 1900s, Indian medicines were very popular in the United States. At a time before antibiotics, when "conventional" medicine had limited success, Native Americans were thought to know the age-old secrets of herbal medicine. Quacks and charlatans jumped on the bandwagon and gave their ineffective and, at times, dangerous tonics and elixirs Indian-sounding names to make them more attractive.

Meridas sold his products all across the country by mail order too. His business grew fast, and he soon had a fleet of delivery trucks, ten cars, his own chauffeur, and even a plane. He had to build a laboratory to keep up with the demand!

Chief Two Moon Meridas started in a small way, selling herbal potions from street corners. In 1914, he set up home with his wife, Helen, in Waterbury, Connecticut. During the terrible influenza pandemic of 1918, when 50 million people died worldwide, at least half a million of them in the United States, Meridas's customers all survived, and business boomed as a result. By 1921, he moved to a new house in Waterbury with a store attached.

His bestselling product was "Bitter Oil—The Wonder Tonic," which claimed to relieve headaches, gastric problems, constipation, bil-

> Meridas secretly gave away large sums of money to people in need. The extent of his generosity wasn't discovered until after his death. One of his favorite causes was the Pine Ridge Indian Reservation in South Dakota. He gave them money, cattle, and help with health care. In return, the Oglala Lakota tribal council attended by 8,000 Indians made him an honorary Sioux Chief in August 1930. A month later, he visited Europe and met Pope Pius XI.

iousness, kidney troubles, and bladder problems. Every drugstore worth its salt sold Chief Two Moon Herb Co.'s products, advertised by posters and life-size cardboard cutouts of the chief himself in full tribal dress.

People came from all over the country to see the chief in person. So many cars arrived in the small town on Sunday mornings that extra police officers had to be posted to direct the traffic. To his credit, he didn't charge them to meet him and talk about their health problems. He only charged for the products they bought, and it made him a rich man.

He was prosecuted in New York and Connecticut for practicing medicine and naturopathy without the proper certificates and licenses. In 1932, he brought twenty-six Sioux chiefs from South Dakota to Waterbury to speak on his behalf in one court case. He had to post a $1,000 bond for each Indian who left the reservation, and he paid for their transport and accommodation. Soon after this, he started suffering from stomach pain. His condition worsened until he died on November 3, 1933. An autopsy found a ruptured vein and cirrhosis of the liver. Cirrhosis is a common consequence of heavy

> Years after Meridas's death, it was discovered that he may indeed have been a heavy drinker but hid it well.

At the time of his marriage, Meridas was living in New York and earning his living as a metal worker.

drinking, but he wasn't known to be a drinker and his friends never saw him drunk. His medicines came under suspicion for a while, but no ingredients that could account for his liver damage were found.

His wife carried on running the business after his death until 1969, when she retired and closed it down.

Very little is known about his early life. He was born Chico Colon Meridan to a Mexican father of the same name. His death certificate shows his place of birth as Devil's Lake, South Dakota, but researchers have been unable to find any evidence to support this. His date of birth isn't known for sure either. His marriage license gives his year of birth as 1888.

He claimed Blackfoot and Pueblo Indian heritage. His "Two Moon" name was invented from his mother's name, Mary Tumoon, and for some reason he changed his last name from Meridan to Meridas. He claimed to have learned how to make herbal medicines on the South Dakota reservation where he lived until he was twelve years old. He carried on making and recommending herbal potions while he toured the country with a carnival troupe, and it eventually provided his livelihood.

Some of his critics and business rivals branded him a charlatan, not a genuine Indian at all. He tried to prove his Native American heritage for most of his life, but the Department of the Interior refused to certify him as an American Indian. He wrote to senators and officials asking for their help but never managed to prove the Indian heritage he claimed. He may have been a genuine Native American with a lifetime's experience in making age-old natural remedies, or he may have been an impostor who latched on to a false Indian identity for commercial reasons. No one has been able to unearth the truth about Chief Two Moon Meridas.

FRAUD ALERT: BOGUS BRAVES

Investigators have been exposing fake Indians since the 1930s. And they keep coming.

- *The Rebel Outlaw: Josey Wales* and *The Education of Little Tree* were bestselling Western tales written in the 1970s by Forrest Carter, supposedly a Cherokee. The Clint Eastwood film, *The Outlaw Josey Wales*, was based on Carter's book. However, Forrest Carter was later revealed to be Asa Earl Carter, oddly a former Klansman and speechwriter for the segregationist Governor of Alabama, George Wallace.

- In 1998, *Esquire* magazine received a handwritten article from a Navajo man named Nasdijj. It told the story of his son, Tommy Nothing Fancy, who suffered from fetal alcohol syndrome, which the writer said was an issue for Native Americans. *Esquire* published the article, and it was so well received that it came within a whisker of winning a national magazine award. The author, Nasdijj, went on to write three successful books in the early 2000s to great acclaim. In fact, Nasdijj didn't exist. In 2006, the author's real identity was discovered—Timothy Patrick Barrus, a writer from Lansing, Michigan.

- Margaret B. Jones's critically acclaimed book, *Love and Consequences: A Memoir of Hope and Survival*, described her upbringing as a half Native American girl and Los Angeles Bloods gang member. When a photograph of Jones appeared in the *New York Times*, the book's publisher received a phone call from the author's sister. She revealed that Jones wasn't half Native American, wasn't a gang member, and wasn't even named Margaret B. Jones. Her real name was Margaret Seltzer.

► chapter ◄

7

FABULOUS FANTASISTS

Pretending to be someone else is a common feature of children's play, but some people never grow out of it. They invent exotic identities that are more exciting and interesting than their real lives. They are fantasists, and they've been with us for hundreds of years.

In past centuries, when few people traveled further than the next town, a favorite ploy was to masquerade as a native from the other side of the world or an explorer of faraway places that most people had barely heard of. George Psalmanazar, Princess Caraboo, and Louis de Rougemont had a ready audience for their stories of unknown lands, strange customs, and bizarre creatures. They often threw in a bit of cannibalism for good measure.

Today, there is hardly a square inch of the world that scientists, filmmakers, and photographers have not visited and recorded in

The most famous fictional fantasist is Walter Mitty, the creation of American writer James Thurber in the 1930s. Mitty is a mild-mannered man with a heroic fantasy life. His story became so well known that a psychological condition was named after him—Walter Mitty Syndrome. Sufferers fantasize about being more important than they really are.

glorious high definition or 3-D, so stories of monsters and mermaids are less convincing now. Fantasists have had to move on to new territory. In the wake of the 9/11 attacks in the United States, dozens of people made fraudulent claims to have escaped from the falling buildings, to have rescued others, or to have been rescued themselves after being buried in the rubble. One by one, they were exposed as phonies craving sympathy and attention. And the military community is constantly on guard against the uniform junkies who keep trying to infiltrate its ranks. We'll check out a few of these fantastical falsehoods in this chapter.

THE GREATEST LIAR ON EARTH

Between August 1898 and May 1899, *The Wide World Magazine* in England serialized the extraordinary story of a European man who claimed he'd spent thirty years living among Aboriginals in the wild Australian outback.

The man was Louis de Rougemont. His fantastic tales of flying wombats, gold reefs in the desert, and cannibalism among Aboriginals caused a sensation. De Rougemont was invited to give lectures about his experiences. He claimed to have been born in Paris in 1844 and brought up in Switzerland by his mother after his parents separated. When he was nineteen, he set out on a marathon tour of the Far East to avoid having to serve in the French army as his father wanted. He claimed to have worked as a cook on a pearl-fishing boat in Batavia (Jakarta today) and described horrifying attacks on the pearl-divers by sharks and giant octopuses big enough to pull a whole boat down. He survived attacks from bloodthirsty natives and a terrible storm at sea that swept away everyone except himself and the captain's dog, a terrier named Bruno.

As the boat drifted past islands in the Timor Sea, natives on the islands attacked it by throwing boomerangs at it. A storm eventually hurled the boat onto a reef. Bruno dragged de Rougemont onto the shore of a deserted island, where they spent the next two and a half years.

From time to time, he saw ships passing by on the horizon, but none of them spotted him. Natives arrived on the island one night, blown off course by a storm, and took him back to the Australian mainland with them. He learned how the natives caught emus, kangaroos, snakes, and birds. He also described cannibal feasts following bloody battles with neighboring tribes. He tried to return to civilization by sea but was beaten back by a storm. Then he set out overland to the south on foot, accompanied by a native woman named Yamba and Bruno the dog.

De Rougemont carried on across the continent and claimed to have found a region rich in gold and gemstones. At about this time, his companion Yamba fell ill and died. He was finally rescued after walking into a gold prospectors' camp near Mount Margaret in Western Australia. He eventually reached Brisbane, where he caught a ship bound for New Zealand. From there, he sailed on the SS *Waikato* to London, arriving in March 1898.

Part of de Rougemont's story sounds very similar to Daniel Defoe's tale of Robinson Crusoe's adventures, first published in 1719. De Rougemont's island was smaller than Crusoe's, with no animal life apart from visiting birds. He described it as one hundred yards long, ten yards wide, and barely eight feet above sea level. Like Crusoe, de Rougemont stripped his wrecked boat, still stuck fast on the reef, for materials and supplies. He claimed to have built a shelter from oyster shells and to have grown corn in upturned turtle shells fertilized with turtle blood. He supplemented his diet with fish stolen from pelicans that visited the island and amused himself by riding on the backs of turtles.

Testing Times

The *Daily Chronicle* newspaper carried readers' letters arguing over de Rougemont's claims for months. His supporters pointed to the case of Paul du Chaillu, an explorer who had returned from equatorial Africa with stories of huge, hairy, manlike apes and tiny people. He was ridiculed. However, his reports of what turned out to be gorillas and pygmies were later verified by other explorers. So de Rougemont's claims could potentially be true. De Rougemont's opponents cited the

During de Rougemont's extraordinary trek across Australia, he claimed to have met the explorer Alfred Gibson, who fell ill and died while de Rougemont was with him. Gibson was part of the Giles Expedition of 1873 that attempted to cross Australia from the Darwin-Adelaide telegraph line to the west coast. When Giles and Gibson were forced to turn back, Gibson left on their last remaining horse while Giles followed on foot. Gibson lost his way and was never seen again, but Ernest Giles survived and named the region the Gibson Desert after his missing companion.

case of George Psalmanazar, an impostor and teller of tall tales about his fictitious life and times in Formosa (Taiwan today).

When news of de Rougemont's adventures reached Australia, the Sydney *Evening News* reported that the story confirmed that the British public was one of the most gullible in the world. Just as de Rougemont was preparing to take the leading role in a play about his exploits, the *Daily Telegraph* newspaper in Sydney published a dramatic story that changed everything. After it printed a sketch of de Rougemont, several people recognized him and gave them the man's name. It wasn't Louis de Rougemont. It was Henri Louis Grien. He was known for telling incredible tales of exotic places he claimed to have visited, including a story about capturing turtles and riding on their backs. A woman named Elizabeth Jane Ravenscroft recognized him as the husband who had deserted her and their children in Australia in 1897 after fourteen years of marriage. They had seven children, but only four survived. If this was true and de Rougemont was Grien, he plainly couldn't have spent thirty years in the outback.

In due course, the truth was untangled. De Rougemont was indeed Henri Louis Grien. He was born into a farming family in Gressy, near Lake Neuchâtel in Switzerland, as Henri Louis Grin on November 12, 1847. When he was ten years old, his family moved to the nearby town of Yverdon. When he was sixteen, he fell out with his parents and left home. After holding down various small jobs, including a travel courier and valet, he tried his hand at seamanship. He bought an eleven-ton cutter named

Ada and worked as its master. To register the boat, he had to become a British citizen. He changed his name to Grien at the same time.

He hoped to make his fortune from pearl fishing, but the enterprise proved to be a failure. In desperation, he hired two men to kidnap Aboriginals and imprison them onboard the *Ada*. Then once they were at sea, the unfortunate men were forced to work as pearl divers. After two months, one of the hired men walked into a police station and claimed that he had killed one of the divers in self-defense. However, when Aboriginals who had witnessed the event were found and interviewed, the killer was charged with murder. He was found guilty of manslaughter and sentenced to five years in prison. When Grien heard about this, he made off into the Timor Sea to avoid arrest. Two months later, in April 1877, he turned up at the Cape York Peninsula on the other side of Australia. He got rid of the *Ada* as soon as he could.

When Grien vanished after more failed schemes, he had in fact gone to New Zealand. After even more failed jobs and money-making schemes, he hit on the idea of selling his fabulous stories. The tales he told about his pearl-fishing adventures were now embroidered with extra thrills and dramas invented from books he had read (some factual, some not) and notebooks written by an explorer named Harry Stockdale. His brother in Switzerland suggested that distance would make his stories more marketable, so perhaps he should think about publishing in England. This is what brought Grien, as de Rougemont, to London on the SS *Waikato* in 1898.

Grien tried his luck as a doctor in the Palmer goldfields in north Queensland, but he wasn't up to the job—probably because he had no medical training! He then bought a camera and became a photographer. When this too failed, he took a job as a cook on a pearl-fishing boat.

A Liar Onstage

After he was outed as an impostor, he disappeared from England. He turned up in South Africa toward the end of 1899, touring the music halls as "The Greatest Liar on Earth." Fortunately for de Rougemont, the Second Boer War had broken out. It guaranteed him large audiences of off-duty troops looking for entertainment. And reporters sent to cover the war also reported on de Rougemont's theatrical performances. After a year or so in South Africa, he made the extraordinary decision to take his stage act to Australia. Again and again, he was heckled mercilessly and booed off the stage. He beat a hasty retreat to London.

In 1915, although still married to his first wife, he married Thirza Ann Wolf. Britain was at war and experiencing a food shortage. De Rougemont claimed to have invented a food substitute that could replace meat, but as usual he could find no one to invest in it. His marriage failed too, and Thirza left him. He spent his last few years in poverty, selling matches on the streets and working as a handyman. He was going by the name of Louis Redman to avoid publicity and ridicule. He died on June 9, 1921, after a short illness.

> In London in 1906, de Rougemont appeared at the Hippodrome theater in a swimming costume! In front of him, a live turtle and a huge tank of water! He told the audience that he had been ridiculed for his stories of riding on the backs of turtles. Then he pushed the turtle into the water and climbed onto its back. He rode the turtle back and forth across the tank. His supporters contended that if this part of his story was true, it was perfectly possible that the rest was true too, but others were unconvinced.

DEAD MAN WALKING

When English aristocrat Lord Buckingham arrived at a British port, immigration officials had a problem—they knew he couldn't possibly be Lord Buckingham!

Dover is a busy seaport on England's south coast, where passenger ferries from Europe dock every day. On January 15, 2005, the port's police officers received information from Calais, France, that a passenger calling himself Lord Christopher Buckingham had boarded a ship and was on his way to Dover. The problem was that their routine checks showed that Christopher Buckingham was dead!

Buckingham, looking remarkable well for a dead man, was stopped by police officers as he drove off the ship. He was carrying a Swiss driver's license and a photocopy of his British passport. He was taken into custody while further checks were made. He claimed to be a member of the House of Lords, the upper house of the British Parliament, but his name did not appear in its list of members. There was once a genuine Lord Buckingham, but the title had died out in the seventeenth century. During questioning, Buckingham insisted he was telling the truth and his passport was genuine. In addition to his British citizenship, he also claimed to hold Swiss and German passports, but checks in Switzerland and Germany failed to turn up passport records in his name.

The police were convinced that he was lying, but they had too little evidence to hold him. He was charged with obtaining a British passport by deception. The passport was canceled, and he was released on condition that he must return a week later for further questioning.

In the meantime, the police gathered information about the real Christopher Buckingham and checked everything the bogus Buckingham had told them. They found that the school he claimed to have attended, St. Christopher's in Westminster, London, didn't exist. The information he gave them about his family didn't check out either.

No Comment

The police didn't expect Buckingham to return at the agreed time. They assumed he would ditch his Buckingham identity and go underground, but amazingly he kept his appointment. Police officers challenged him with the information they'd uncovered and asked who he really was. His answer? "No comment." He was kept in custody and put before a judge in the morning. To the astonishment of the police, who argued that Buckingham should be kept locked up until they could establish his identity, the judge released him on bail. As they took him to his car, it occurred to one of the officers that Buckingham could be a British spy, because secret agents traveling under false identities were occasionally intercepted at the port. Buckingham was evasive. Later, the officer checked with the intelligence service. They had no record of anyone matching Buckingham.

Then the police found his ex-wife. When they rang her, she asked, "Have you found out who he is?" She had discovered that he was lying about his past but was never able to find out who he really was. They had met while they were both working in a hotel in Germany. They married in 1984. Soon afterward, they moved to England. They had two children, a boy and a girl. Buckingham worked in IT and computer security. He sometimes disappeared for a few days at a time without explanation. His wife began to suspect that he was having an affair. He was also very secretive about his past. The strain drove the couple apart, and they separated in 1996. His wife investigated him, but she failed to uncover any information about his life before she met him. She gave up after their divorce in 1997.

The police found the real Christopher Buckingham's mother. DNA tests proved that the bogus Buckingham was not related to her. DNA databases in Britain and Switzerland were checked, but there was no match to any known criminal. All the leads went cold.

When Buckingham appeared in court on the passport charge, he asked to be allowed to return to Switzerland, where he would be able to produce evidence of his identity. When the judge denied his request, he entered a guilty plea. The police were convinced that there was more to Buckingham than a minor passport offense, but the investigation stalled.

Caging the Jackal

The police released his photograph and asked the public for help. They also sent his fingerprints to several countries he might have had links with. Newspapers dubbed him "The Jackal" after a character in the Frederick Forsyth novel *The Day of the Jackal*, who,

While "Buckingham" was in prison, the police discovered that he had a girlfriend in Zurich. She had been a nurse who looked after him while he was recovering from a car accident. Buckingham claimed that she could produce documents to prove his identity, but she was unable to help.

like Buckingham, had stolen the identity of a dead baby. Meanwhile, Buckingham's trial had ended with a guilty verdict and a prison sentence of twenty-one months, which was reduced to nine months on appeal.

When he was released from prison, the authorities had a problem. No one knew who he was or where he was from, so what was to be done with him? If they could prove he was a foreign national, they could deport him, but as a stateless person, he was held in custody by the Immigration Service.

End Game

Then the case took a surprising turn. Buckingham's daughter was contacted by a man named Kevin Stopford, who claimed to know who her father was. He sent her a photograph that appeared to show Buckingham as a young man. He said Buckingham's real name was Charles Albert Stopford, Kevin Stopford's brother. He advised the British authorities to send Buckingham's fingerprints to the United States. This they did, and it did indeed confirm his identity as Charles Albert Stopford, a former U.S. Navy serviceman. Stopford had vanished at the age of twenty-one in 1983, the same year that Buckingham appeared.

When Buckingham was told what the police had discovered, he insisted that he had lost his memory after his car accident and didn't remember anything about his life or family in America. The British authorities immediately began the deportation process to send him to the United States. In July 2006, he was flown to Orlando, Florida. There, he continued to call himself Christopher and spoke with an English accent. He continued to claim that he was suffering from amnesia and so couldn't explain why he had left the United States and adopted the identity of an English aristocrat.

THE FAKE FORMOSAN

In 1703, London was buzzing with news of an extraordinary arrival. A man named George Psalmanazar was regaling people with stories of his native country, the far-off island of Formosa (Taiwan).

George Psalmanazar relished the role of exotic celebrity foreigner, the civilized savage. Most people believed his stories without question, but a few were suspicious of the white-skinned, blond-haired man who spoke without any discernible Asian accent.

The great scientist Sir Isaac Newton, who was the president of the Royal Society, chaired an interrogation of Psalmanazar. Edmund Halley, after whom Halley's Comet is named, asked Psalmanazar a telling question. He wanted to know if the sun ever shines down to the bottom of chimneys in Formosa. Psalmanazar said no, and Halley thought he had exposed him as a fraud. Formosa lies between the tropics, so at times the sun would be directly overhead and would therefore reach the bottom of chimneys. However, Psalmanazar outwitted him by saying that the chimneys on Formosa bend and twist, so sunlight never reaches the bottom.

When Psalmanazar was asked about the whiteness of his skin, he claimed to be of noble birth

A Jesuit astronomer named Father Jean de Fontaney, who had some personal knowledge of southeast Asia, described Psalmanazar as "the pretended Formosan" and suggested that he was actually more likely to be Flemish or Dutch. Fortunately for Psalmanazar, the opinion of a Jesuit counted for little in anti-Catholic England at that time—the last Catholic king of England, James II, had been deposed only five years earlier.

and therefore he spent his days indoors instead of working in the fields. Despite his clever answers, the members of the Royal Society were unconvinced by him, but they kept their thoughts to themselves because Psalmanazar had become so popular with the public.

Keeping the Readers Happy

He capitalized on his fame by writing a book called *An Historical and Geographical Description of Formosa* in 1704. The next year, the Bishop of London sent him to Christ Church College at Oxford University to study divinity and give lectures about Formosa, but he left after just one term. At this time, he also prepared a second edition of his book with more sensational accounts of devil worship and cannibalism to keep his readers happy. As his stories became evermore extreme, people finally began to realize that he was a fraud. He tried to revive his fortunes, unsuccessfully, by writing a pamphlet called "A Dialogue Between a Japanese and a Formosan."

Then an extraordinary publication by anonymous authors appeared. It was entitled (take a deep breath!) "An Enquiry into the Objections against George Psalmanazar of Formosa: In Which the Accounts of the People, and Language of Formosa by Candidius, and other European Authors, and the Letters from Geneva, and from Suffolk, about Psalmanazar, Are Proved Not to Contradict His Accounts"! The unnamed authors described themselves as plebeians with little education, but there are suspicions that the real author may have been Psalmanazar himself. It concluded that nothing Psalmanazar had said had been proven wrong and therefore he could be who he said he was. However, his short spell of fame had passed.

By the 1720s, he seems to have tired of his fake identity. He also appears to have been affected by reading a book called *A Serious Call to the Devout and Holy Life*. It invited the reader to look back on his life and think about what use he has made of it. He worked in the literary treadmill of Grub Street for forty years, contributing to many, many books. In one of them, *A Complete System of Geography*, he included a piece about himself. He described himself as a pretended native of Formosa, who had been encouraged to tell his fabulous tale by people who took advantage of his youthful vanity. It also said that he intended to leave an account of the truth to be published after his death. And he was as good as his word. A year after his death in 1763 at the age of eighty-four, his memoirs were published.

Unable to make a living as a celebrity foreigner any more, Psalmanazar tried using his name to promote commercial products and medicines, but without success. He tried a succession of jobs including painting fans, teaching languages, and working as a clerk to a regiment of dragoons. A clergyman took pity on him and raised twenty pounds a year from his few remaining supporters to save him from utter destitution. He eventually found a job working as a hack on Grub Street—a community of freelance writers, editors, and booksellers in London who worked on the fringes of the literary and journalistic scene.

Becoming Psalmanazar

Psalmanazar was born in France in 1679. When he left school, he made his own way in life, working for a while as a Latin tutor, but he earned so little that he fell into poverty and was reduced to begging. He decided to go to live with his mother, who was separated from his father. With the help of a cloak stolen from a church, he masqueraded as an Irish Catholic on a pilgrimage to Rome, presumably because it enabled him to beg for alms (money and food) on the way. Traveling as a pilgrim was also less risky, because pilgrims had nothing worth stealing.

His mother was unable to support him, so he set off on foot for his father's home in Germany. When he fared no better there, he decided to try his luck in the Netherlands. He was still only about fifteen years old. For this journey, he decided to pretend to be a traveler from Japan, mainly because so little was known about Japan that he was unlikely to be found out. Japan had been closed to foreigners since 1640.

On the way, he took a series of menial jobs and was briefly imprisoned as a spy. He enlisted in a German army regiment that was fighting alongside the Dutch against the French. Europe was frequently at war. This time it was the War of the Spanish Succession. When the Spanish king died, his throne was set to pass to the French king's grandson. This would have united England's two most powerful enemies. England joined a grand alliance of European powers to fight this Franco-Spanish union.

When Psalmanazar's regiment reached Sluis in the Netherlands, he met Reverend Alexander Innes, a chaplain with a Scottish regiment fighting nearby. Innes tested Psalmanazar. He asked him to translate a piece of Latin text into Japanese. Later, he asked him to translate the same Latin passage again. When he compared the two translations, they were completely different. Psalmanazar realized that he had been found out, but he was amazed when Innes simply told him to be more careful in future. Innes wanted to use Psalmanazar to further his own career, and he didn't care if Psalmanazar was a fake.

Innes wrote to the Bishop of London about Psalmanazar. He said that Jesuits had kidnapped him and brought him to Avignon in France. He had resisted their attempts to convert him to Catholicism. Innes said he had successfully converted Psalmanazar to Anglicanism and baptized him. The story appealed to the anti-Catholic bishop, who invited them to an audience with him. On their way to London, Psalmanazar changed his fake origin from Japan to Formosa. The name George Psalmanazar may have been invented by Innes too—inspired by the biblical Assyrian king Shalmaneser.

The one puzzle his memoirs didn't resolve was—who was he? He never revealed his real name. To this day, no one knows who George Psalmanazar really was.

THE FANTASY PRINCESS

While some impostors are driven to a life of pretense to claim a throne, steal an inheritance, or simply make a living, others adopt an exotic false identity to garner sympathy and assistance that they wouldn't otherwise attract. Such was the case of a woman known as Princess Caraboo, one of the most colorful and exuberant impostors.

On the evening of Thursday, April 3, 1817, a strange woman turned up in Almondsbury, a small town near the thriving city port of Bristol in Gloucestershire, England. She was in her twenties, about five feet two inches tall, and clean but poorly dressed in a black gown with a frill around the neck and an untidy turban made from a shawl wound around her head. She had been knocking on doors looking for somewhere to stay. She used hand gestures to make herself understood, as she didn't appear to be able to speak English.

It was just two years since the end of the Napoleonic Wars, so mysterious foreigners were treated with great caution as potential spies. A couple whose cottage the woman called at were so worried that they informed the overseer of the parish poorhouse about her. He asked a magistrate, Samuel Worrall, what should be done. Worrall sent the overseer to collect the woman. He brought her to the magistrate's residence at Knole Park. Neither Worrall nor his Greek valet could understand the strange language she spoke, and she wasn't carrying any papers that might identify her. She was a mystery.

Worrall's wife, Elizabeth, was especially intrigued by the woman. She asked her maid and footman to take the woman to the village inn with a request to the landlady to give her a room and a good supper. When they arrived, the woman spotted a picture of a pineapple on the wall and pointed at it excitedly as if she recognized it. When she was taken to her room, the landlady's daughter had to show her what the bed was for or she would have lain down on the floor to sleep.

Early the next morning, Mrs. Worrall went to the inn to see the woman. A local clergyman arrived with some books containing pictures of foreign lands. The woman looked through them and appeared to recognize pictures of China.

Mrs. Worrall decided to bring her back to Knole Park, but suspecting that she might be a fraud, Mrs. Worrall said, "My good young woman, I very much fear that you are imposing upon me, and that you understand and can answer me in my own language; if so, and distress has driven you to this expedient, make a friend of me; I am female as yourself, and can feel for you, and will give you money and clothes, and will put you on your journey, without disclosing your conduct to anyone; but it must be on condition that you speak the truth. If you deceive me, I think it right to inform you, that Mr. Worrall is a magistrate, and has the power of sending you to prison, committing you to hard labor, and passing you as a vagrant to your own parish."

The woman didn't appear to understand and started talking in her own language. Mrs. Worrall then wrote her name on a piece of paper and said it. The woman pointed at herself and said, "Caraboo."

The next day, Caraboo was taken to Bristol and examined by the mayor. Unable to find out who she was or where she came from, he sent her to St. Peter's Hospital, a pauper's workhouse where Bristol's vagrants were held. By then, her circumstances had become more widely known. People started arriving at the hospital to see her, often with friends from other countries in the hope that they might discover where she was from, but none was successful.

Mrs. Worrall rescued her from the hospital and took her to her husband's office in Bristol, where she was cared for by the housekeeper. Visitors continued to call on her, and eventually one of them appeared to understand her. He was a Portuguese sailor named Manuel Eynesso. He listened to her and said she was a princess from the East Indies. She had been brought to England against her will and abandoned. He said the language she spoke was not a pure dialect but a mixture of languages from Sumatra and other islands. After she heard this account, Mrs. Worrall seemed convinced that Caraboo was genuine and brought her back to Knole Park.

Caraboo's Story

Captain Palmer, a sailor who had made several voyages to the East Indies, began to take an interest in Caraboo's story. He met her and, like Eynesso, claimed to recognize the language she spoke. He wrote down a detailed account of her story. According to this, Caraboo was the daughter of a man of Chinese origin, named Jessu Mandu, and a Malay woman. She called the island where she lived Javasu.

While she was walking in her garden, she was seized by pirates led by a man named Chee-min. They tied her up and gagged her before carrying her off to Chee-min's boat. The pirates sold her to the captain of a ship called the *Tappa Boo*, which sailed for Europe. Eleven weeks later, the *Tappa Boo* entered the Bristol Channel, and Caraboo made her escape by jumping overboard and swimming to the shore. Until then, she had been wearing a fine dress embroidered with gold thread, but she exchanged it for the clothes she wore when she called at a house for help. She wandered the country roads for six weeks before reaching Almondsbury.

During her time at Knole Park, she prepared all her own meals. She liked curry and preferred rice to bread, and she drank only water or tea. She fasted every Tuesday. She often exercised in the garden with a bow and arrows and by using a stick as a sword. She appeared to be a skilled fencer. She built an arbor in the garden and used it as a place of worship. The farmers and tenants around Almondsbury got to know her and grew fond of her.

When Captain Palmer visited her, he brought a Malay dagger called a crease with him and explained that the point would have been dipped in vegetable poison. Caraboo took the dagger, rubbed the leaves of a nearby plant on the blade, touched it to her arm, and pretended to swoon as if she knew about this custom.

When Caraboo was shown Chinese items, such as a purse, a fan, and a Chinese puzzle, she appeared to recognize them. When she was given a scarf, she showed how it was worn, first in the Chinese style and then in the style of her own island, Javasu. She identified other items, including coconut, pepper, and coral, as belonging to her mother's Malay country. She also showed the way her people wrote.

She disappeared one day and returned in the evening with mud-spattered clothes. She fell ill after her return, and a physician, Dr. William Mortimer, was called to attend her. Mortimer was suspicious of Caraboo because her skin was white and her features European. He returned later with another doctor. In Caraboo's presence, one of the men said that Caraboo was dangerously ill and probably wouldn't survive. At this, her face turned bright red. As she had shown no understanding of English up to this point, they thought they had exposed her as a fraud, but the maid who had been looking after her said she had become flushed in the face like this several times before.

A Bath doctor by the name of Charles Hummings Wilkinson met Caraboo and was so impressed by her that he wrote to the *Bath Chronicle* about her. The Worralls started receiving letters from all over the British Isles with theories about her possible origins. One day, she disappeared again. This time, she was spotted in Bath by someone who had read Dr. Wilkinson's letters in the *Bath Chronicle*. He contacted Wilkinson to let him know where she was. Wilkinson found her in the Pack Horse Inn. So many people were arriving to see her that Wilkinson urged two ladies to take her to their home for her own safety. Then he contacted Mrs. Worrall, who went to Bath to collect her. When Caraboo saw Mrs. Worrall, she fell to her knees sobbing. Now able to speak a few words of English, she told Mrs. Worrall that she desperately wanted to return to Javasu to see her parents and so she had run away. Mrs. Worrall persuaded her to return to Knole Park.

Uncovering the Truth

One day, Mrs. Worrall told Caraboo they were to go to Bristol for a final sitting with an artist named Edward Bird, who had been painting Caraboo's portrait. However, instead of going to Bird's studio, Mrs. Worrall actually took Caraboo to Dr. Mortimer's house. While she was shown into one room, Mrs. Worrall went to another room to meet a Mrs. Neale. Mrs. Neale had read the newspaper reports about Princess Caraboo and thought she recognized her.

She kept a lodging house in Lewin's Mead, Bristol. A few months earlier, a woman matching Caraboo's description had come to stay there. She was English but sometimes spoke in a made-up language. The last time they saw her, she was wearing a turban matching the one described in the newspaper reports. After hearing Mrs. Neale's story, Mrs. Worrall confronted Caraboo with what she had learned. Initially, Caraboo burst into tears and spoke in her mysterious language, but Mrs. Worrall persisted. Realizing that the game was up, "Caraboo" finally spoke in English with a strong north Devon accent. She told the truth for the first time. And it was quite a story.

She said she was born Mary Willcocks in Witheridge, Devon, in 1791 and worked as a wool spinner from the age of eight. At the age of sixteen, she went to work for a family, looking after their children and doing jobs around their farm, but she was paid so little that she left. She found work in Exeter, but she had to work so hard for so little money that she left after only two months. She wandered the streets of Exeter begging for money. She was so unhappy that she decided to hang herself from a tree. However, at that moment, she said she heard a voice saying, "Cursed are they that do murder and sin against the Lord." So she carried on walking. She met a man who took pity on her and gave her five shillings, which she used to find lodgings in Taunton for a few days.

From there, she went on to Bristol. She begged on the streets for money for lodgings. While she was going from door to door begging in a village near Bristol, a constable arrested her and intended to put her in front of a magistrate in the morning, but she escaped through a window. She got away from the area as fast as she could and kept traveling, getting to within thirty miles of London. By then she had fallen ill and was taken to a hospital by two kind women who stopped to pick her up.

A New Start

When it was finally time for her to leave the hospital, she had nowhere to live. After accidentally going to a brothel she mistook for a convent, she eventually ended up in London, where she took lodgings with a fishmonger named Mrs. Hillier.

One day while she was shopping, a well-dressed gentleman spotted her. Mary later gave a variety of different names for him—John Henry Baker, Beckerstedt, Bakerstehndt, and Beckerstein. Take your pick! He was a half-Malayan ex-sailor and must have cut quite a dash. He inquired after her, and when he discovered her name and address, he wrote to her and sent her flowers. He called to see her when Mrs. Hillier was out. After only two months, they married. John Henry taught Mary a few words of the Malay language, which she would use later to her advantage. The couple moved from town to town looking for work without success. John Henry left for Calais and sent Mary back to London, saying he would send for her, but she never heard from him again. And now she was pregnant. To support herself, she worked at the Crab Tree, a coaching inn on Tottenham Court Road in London, until she went into labor.

She had the baby, a boy, at the City Road Lying-In Hospital and named him John Henry after her husband. When she left the hospital, she took the baby to the Foundling Hospital and gave him up, as she was unable to support him.

Mary visited the Foundling Hospital every Monday to ask about her baby. One day, she was told that her son had died. She returned home to Witheridge soon afterward. In due course, she moved on to Bristol and stayed at Mrs. Neale's. Then one day, as a joke, she dressed in her turban and went begging as if she were a foreigner. By then, she had made an arrangement with a ship's captain to take her to America. He was due to leave in fifteen days, so she had to raise the five pounds' cost of her passage by then. This is what took her to Almondsbury and the Worrall's house.

On the day when she disappeared from Knole Park and returned with muddy clothes, she had cut across the fields to her previous lodgings with Mrs. Neale in Lewin's Mead. There, she had packed her trunk and gone to the quay to find the ship that would take her to America. But when she arrived, the ship had already sailed and so she returned to Knole Park.

Liar, Liar

Having been duped once, Mrs. Worrall didn't automatically believe everything Mary told her. She determined to find out how much of Mary's story was true. She asked Captain Palmer to go to Witheridge and look for Mary's parents. Palmer visited the recently retired vicar

The Foundling Hospital was established in 1741 by a businessman and philanthropist named Thomas Coram as a children's home for the "education and maintenance of exposed and deserted young children." He was moved to establish it by the sight of abandoned babies and young children starving and dying on the streets of London. Today, part of the site the Foundling Hospital stood on is a children's playground near the world-famous Great Ormond Street Hospital for Children. The Foundling Hospital itself has gone, but the charitable organization behind it still exists, now known as the Thomas Coram Foundation for Children, or simply Coram.

of Witheridge, Mr. Dickins, who lived in Tiverton. The vicar knew the family well and expressed great surprise that an uneducated girl like Mary Willcocks could have been so successful in a life of such duplicity. He spoke well of her parents, whom he had known for twenty-five years. He had read of the strange events in Almondsbury but never suspected that the girl at the heart of it all was the Willcockses' daughter. The vicar accompanied Palmer to Witheridge. They met Mary's parents and asked them what they knew of Mary's circumstances.

When the Willcockses were told what their daughter had been doing, they were very upset and hoped Mrs. Worrall would forgive her. Captain Palmer returned to Bristol and confirmed to Mrs. Worrall that the parents' story of Mary's life tallied in most respects with the account Mary herself had given. Mrs. Worrall then offered to pay Mary's passage to America and she accepted. She sailed for Philadelphia under the protection of three women traveling to America to work as teachers. She traveled as Mary Burgess, as she was too well known as Willcocks or Baker.

Mary never explained why she wanted to go to America, except for telling one of her many visitors that she expected to return in a carriage with four horses. So perhaps she thought she could make her fortune in a new land. No one is certain what happened to her, but according to one story, she returned to England, though not in a carriage with four horses. There were reports of her being seen in London, still

Mary's father was a cobbler. He was a strict disciplinarian. who had flogged his daughter with a strap on several occasions. He said he thought his daughter was not right in her head following a bout of rheumatic fever at the age of fifteen. His wife was in poor health and suffered from a troublesome cough. They'd had eleven children, but seven of them died in infancy.

The family had been reasonably prosperous until "the Enclosures." These were a series of acts of Parliament that enclosed land that had previously been open. Until the Enclosure Acts, local people had been able to use this common land for grazing animals and collecting firewood. More than a fifth of the land in England was enclosed by these acts to bring it into more productive use by farmers and landowners. Whole villages that had previously been self-sufficient were driven into poverty as a result. The impoverishment of Witheridge by the Enclosure Acts rendered most of Mr. Willcocks's usual customers unable to afford new footwear. After this, everyone in the village fell on hard times, except for the squire, who benefited from the land enclosure.

masquerading as Princess Caraboo. She settled in Bristol and gave birth to a daughter there in 1829. She is said to have made her living by selling leeches to Bristol Infirmary Hospital until her death in 1864. She was buried in an unmarked grave in the Hebron Road Burial Ground in Bristol, where she still lies today.

THOM'S LAST BATTLE

John Nichols Thom was a very strange man indeed. He declared himself to be the king of Jerusalem and savior of the world! He achieved the distinction of commanding one side in the last battle fought on English soil.

Thom was born in Cornwall, England, in 1799. His mother died in an insane asylum, and his own mental state seems to have been fragile. He is described as often lapsing into fits of melancholy and eccentric behavior. He started his working life with a wine merchant in Truro. When the business failed, Thom set up his own business as a wine merchant, maltster (dealer in malted grain), and hop dealer. By all accounts he was very successful, but at the end of 1831, he appears to have suffered some sort of psychiatric problem, described as apoplexy or derangement of the intellect. He was treated by bloodletting, a common procedure at that time.

Draining blood from the body was a standard "cure" for all sorts of conditions for about two thousand years up to the late nineteenth century. It was done in the mistaken belief that the human body was filled with four substances called humors, which had to be in balance for good health. Illness was thought to be an indication that the humors were out of balance, and in some cases this could be rectified by draining blood.

Going Astray

In May 1832, Thom set sail with a cargo of malt bound for Liverpool, but he disappeared.

In the autumn of 1832, he turned up in Canterbury, Kent, dressed as a Turk and claiming to be Count Moses R. Rothschild. After a few weeks, he changed his name to Sir William Percy Honeywood Courtenay of Powderham, heir to the Earl of Devon, King of Jerusalem, and Knight of Malta! He stood for election to Parliament in 1832 but was unsuccessful.

Although he was popular and drew large crowds for his speeches, his bizarre dress and behavior led some people to believe he was insane. In 1833, he gave evidence as a witness in a criminal trial, but his account was so clearly invented that he was charged with perjury and put on trial himself. He was found guilty and sentenced to a term of imprisonment followed by transportation to Australia. His friends persuaded the authorities that he was insane, and instead of prison, he was sent to an asylum. It was four years before he was considered well enough for release. However,

When Thom disappeared in 1832, he claimed he had gone to Beirut in pursuit of Lady Hester Stanhope, with whom he had become infatuated, only to suffer her rejection. However, records suggest he was actually living in London under the name of Squire Thompson.

he evidently wasn't completely recovered, because he claimed that he didn't recognize his wife or father.

The End is Nigh

When he left the asylum, he called himself Sir William Courtenay again, claimed he was the savior of the world, and became a traveling preacher. He also claimed that his sword was King Arthur's legendary Excalibur. Then, his ill-fated military career began. He convinced about a hundred followers that blades and bullets would not harm them because their faith made them invincible. He also claimed that he could kill 10,000 men simply by clapping his hands and that, in the unlikely event of him being killed, he would come back to life three days later.

Though Thom's run for Parliament was unsuccessful, he must have made quite an impression with the voters. He wore a red velvet suit embroidered with a golden Maltese cross, with a broad-brimmed Spanish sombrero resting on his long, wild black hair. And he carried a sword. He polled a respectable 375 votes, nearly half the number polled by the winning candidate.

Thom and his supporters paraded through the countryside and towns of Kent. A farmer who lost workers to Thom's "army" asked magistrates to arrest the workers. A constable was dispatched to detain them. Thom shot him dead and then led a group of thirty to forty of his men to Bossenden Wood. He encouraged his followers by promising each of them forty or fifty acres of land.

The authorities decided it was time to end Thom's activities. A force of one hundred soldiers of the 45th Foot Regiment was sent to arrest Thom and his followers. They surrounded the wood and demanded Thom's surrender. Thom's response was to shoot one of the officers, Lieutenant Bennett, who died. At this, the soldiers opened fire, killing Thom and several of his followers. The remaining members of Thom's force scattered. The soldiers rounded up twenty-five of them. The skirmish is known as the Battle of Bossenden

Wood, the last battle fought on English soil. An inquest was held into Thom's death. When the coroner heard about his claim that he would rise after three days, he ordered Thom's heart to be removed and pickled...just in case!

FRAUD ALERT: RANK OUTSIDERS

The right to wear a military uniform has to be earned. Service personnel take a dim view of anyone who wears a uniform he or she is not entitled to. It dishonors those who have a legitimate right to wear the uniform and especially those who have been wounded or killed in service.

Veterans' organizations are constantly on the lookout for bogus war heroes and keep finding them. Wearing uniforms or honors that have not been earned is illegal in many countries too. The United States takes this matter particularly seriously. The Stolen Valor Act of 2005 made the wearing of unearned medals a federal offense punishable by up to a year in prison, depending on which medal is claimed. Even so, the admiration and respect generated by a distinguished military career is too tempting for some people. Here are a few interesting examples.

- Elite troops and special forces are a particular draw for impostors. In 2002, more than 1,000 men who claimed to be U.S. Navy SEALs were checked out. Only three of them were found to be telling the truth! So, for every genuine Navy SEAL, there are more than 300 impostors! In 2002, Joseph A. Cafasso gave the Fox News Channel the benefit of his experience and military contacts as a lieutenant colonel in the Special Forces to inform its reports on the war in Afghanistan. In fact, records subsequently showed that his military service amounted to forty-four days of boot camp at Fort Dix, New Jersey, in 1976 and an honorable discharge as a private, first class. Reporters, executives, and genuine military officers had all been taken in by him.
- A distinguished war record can help a political career. Douglas R. Stringfellow (1922–66) was elected a U.S. Congressman for Utah in 1952, in part because of his

distinguished war record. He had served with the Office of Strategic Services (OSS) during World War II. The OSS was an intelligence agency, the forerunner of the CIA, which ran espionage operations behind enemy lines during the war. Stringfellow described the part he played in seizing atomic scientist Otto Hahn and bringing him to England. In 1945, Hahn and nine other German physicists were indeed located by a secret operation called Alsos and brought out of Germany to prevent them from falling into Soviet hands. Stringfellow claimed to have been captured and held in the Belsen concentration camp. While there, he was tortured so brutally that he left as a paraplegic. He received the Silver Star. He recounted his story in speeches and on national television when he appeared in the popular *This is Your Life* program.

▸ However, while Stringfellow was standing for reelection in 1954, his war record was exposed as untrue in an article printed in the *Army Times.* Initially, Stringfellow claimed that reports questioning his record were the malicious work of political opponents. However, a few days later, he made a tearful confession on television. He hadn't worked for the OSS, didn't win a Silver Star, and wasn't even paraplegic. He had been a private in the Army Air Forces, so his stories of secret missions as an agent behind enemy lines were invented. His injuries were caused by a mine explosion during routine service in France, after which he walked with the aid of a cane. Having trashed his political fortunes, he returned to his previous career as a radio announcer in Utah. He died after a heart attack in 1966 at the age of only forty-four.

- Lafayette Keaton was well known for the lectures he gave Oregon schoolchildren and war veterans about his military service in World War II, Korea, and Vietnam. The eighty-year-old veteran claimed to have won a Silver Star in Korea and to have served as a Ranger on three tours of duty in Vietnam. However, a local TV station in Portland, Oregon, exposed his claims as lies in 2010. In fact, he didn't join the military until after World War II, he wasn't posted to Korea until after the war ended, and he didn't serve in Vietnam.

- Sometimes, bogus military personnel give themselves away by covering their chests with the wrong medals or by tell-tale errors in behavior. While FBI Special Agent Thomas A. Cottone Jr. was attending a military funeral in 2005, a Marine captain among the mourners caught his attention. Cottone's day job included the investigation of military impostors. He was immediately suspicious of the medals and ribbons on the captain's chest, but the clincher was the captain's behavior when the band started playing the Marine Corps hymn. A genuine Marine would have snapped to attention, but this captain didn't react. The man turned out to be a New Jersey bus driver, Walter Carlson, who had never served in the military. He had bought the uniform and medals.

- Even genuine serving military personnel occasionally claim bogus service or medals. In 2004, U.S. Navy captain Roger D. Edwards was found guilty of wearing ribbons and medals he wasn't entitled to, including a Silver Star, four Purple Hearts, a gold star on a Defense Meritorious Award, a gold star on a Meritorious Service Medal, a Joint Service Commendation Medal, a Combat Action Ribbon, an Armed Forces Expeditionary Medal, Parachutist Wings, and a Distinguished Flying Cross.

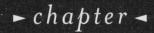

► *chapter* ◄

8

SPOOKS AND COPS

Who wouldn't want to be James Bond? A globetrotting lifestyle, Savile Row suits, a license to kill, and a fantastic car (Aston Martin of course)? Not to mention hot (and cold) Bond girls and dodgy budgie-smugglers (tight Speedos). It's a life to die for, except that James Bond never dies. Unfortunately, the real world of spies is less glamorous than Bond's fictional one. Even so, some men (and they are usually men) can't stop themselves from pretending to be spies, but then they do what no real spy would do—they try to impress people by talking about their secret work.

The real world of espionage always involves a degree of lying, deception, and subterfuge, so all real spies are impostors to some extent. They are more properly the subjects of a book about spies. However, deep-cover police officers and secret service agents who adopt a false identity over a period of several years to infiltrate groups of activists or assassinate enemies do warrant inclusion here, so we'll take a look at a few of those. There are also people who pretend to be spies and agents for the purpose of personal gain or vanity.

In a Los Angeles court in 2007, Larry Lee Risser pleaded guilty to an extraordinary deception. Risser had made a phone call to a friend, a gun shop owner, claiming that he'd been wounded during a secret CIA mission. Military radio messages hissed and crackled in the background. Risser said he urgently needed $10,000 to pay for a rescue helicopter. His friend transferred the money straight away and later heard that Risser was recovering in Germany. It was a lie. Risser had started constructing his false identity during visits to a shooting range and the gun shop. He told the regulars a string of yarns— he'd made millions in the security business, he exported bulletproof cars to the Philippines, he was Angelina Jolie's bodyguard, he'd been awarded the Silver Star, and, finally, he worked for the CIA. Risser had also tried to get $14,000 out of the shooting range owner, who initially wrote out a check but got suspicious, canceled it, and called the police. Another man gave Risser $10,000 to pay for specialist training to help him get a promotion. The FBI brought Risser's bizarre activities to an end.

For those who don't aspire to be bogus secret agents, the lure of a uniform and the ability to order people about is more attractive. People often see the uniform but not the person inside it, and they respond to the authority of the office-holder. Norwegian far-right murderer Anders Behring Breivik wore a police uniform to get close to his victims. By the time they realized he wasn't really a police officer, it was too late. After killing eight people and injuring more than two hundred with a bomb explosion in Oslo on July 22, 2011, he roamed the island of Utøya, shooting people attending a summer camp, killing another sixty-nine and wounding more than one hundred before being caught.

Fortunately, most bogus police officers do no more than tell tall stories about invented adventures or pull over motorists for a lecture on bad driving—still a serious offense. In summer 2011, London and several other English cities suffered riots involving hundreds of people looting shops and burning buildings. A blogger wrote about his experiences as a police officer on the front line during the riots. National newspapers picked up his work, and one paid him to write a column. He turned out to be a serial impostor of police and army officers.

Most people have a generous nature. They like to help others if they can. It's an admirable quality that's ripe for exploitation by impostors.

In the United States, police think two people shot dead on Mississippi highways in May 2012 may have been attacked by a bogus officer who pulled them over. A police officer shot in San Antonio in October 2012 is also thought to have been shot by a fake officer.

When the good people of Michigan were approached by a man flashing an FBI badge, saying he was about to be posted to Haiti after the 2010 earthquake and he was collecting money to help the victims, especially children, they dipped in their pockets and gave generously. The man, Kevin Balfour, is said to have collected several thousand dollars. Balfour sometimes turned up at parties wearing an FBI vest and badge and carrying a firearm. However, Balfour wasn't an FBI agent and wasn't going to Haiti. When the FBI was alerted, he was arrested.

Even police officers can be taken in by a convincing uniform. In 2012, an officer working at the Perth Watch House in Australia was found to be an impostor, triggering a major security alert. At the beginning of 2013, a man was charged with impersonating an assistant commissioner of police in Kenya—he had been undetected for five years!

When agents searched Balfour's home and car, they found sixteen firearms, one thousand rounds of ammunition, a bulletproof vest, an FBI badge, Chicago police badges, and a variety of other police and military equipment. Even his wife thought he was part of an FBI team. His record showed that he had a history of this sort of activity. Among nine convictions in two states for crimes including armed robbery, assault, and auto theft, he had a previous conviction for impersonating a police officer in Illinois. At the end of his trial, Judge Nancy Edmunds sentenced Balfour to three years' imprisonment and banned him from owning any law enforcement paraphernalia, including clothing.

THE EYE OF THE DAY

On October 15, 1917, Margaretha Zelle was awakened at 5:00 a.m. She knew immediately what was about to happen. Outside, she saw the twelve men who had come to kill her.

Mata Hari claimed to be a Javanese princess and temple dancer, but her true origins were very different. The woman who would become Mata Hari overcame a series of cruel setbacks and losses in her life by reinventing herself as a different person. Her story begins, not amid the palaces and temples of the Far East, but in the Dutch town of Leeuwarden. She was born on August 7, 1876, as Margaretha Geertruida Zelle. Her father Adam was a prominent businessman. Margaretha had a very happy childhood until she was twelve years old, when her father stunned the family by announcing that he was bankrupt. He left home to look for work and divorced his wife, Antje, a year later.

Margaretha suffered a second terrible loss in 1891 when her mother died at the age of forty-nine. Margaretha and her three brothers were split up and sent to live with different relatives. She was heartbroken when she was not allowed to live with her father but was sent to live with an uncle in a small town called Sneek. She was a headstrong girl who was difficult to handle, so she was sent to a school in Leiden to train as a teacher. A year later, she was forced to leave in disgrace amid rumors of an inappropriate relationship with the school's married headmaster. She was a teenager, while he was in his fifties. She moved in with an uncle in the Dutch capital, The Hague.

While she was living in The Hague, the eighteen-year-old Margaretha answered a newspaper ad from an officer seeking a wife. The officer was Rudolf MacLeod. He was a career soldier who had entered

In The Hague, Margaretha would have been accustomed to seeing handsome military officers in smart uniforms. During the nineteenth century, the Dutch fought several wars in the territory known then as the Dutch East Indies (Indonesia today) to exercise its control over the reluctant colony. The Netherlands was then a highly militarized nation, and The Hague was the hub of its military command network.

the military academy at the age of only sixteen and was posted to the Dutch East Indies five years later. He was home on medical leave from active service. The nature of his illness is unknown. It could have been diabetes, rheumatism, beriberi, or syphilis. Syphilis was very common among soldiers serving in the Indies.

Marriage and Motherhood

When they met, MacLeod, who was thirty-eight, was instantly attracted to the tall, slim Margaretha. They were engaged within a week and married a few months later, but the marriage began badly. MacLeod was in debt and couldn't support his wife, so they had to live with his sister, Louise, who disapproved of her brother's attractive young wife. Within a year, Margaretha was expecting their first child, a boy named Norman John. In 1896, when the boy was just a few months old, the family left the Netherlands for the Dutch East Indies, where Rudolf was to resume his military service. They took up residence in a spacious home attended by servants. Margaretha had a second child, a girl named Jeanne Louise and nicknamed Non, but the marriage continued to deteriorate. Rudolf and Margaretha argued and suspected each other of taking lovers. The attractive and flirtatious Margaretha enjoyed the admiring glances of young officers, which infuriated Rudolf.

In June 1899, both of the children fell ill. Their two-year-old son lapsed into a coma and died. Poisoning was suspected but couldn't be proven because Rudolf refused to give his permission for an autopsy. Their daughter survived.

In 1900, Rudolf came to the end of his military service and was discharged from the army. He was still deeply in debt, and now his income was slashed to a small military pension. His anger and frustration at his reduced circumstances led to violent outbursts.

Home Alone

Margaretha longed to return to the Netherlands. She got her wish in March 1902. A few months later, she obtained a legal separation from

Rudolf. He responded in an extraordinary and vindictive way. He placed ads in local newspapers telling people not to supply his wife with credit or merchandise because he was no longer responsible for her. She turned to prostitution to earn some money. A brief attempt at a reunion with Rudolf failed. When they parted for good, their daughter stayed with Rudolf.

Margaretha was now on her own with no home, no work, and no money. After failing to find work in Amsterdam and The Hague, she moved to Paris. It was here that she created her famous alter ego, Mata Hari. She invented dance routines, wearing very revealing costumes loosely based on those of genuine Javan dancers. Risqué dance was not unusual in Paris in the early 1900s, but Margaretha's performances stood out because she claimed they were traditional sacred dances from the mysterious Orient.

At first, she performed in people's homes. News of her performances spread, and she was invited to dance at a museum of oriental art. It was the museum proprietor, Émile Guimet, who suggested that she should adopt a name as exotic as her stage persona. She chose Mata Hari, a Malay phrase that means "the eye of the day," or sunrise. She gave her first public performance as Mata Hari at the Musée Guimet on March 13, 1905. The audience included the most important and influential Parisians of the day. The performance caused a sensation. Glowing, admiring accounts appeared in newspapers. When reporters asked about her life, she invented a fictitious past as a temple dancer in Java. She was hired to dance in theaters and private homes, onstage, and at parties. By now, she not only danced as Mata Hari, but also lived as Mata Hari.

Meanwhile, in the Netherlands, Rudolf wanted to remarry, so he needed Margaretha to agree to a divorce. His lawyer threatened to produce a photograph of her dancing naked if she contested the divorce or tried to win custody of their daughter. She agreed to everything, and the divorce was granted in 1906.

Fame and Fortune

Mata Hari's fame continued to spread. She was paid large sums of money to dance in Paris, Madrid, Monte Carlo, Berlin, Vienna, and Milan. And she had frequent liaisons and romances with wealthy men including diplomats, bankers, and military officers. She used them to provide the money she needed to maintain her extravagant lifestyle. And they were only too happy to pay her and shower her with expensive gifts.

When World War I broke out, she was working in Berlin. She was anxious to return to France, but when she tried to make the journey by train, German border guards refused to let her pass. They seized her luggage and sent her back to Berlin. A few days later, she managed to get to The Hague. There, she received a visit that set her on the course that would lead inexorably to her death. A German diplomat named Karl Kroemer called to see her. He paid her a large sum of money to spy for Germany. She accepted the payment but later said that she had no intention of working as a spy. She said she took Kroemer's money by way of compensation for the belongings German officials had confiscated.

Raising Suspicions

In 1915, she traveled from The Hague to France by sea via Folkstone, England. In Folkstone, she was questioned by British secret service agents, who were suspicious of her.

The British passed on their suspicions to their French ally. Margaretha continued her travels to Spain and Portugal and back to the Netherlands. Meanwhile, the British had found out about the payment she received from Kroemer, who was known to have recruited spies. It seemed to confirm their belief that she was a German agent.

In 1916, she wanted to travel from The Hague to France via England again, but the British authorities refused her visa application, so she had to travel via Spain instead. Soon after she arrived in Paris, she noticed that two men were following her. They were police officers who

The British agents' suspicions appear to have been based on nothing more than her being a glamorous, intelligent, multilingual, independent woman traveling internationally on her own during wartime. This marked her out as a very rare individual.

watched where she went and who she met. They recorded details of her meetings with men—quite a few men. She treated most of these men as sources of money, but she was particularly fond of one of them, a Russian army officer named Vadim de Masloff. He was twenty-one and she was thirty-nine.

After Vadim returned to the front, she wanted to visit the town of Vittel, near where he was recovering from a gas attack. Vittel was in a military zone, so it was necessary to get permission to travel there. While she was applying for a permit to travel, she met a French official named Georges Ladoux. He worked in counterespionage and was aware of the British concerns about Mata Hari. And now this suspected German spy who had multiple liaisons with military officers from different countries was asking for permission to travel into the French war zone. Ladoux was convinced that Mata Hari must be a German spy. He tried to turn her into a double agent by inviting her to spy for France. She decided to accept his offer in the hope of earning a large sum of money, perhaps as much as a million francs, which would enable her to end her relationships with other men and marry Vadim.

Her visit to Vittel was approved. She spent a week with Vadim before he had to return to the front. To justify the fortune she wanted from Ladoux, she had to deliver a huge intelligence coup. She planned to travel to Belgium and seduce General Moritz Ferdinand von Bissing, who oversaw the German occupation forces there. She was certain that she could persuade him to reveal some military secrets in the bedroom. But she couldn't travel directly to Belgium. She would have to go via Spain, Britain, and the Netherlands. However, she didn't get any farther than Britain.

The British were searching for a known German spy named Clara Bendix, who bore a resemblance to Mata Hari. They suspected that

Margaretha Zelle, Mata Hari, and Clara Bendix were the same person. When they found Mata Hari onboard a ship in Falmouth, they arrested her and took her to London for questioning. She denied that she was Clara Bendix. After two days of interrogation, she revealed that she was working as a spy for the French secret service. The British confirmed this with Ladoux. After four days, they released her but refused to let her continue her journey. They sent her back to Spain. In Madrid, with very little money, she wired a request to a former lover, Baron Edouard Willem van der Capellen, for funds. Meanwhile, she arranged a meeting with a high-ranking German official, Major Arnold Kalle. During their conversation, he revealed that a submarine was due to land German and Turkish officers on the coast of Morocco. In return for this information, she gave Kalle some French "secrets"—not secrets at all, but information that was circulating openly in France.

She returned to France and went to see Ladoux in the hope of receiving payment. When he eventually agreed to see her, he refused to pay her anything. He said the information was useless as it was already known to the French, because they were able to decode German radio messages.

In the middle of January 1917, Vadim managed to get some leave and traveled to Paris to see her. He revealed that his commanding officer had told him not to contact her again, because he said she was only interested in him for his money. When Vadim left, she tried to go to the Netherlands, but she couldn't obtain the necessary permit to travel.

> Kalle paid Mata Hari, but she appears to have treated this as one of the many payments she received from men she had romantic liaisons with, not a payment for espionage.

Arrest and Trial

She was arrested in her hotel room in Paris on February 13, 1917. She was interrogated again and again over the next four months by a dogged investigator named Pierre Bouchardon. He was convinced that she was guilty, but she insisted that she was not a double agent and had only ever acted on behalf of France. Between interrogations, she was held in the filthy, rat-infested conditions of Saint-Lazare prison—a world away from the luxury and grandeur she was accustomed to. Her health and her mental state both deteriorated as the weeks went by. She had a fever, coughed up blood, and cried for long periods. Her lawyer repeatedly requested that she be released or at the very least transferred to a hospital room, but every request was denied.

The only visitor she was allowed was her lawyer, Edouard Clunet. He was yet another former lover. As a corporate lawyer, the seventy-four-year-old Clunet was not the best person to defend her in such a serious criminal case. In addition, her defense was severely limited by the rules of the military trial she would face. During her imprisonment, Vadim was writing to her, but his letters and postcards were intercepted by the police and kept from her. He didn't know she had been arrested, and he became increasingly disturbed by her silence.

At this late stage, Georges Ladoux produced the "evidence" that would seal Mata Hari's fate. While he was reading through transcripts of German radio messages that had been intercepted several months earlier, he found messages from Mata Hari's former German lover, Major Kalle, about an agent code-named H21, who was passing information about France to Germany. The agent's movements between Madrid and Paris matched Mata Hari's. Strangely, these messages had been sent using a code the Germans knew the French had broken. In other words, the Germans wanted the French to read them. It may be that the Germans knew Mata Hari wasn't going to be any use to them, or they had learned that she was working as a double agent and decided to sacrifice her to protect more valuable agents.

The French had not informed the Dutch authorities that they were holding a Dutch national. When Mata Hari herself wrote a letter to the Dutch Consul, the French sent it through the ordinary postal system, not through diplomatic channels, to delay it as long as possible. Surprisingly, when it finally arrived, the Dutch seemed unconcerned about Mata Hari's treatment.

The easiest way to "neutralize" her was to reveal her as a German spy to the French. Another possibility is that the messages—or at least some of them—were not genuine but instead fabricated, possibly by Ladoux, to incriminate Mata Hari.

Finally broken, Mata Hari told Bouchardon about the visit she had received in 1915 from Karl Kroemer, who had asked her to spy for Germany and paid her. She admitted accepting the money but insisted she had done nothing in return. She said she had only worked for France after Ladoux had recruited her. However, Ladoux denied ever offering to pay her to work as a spy.

Her trial began on July 24, 1917. Public and press crowded into the courthouse to see the famous dancer and sex symbol. However, the prosecution's request that the trial should be held in secret because of national security was accepted, so the court was cleared.

The trial took only two days. The prosecution witnesses were heard on the first day. They included one of the police officers who had tailed Mata Hari in Paris. He spoke of the many men she had met. However, nothing in any of the five prosecution testimonies amounted to evidence of espionage. Even so, it didn't stop the prosecutor, André Mornet, from describing Mata Hari as "perhaps the greatest woman spy of the century."

On the second day, it was Clunet's turn to present the defense case. Several influential men who had been Mata Hari's lovers confirmed that she had never shown any interest in the war or military matters. In a final statement, Mata Hari asserted her right to have friends from other countries, even countries that were at war with France. The judges retired and took only forty-five minutes to find her guilty of all charges. She was sentenced to death, and her belongings were ordered to be sold to recover the cost of her trial. She was returned to Saint-Lazare prison to await execution. An appeal against the death sentence was rejected. A further appeal to the Supreme Court was rejected too. The Dutch government sent a request for clemency, but this was rejected.

Execution

Mata Hari was awakened at 5:00 a.m. on October 15, 1917. She dressed and then was escorted to the execution ground. She was met with the sight of twelve soldiers—a firing squad. She refused to wear a blindfold. As she stood alone, a sergeant major raised his saber and gave the command to aim and fire. The rifle shots rang out, and Mata Hari sank to the ground. The sergeant major walked up to her and shot her in the head. Her body was not claimed by her family and was used for medical research. Her head was known to have been kept by the Museum of Anatomy in Paris, but it disappeared and has never been found.

THE SPY WHO CAME IN FROM THE COLD SEA

One of the most bizarre impostor cases is that of Major William Martin of the Royal Marines. He was already dead before he became a secret agent who was sent on a vital mission for the Allies during World War II!

In 1942, the Allies were planning to invade southern Europe from North Africa. It was vital to take control of Sicily to eliminate Luftwaffe bases on the island and keep the Mediterranean sea routes open. The Allies assumed that German commanders would come to the same conclusion and would defend Sicily with massive force. It was essential to find a way to confuse them so that they might move some of their forces elsewhere. The British came up with an extraordinary ruse codenamed Operation Mincemeat.

They planned to have the Germans discover faked documents suggesting that the Allied invasion would target Greece and Sardinia instead of Sicily.

Having come up with the plan, the next problem was how to get the documents to the Germans in a believable way. During World War I, the British had used a similar trick. In that case, they arranged for a bag containing false battle plans to fall into enemy hands. It is said to have

helped them win the Battle of
Beersheba in 1917.

However, the British couldn't
just drop the documents somewhere where German troops

Interestingly, this idea is said to have
originated from a naval intelligence officer named Ian Fleming, who would later
write the James Bond novels.

would find them. The mysterious appearance of secret battle plans
on their doorstep would have raised suspicions. Instead, the British
planned to place the documents on a dead body that would be washed
up from a plane crash at sea off the coast of Spain. Spain remained
neutral during the war, but the Franco regime was sympathetic to Nazi
Germany. If the documents were to fall into Spanish hands, it was very
likely that German agents would learn of their contents.

The next problem was the body. Obtaining a body during one
of the largest military conflicts in history may not seem problem-
atic. However, the body had to be obtained secretly and the cause
of death had to look like hypothermia and drowning after a plane
crash. The age and build of the body were important too. The man
had to look like a convincing Royal Marines major. The coroner
of St. Pancras in London was told what to look out for. Eventually,
on January 28, 1943, he found the perfect body. A thirty-four-
year-old Welshman, later revealed to be Glyndwr Michael, had
been found dead in a warehouse in King's Cross. He was home-
less, jobless, and had no friends or family. He wouldn't be missed
by anyone. He had committed suicide by eating rat poison. The
poison had dissipated, leaving no trace, so he could pass for someone who had died at sea.

Researchers later argued that Michael's body may not have been used in
the end but was replaced with the body of a sailor who had died in an accident onboard the British warship HMS *Dasher*. However, the Royal Navy and
Ministry of Defense both denied this and confirmed that Michael's body was
used for Operation Mincemeat.

Making Martin Real

The British then set about creating an identity for the dead man. They filled his pockets with the paraphernalia of everyday life—bills, photographs, tickets, letters, keys, and so on. One problem was that Major Martin needed identity papers bearing his photograph, but Glyndwr Michael had never been photographed while alive. Fortunately, they found an MI5 intelligence officer who looked remarkably like him, so he was photographed instead. Major Martin's body was kept in cold storage while this preparatory work was under way.

The final problem was how to get him ashore in Spain. The body was

> Major Martin was buried in Huelva Cemetery with full military honors. The names of British casualties were routinely listed in the *Times* newspaper, so Major Martin's death was included in the list published in the June 4 issue, just in case a diligent German intelligence officer checked.

packed in dry ice inside a specially built canister. It was loaded onboard the British submarine HMS *Seraph* and stored in one of the sub's torpedo racks. Only the commanding officer, Lt. Bill Jewel, knew what the top-secret cargo was. The submarine slipped out of the Holy Loch in Scotland

on April 19, 1943, and headed south. Eleven days later, at 4:30 a.m., Commander Jewel read the 39th Psalm as Major Martin's body was taken out of the canister and lowered into the sea. The tide carried it toward the shore at Huelva. Before it washed up, it was spotted and picked up by a local sardine fisherman, who handed it over to the Spanish authorities. They alerted a German spy, Adolf Clauss. He was the very spy the British hoped would become involved, because he was known to be gullible. While Spanish officers opened the briefcase chained to the dead man's belt, his body was autopsied. The cause of death was found to be drowning.

The contents of the briefcase were handed over to the German Embassy in Madrid for one hour, just enough time for them to be photographed. They included top-secret letters being carried by hand from one general to another. One of them referred to the forthcoming Allied invasion of Greece. To make their loss seem more authentic, the

British sent messages to their naval attaché in Spain urgently requesting that papers lost in a recent plane crash at sea should be located at all costs without alerting the Spanish authorities to their importance. They hoped that German intelligence would intercept the messages or become aware of British attempts to get the documents back.

Mincemeat Swallowed

When Major Martin's briefcase was returned to the British, officers examined the contents and confirmed that they had been opened. The German Embassy in Madrid had passed everything on to Berlin. German intelligence officers carefully analyzed the contents, even the dates on the major's ticket stubs, in their search for any clue that this was a planted body. The British secret service sent Prime Minister Winston Churchill a message saying, "Mincemeat swallowed whole."

The operation was a complete success. Sicily was left lightly defended. A force of R-boats (motor torpedo boats) and two panzer divisions were moved to Greece. The Allied landings met less resistance than expected, and the island was quickly conquered. Two weeks after the Allied landings began in Sicily, the German High Command still believed that this was just a diversion and carried on waiting for the main event, the invasion of Greece, which never came. The Allies moved up through Italy. The Italian leader, Mussolini, was removed from power. Faced with a major invasion under way in southern Europe, the Germans canceled a huge offensive against Russia. The war began to turn in the Allies' favor.

A film called *The Man Who Never Was*, made in 1956, was based on a book written by one of the naval intelligence officers in charge of Operation Mincemeat, Captain Ewen Montagu. Many of the details of the real events were still classified, so some aspects of the book and film were deliberately fictional. Montagu himself played a minor role in the film. In one scene, the real Captain Montagu is seen talking to the character Captain Montagu, played by actor Clifton Webb.

Operation Mincemeat was probably the most successful military deception ever pulled off. It changed the course of the war and saved thousands of Allied lives. And it was achieved by an impostor who knew *nothing* about his vital role.

KING CON

If a complete stranger told you he was a secret service agent and you were in danger, would you believe him? Would you go into hiding if he told you to? Would you cut yourself off from all your friends? Would you hand over money to him?

In 2002, a joint undercover force of London Metropolitan Police detectives and FBI agents closed in on their target at Heathrow Airport. The man, Robert Hendy-Freegard, had been lured to the airport to collect a $20,000 payment from the mother of one of his victims. He was arrested and charged with more than twenty counts of kidnapping, theft, and deception stretching over the previous ten years.

The story began in Newport, Shropshire, at the beginning of 1993. While Robert Freegard was working in the Swan pub there, he befriended three students from a local agricultural college and convinced one of them that he was actually working undercover for the British military intelligence agency, MI5. He said he was monitoring a terrorist cell at the college. It sounds outlandish, but the IRA was active in Britain at the time. There had been bombings in London and Manchester, and a student at the college in Newport had been exposed as an IRA gunrunner, so the idea that MI5 might be watching the college students was perfectly believable.

Then Freegard told the student that his cover had been blown and that both of them were now in danger. He persuaded the man to tell his two female friends that he was suffering from cancer and to ask them to go away with him for his last holiday. Once they were away, Freegard told the women the "real" reason for getting them away from the college was to protect them from IRA killers who were on their trail. He told them it was essential that they didn't tell their families where they were or the killers would be able to track them down.

He told them they'd have to get money from their families to pay for the security operation. One of the students, John Atkinson, handed over almost £400,000. Another, Sarah Smith, handed over £188,000. He told them the government would eventually refund it all. Meanwhile, they were in hiding, doing menial jobs in Sheffield and paying their earnings to Freegard. In 1994, one of the women, Maria, gave birth to Freegard's child. She was living separately from the other two students, John and Sarah. He then separated John and Sarah from each other, sending John to Derbyshire while Sarah stayed in Sheffield. Maria had a second child by Freegard. While the students lived in fear and poverty, Freegard lived the high life, funded by his victims.

Jekyll and Hyde

In the mid-1990s, he met and seduced several women. One of them, Elizabeth Bartholomew, took out loans totaling £14,500 and handed over the money to him. He was particularly cruel to her. She later said that he had a Jekyll and Hyde personality—charming one moment and terrifyingly angry the next. He persuaded her to change her name and cut off all contact with her family. He changed her appearance and made her live on the streets for weeks at a time.

In 1998, John Atkinson was finally persuaded by his family to escape from Freegard and return home, but he didn't go to the police, because he still believed that his life was in danger. By 2000, while Freegard was working as a car salesman, he met his next victim, Renata Kister. He told her he was an MI5 agent watching someone at the dealership. Once again, he persuaded her to take out a large loan for him. He also persuaded her to house one of his first victims, Sarah. He told Kister that Sarah was in a witness protection program and couldn't speak English, while he told Sarah to pretend she couldn't understand English for security reasons. They both played along perfectly, never suspecting a thing.

Freegard's relationship with Maria ended in 2001. Like John, she escaped to her parents. Freegard moved on to a new relationship with lawyer Caroline Cowper. She believed they were going to be married. The wedding day was set for February 2, 2002. Instead, he stole thousands of pounds from her. Realizing that she had been conned, she reported Freegard to the police. This set off a chain of events that alerted the police to one victim after another. The police now realized they were dealing with an extraordinary series of crimes with multiple victims. By now, Freegard had changed his name, adding Maria's surname, Hendy, and began calling himself Robert Hendy-Freegard.

The Last Victim

Freegard's last victim was American child psychologist Kimberley Adams. He met her in March 2002. By August, they were engaged. He convinced her that he had infiltrated a dangerous network of criminals. Like all his other victims, she was taken in completely. He took over her life and started cutting her off from her family. Then he found out that her stepfather had won a multimillion-dollar lottery prize, so he made Kimberley ask him for money, because he said she would have to leave her job and undergo expensive training to become a spy if she wanted to continue her relationship with him. Her parents and stepfather became suspicious. The FBI and London's Metropolitan Police, now working together, monitored their phone calls. The calls enabled them to analyze Freegard's strengths and weaknesses, much as he had done with his victims.

The police learned that Freegard had a habit of hiding his victims. They were concerned that they might be able to arrest him but be unable to find Kimberley, so they decided not to detain him until they were sure that Kimberley was safe. With police and FBI knowledge, Kimberley's mother arranged to meet Freegard at Heathrow Airport and personally hand over money to him. Several surveillance teams were stationed at the airport, all looking for him. Kimberley's mother had been flown into London the day before the meeting and had undergone intensive preparation for the forthcoming operation. The surveillance teams watched her as she met Freegard. She was told not to hand over any money until she had seen Kimberley. She went with him to a car park where Kimberley was waiting in a car. As soon as the officers saw her, they moved in and arrested Freegard.

They had Freegard and Kimberley, but other victims were still missing, still believing they were in hiding from the IRA. Officers searched Freegard's belongings and found passports, letters, and other documents that eventually led them to Sarah, Elizabeth, and Renata. When Sarah was found, she was still living with Renata and working as a cleaner. Neither woman knew the other was a victim of Freegard's. Sarah had been brainwashed so effectively that, at first, she didn't believe the story police officers told her.

As the police worked through all the documents and information and followed all the leads, they discovered more victims. There was a civil servant who had given Freegard thousands of pounds and even sold her car to raise cash for him. There was a watchmaker who carried out a variety of bizarre tasks and missions dreamt up by Freegard.

Freegard's victims were not stupid people. He appeared to be able to pick up on any flaw or weakness in a potential victim and then exploit it for all it was worth. Case-hardened FBI agents, who thought they'd seen everything, said they had never come across a con artist as accomplished or as ruthless as Freegard. He is thought to have tricked at least a dozen victims out of £1 million.

Freegard was born on March 1, 1971, and brought up in Derbyshire. Even at primary school, he stood out as different. One of his teachers described him as very charming and good-looking, but also very odd. He left school at fifteen with no qualifications and worked as a manual laborer. In 1992, his first girlfriend left him after he stole money from her. A year later, he was working in the Swan pub in Newport, where his life as a bogus MI5 agent began.

In October 2004, Freegard pleaded not guilty to twenty-four charges. At the end of an eight-month trial, he was found guilty on two counts of kidnapping, ten counts of theft, and eight counts of deception and was given a life sentence. He appealed and, amazingly, managed to overturn the kidnapping charges on the grounds that he had not physically restrained any of his victims. As a result, his sentence was reduced to nine years, enabling him to be free after only five years—half the length of time he had spent destroying his victims' lives.

HIT SQUAD

In January 2010, more than twenty of the many tourists and business travelers arriving in Dubai hid a lethal secret. They were all impostors, a team of killers converging on their unsuspecting target.

Mahmoud al-Mabhouh was a senior member of the military wing of the Palestinian group Hamas. Israel held him responsible for the murder of two of its soldiers in 1989, and Mabhouh had admitted his involvement in an interview broadcast on Al Jazeera, the Qatar-based television channel. Although his identity had been hidden, his voice was recognized. In the 1990s, he became involved in procuring weapons for Hamas. He had already survived two assassination attempts by the time a team, thought to be an Israeli hit squad, closed in on him in Dubai.

One of the prime activities of the Institute for Intelligence and Special Operations, more commonly known as the Mossad, is "planning and carrying out special operations beyond Israeli borders." This is widely believed to include the assassination of Israel's enemies.

Mabhouh traveled extensively. Of the many places he visited regularly, including Iran, Syria, and China, Dubai was selected as the best place to attack him, because it was the easiest to enter and move around in freely without raising suspicions. Mabhouh usually traveled with bodyguards, but on this occasion he was on his own, transiting through Dubai on his way to China.

The Operation

The hit squad started arriving in Dubai on January 18, 2010, the day before Mabhouh's arrival. They had known about his travel arrangements for at least a week. They arrived in small groups from Paris, Zurich, Rome, and Frankfurt. The team numbered at least twenty-six agents. The passports they presented to immigration officials were false, but some of them were in the names of real people, and all were from countries that do not need visas for entry to Dubai—twelve British, six Irish, four French, three Australian, and one German.

The twenty-six impostors went about their business efficiently. When Mabhouh arrived on Emirates flight EK912, some of the agents followed him to his hotel. There, other members of the team followed him to his room. Once they knew his room number, another agent booked a room on the opposite side of the hallway.

After Mabhouh was seen leaving the hotel at 4:23 p.m., four members of the team went to his room, where they were joined by another two agents. While they were attempting to open the door's electronic lock, a hotel guest appeared unexpectedly in the hallway. One of the agents pretended to be a member of the hotel staff and directed him to his room. Mabhouh returned to the hotel at 8:24 p.m., unaware that the killers were waiting for him inside his room. No one knows exactly what happened next.

Natural Death or Murder?

The next morning, a hotel cleaner was unable to enter the room. Hotel security staff opened the door and found Mabhouh's body lying on the bed. At first, officials thought he had died of natural causes. Apart from a couple of broken bed slats, there was no sign of a struggle in the room. However, ten days later, after forensic tests, the authorities announced that Mabhouh had been murdered. It is thought that he was injected with a powerful muscle relaxant called succinylcholine and then suffocated.

By the time the murder had been detected, the hit squad was long gone. Its members had started leaving for various destinations within minutes of the operation's successful conclusion. Suspicions fell on a rival Palestinian group, but photographs of the suspects showed people who were clearly not Palestinian. The suspects were identified from their payment and phone records and from hotel security recordings, but these identities quickly proved to be false. In most cases, their passport details were traced to innocent people. As some of the passports belonged to people with dual Israeli nationality, and Israeli agents had made use of this type of passport before, suspicion shifted to the Mossad.

The countries whose citizens' identities and passports had been hijacked for the operation made official complaints to Israel. In March 2010, Britain expelled an Israeli diplomat after discovering evidence that Israel had used forged British passports. Later, Australia and Ireland also expelled Israeli diplomats for the same reason. The European Union and United Nations condemned the use of forged passports belonging to innocent people in an extrajudicial killing. Israel has made no comment on the accusations of Mossad involvement.

THE SECRET CIRCLE'S SECRET SPY

In 1983, a book called *Churchill's Secret Agent* was published. It told the story of a remarkable British spy named Josephine Butler, who worked in occupied France during World War II. The book, a first-hand account by Dr. Butler, describes her missions for a top-secret organization called the Secret Circle that reported directly to Prime Minister Winston Churchill. And her accounts were daring indeed.

Butler describes being brought up in Belgium and France, so she was a fluent French speaker. She studied medicine at the Sorbonne and then worked in cancer research. In 1938, when it became clear that war was imminent, she left for England. When war broke out, she found work driving VIPs around. It seems odd that her medical expertise wasn't made use of in one way or another. Then, strangely, this unknown driver was chosen for secret work involving the analysis of reports from agents in France.

Soon afterward, even more strangely, she was whisked off to meet Winston Churchill, who appears to have handpicked her to be one of Britain's most secret spies—one of only twelve members of his Secret Circle. She was told to disappear from her normal everyday life and sever all contacts with friends and family. She was to be replaced by an identical-looking cousin, so identical that the substitute would fool everyone but her father.

She was sent on dozens of missions into occupied France. She claimed to have spied on, and possibly met, Admiral Canaris, the head of the Abwehr, the German military intelligence service, and to have been held briefly by the Gestapo.

While in custody, Dr. Butler was questioned by a man she later discovered was Klaus Barbie, the notorious "Butcher of Lyon." Barbie was found living in Bolivia in 1971 and extradited to France. In 1984, he was charged with war crimes dating from his time as head of the Gestapo in Lyon. He was found guilty and sentenced to life imprisonment. He died in prison in 1991, a year before Dr. Butler's death.

The problem with Dr. Butler's claims is that there doesn't appear to be any evidence in the extensive records of the Royal Air Force (RAF) or the Prime Minister's office that *any* of it happened. There are no records of any of the fifteen meetings she is supposed to have had with Churchill or of the existence of the Secret Circle. The RAF, which provided the aircraft and pilots to fly agents into and out of France, can't confirm any of her operations. The flight records for airfields she claimed to have flown from don't match her claimed operations. The sheer number of her missions seems fanciful too. Conveniently, the people Butler named in her books had already died, so they couldn't corroborate her story.

Nigel West's book *Counterfeit Spies* dismantled Dr. Butler's claims and tells the stories of many other people who appear to have invented secret lives as wartime spies. Another book, *The Forgotten Service:*

Auxiliary Ambulance Station 3 by Angela Raby, also claims that Dr. Butler's story is just that—fiction.

BOND LITE

Secret service agents work in the shadows, combating crime and protecting the nation, but how can you tell if someone really is an agent when even the police can be fooled?

When British MI5 agent Michael Newitt passed information to the police in Leicestershire, England, about a drugs offense, one of the officers noticed something that didn't seem quite right. Newitt had given his MI5 rank as Commander, the same rank as the fictional spy James Bond. The police officer, who had a military background, was suspicious of this and ran some checks on Newitt.

Newitt carried a leather wallet containing his MI5 ID card, identifying him as an operational firearms officer. He was equipped with several guns, handcuffs, a baton, and police radio sets. His car was fitted with flashing lights and a siren. He'd used the car to stop a suspected drunk driver and then arrested him and handed him over to the local police. He'd had several contacts with the police, who had previously accepted his MI5 identity.

However, checks revealed that Newitt was not a member of MI5 at all. When police officers arrived at his home to arrest him, his wife protested that they had the wrong man. She knew about his MI5 work, because he sometimes disappeared on "special missions." But the police didn't have the wrong man.

Newitt's guns, including a Glock 9mm pistol, were found to be replicas. His ID card had the initials CMG after his name. This stands for Companion of the Order of St. Michael and St. George, the same honor awarded to James Bond. In fact, Newitt was a businessman whose IT company was in trouble. He had first used his secret service alter ego to fight the removal of his boat from a marina. He demanded that the boat be returned and served the marina's manager with a copy of the Official Secrets Act. He claimed to be an undercover officer again to fight the repossession of his car. Pretending to be a spy became a way of life, but Newitt's James Bond fantasy world ended in a prison cell. He was jailed for two years for a series of identity and firearms offenses.

SPY COP

In 2011, a court case against a group of environmental activists in England collapsed sensationally when one of their fellow activists was exposed as an undercover police officer and, it was alleged, an agent provocateur.

In April 2009, members of an environmental protest group gathered at a school in Nottingham, England. They were preparing to occupy the nearby Ratcliffe-on-Soar power station in a protest against global warming. Occupying the coal-fired plant for a week would stop it from releasing more than 160,000 tons of carbon into the atmosphere.

When the protesters heard rumors that the plant was under a heavy police guard, however, they thought they might have to abandon the break-in plan. One of their most trusted members, Mark Stone, was sent to recce the area. When he came back, he said there were no police to be seen and he seemed keen for the protest to go ahead. He even suggested the best way to break in.

Shortly after midnight on April 14, police officers raided the school and arrested 114 activists. Twenty-seven of them, including Stone, were charged with conspiracy to commit trespass. Twenty admitted that they planned to enter the power station and were convicted. Strangely, Stone had refused to use the same firm of lawyers as the rest of those charged. The charges against him, and only him, were subsequently dropped.

> It wasn't the first time this particular power station had been singled out by protesters. In 2007, eleven activists were arrested after entering it. This time, though, the police seemed to have inside knowledge of the protesters' intentions.

Six of the activists claimed that they had not decided yet whether to break into the power station when they were arrested, so they pleaded not guilty and were tried separately from the others. However, by then they had discovered documents that revealed Mark Stone's true identity. He was really Police Constable Mark Kennedy—a police officer working undercover!

When Kennedy was confronted, he admitted that his real name was indeed Mark Kennedy. He had been infiltrating the environmental movement and spying on its activities for the previous seven years and reporting back to the National Public Order Intelligence Unit. The secret seventy-strong unit had been set up in 1999 to investigate politically motivated disorder. Kennedy had been recruited to the unit in 2002. He had taken part in, and on some occasions even helped to organize, some of the most important environmental protests held in Britain, while reporting back to his police handlers.

To maintain security, activists often limited information about forthcoming protests to those members who were directly involved in planning them, especially those responsible for transport. Stone's car and his ability to rent other vehicles ensured him a place in the inner circle, privy to the most secret information. He was involved in, or aware of, protests at the G8 summit in Gleneagles, Drax power station in North Yorkshire, and Hartlepool nuclear power station. His enthusiasm for taking part in one activity after another, his money, his disappearances,

Kennedy was given a new identity, Mark Stone, and a new life history. He played the part of a professional climber. He looked the part, with long hair and tattoos, and was readily accepted. His job explained his occasional absences—he was climbing abroad. Using a fake passport and driver's license provided by the police, he visited environmental, animal rights, and anarchist protest groups in more than twenty countries. He said his work as a climber was very well paid, which enabled him to cover some of the group's expenses. He rented vehicles for them and even sometimes paid their fines when they were prosecuted. It earned him the nickname "Flash."

and the fact that any charges laid against him always seemed to be dropped had started to raise suspicions among some of his fellow activists. Instead of "Flash," his previous nickname, a few of them prophetically started calling him "Detective Stone" behind his back.

When defense lawyers told the Crown Prosecution Service that it was essential to disclose information about Stone/Kennedy's role in order to ensure a fair trial for the defendants, the case was suddenly halted and the charges were dropped. Sensationally, the undercover police officer had changed sides and offered to help the defense. When his cover was blown publicly, he went into hiding for his own safety. His email account, phone numbers, and Facebook account were all closed down. He couldn't continue living as Mark Stone, green activist, anymore, but he couldn't live openly as Mark Kennedy either because of the hundreds of enemies he had made during years of spying on people.

In November 2012, Kennedy announced his intention to sue his former employer, the Metropolitan Police, for up to £100,000 compensation for negligence—specifically, for not preventing him from falling in love with one of the activists. Another ten women and one man are also suing the police for emotional distress following relationships with undercover police officers. Three of the women are said to be former lovers of Kennedy, who was also married during his time as an undercover officer.

CLEANING UP GERALD

The town of Gerald, Missouri, had struggled with drug problems for years when a federal agent arrived in 2008. But he was not quite the godsend the townsfolk of Gerald initially believed him to be.

As soon as federal agent Bill Jakob arrived in Gerald, he got to work on the town's drug problem. Doors were broken down, homes were searched, suspects were cuffed, and arrests were made, sometimes at gunpoint. Reports describe the townsfolk as feeling like a tornado had hit them. "Sergeant Bill," as he became known, was a very effective law enforcer.

Then a local reporter who received complaints about Jakob's behavior made a few inquiries about him. Where had he come from? Why had he been sent to Gerald? Who had sent him? The questions were met with silence and blank stares. There was no record of a federal agent named Bill Jakob. It seems that he was accepted by local officials and officers simply because he looked, sounded, and acted the way they expected a federal agent to look, sound, and act. He also gave them his supervisor's phone number. When they called it, a woman who has never been identified answered, "multijurisdictional task force." Jakob's car was equipped with radios and flashing lights. He had a police uniform, ID card, and all the right gear. However, the reporter simply had to key Jakob's name into her computer to find out the truth about him.

He had been a member of the Missouri Army National Guard, but he had been discharged after faking a promotion and wearing a Ranger pin and air assault badge he wasn't entitled to. Then he got a job with a security company based on a fictitious military service history and a university degree he didn't have.

> Bill Jakob also worked for the Federal Reserve but left after his employer discovered a criminal record he hadn't declared.

Finally, in March 2008, he became the federal agent who arrived in Gerald.

In court, Jakob also admitted to impersonating a Drug Enforcement Administration agent and a U.S. Marshal. The multijurisdictional task force he claimed to belong to during his time in Gerald appears to have been inspired by the movie *Beverley Hills Cop*. The town's police chief, two of his officers, and a sheriff's deputy were fired for being so taken in by this impostor. And the town's authorities now had to deal with civil lawsuits from people Jakob had arrested, questioned, and whose homes he had searched without the appropriate warrants.

Jakob was sentenced to five years for twenty-three charges including wire fraud, mail fraud, false impersonation, and making false statements to the FBI. He was ordered to pay $2,300 in court fees and repay $30,000 relating to another scam. On the upside, he is reported to have signed a movie deal with a production company.

FRAUD ALERT: CYBER DOUBLES

The brave new world of digital communication has made a whole new branch of fakery possible. Millions of Web surfers hide their identity perfectly legitimately and sensibly by adopting a username. But there are others who actively pretend to be someone else and use their online presence for mischief or worse. After all, it's a lot easier to pretend to be someone else when you don't have to meet anyone face-to-face or produce identity documents. With a few clicks of a mouse, you can be whoever you want. Who's to know you're not a tall, dark, handsome airline pilot or a securities trader with a million dollars in the bank? Surprisingly, spies are also using social media networks to fish for information.

- In 2011, a Facebook account was opened by an impostor pretending to be a senior NATO military commander, American Admiral James Stavridis. Military officers were taken in by it. Facebook closed the account when NATO realized it was a fake. Newspaper reports suggested that a foreign intelligence service may have been behind the scam in an attempt to harvest personal information and other tidbits from chatter on the page between the fake admiral and military contacts.

- When former Pakistan Prime Minister Benazir Bhutto was assassinated in 2007, her son, Bilawal Bhutto Zardari, became the Pakistan People's Party chairman. Someone opened a bogus Facebook account using his identity. The site seemed so real that journalists are said to have used information posted on it. Facebook closed the fake account, but the impostor was never identified. Political rivals were suspected.

■ Businesses and their executives have fallen prey to the activities of online impostors too. In 2012, a senior executive of the Commonwealth Bank of Australia was impersonated on Twitter by someone making inflammatory comments about the bank. In the same year, someone impersonating a director at HSBC in Singapore made insulting remarks about Singaporeans in an apparent attempt to damage the bank.

■ In 2011, British actor Daniel Roche heard from friends that they had seen his Facebook page. However, Daniel was then a child actor who was too young to have his own Facebook account. He discovered that the impostor behind the page had used it to chat to his school friends. Unable to get the page closed down, he made a video saying that it had nothing to do with him and posted it on the page. The impostor repeatedly removed it. The page was eventually closed down after several months when a national newspaper got involved.

►*chapter*◄

9

A MISCELLANY OF MIMICS

We've looked at many specific types of impostors so far, but in the end, there are some impostors who just don't fit easily into any category. Some were trying to escape the difficulties of their real lives. Some, like Chung Ling Soo, the Chinese magician, were performers who adopted a more exotic identity for the stage. But in other cases, it is unclear why these pretenders assumed a false identity.

Inventions that change the way we communicate with each other offer impostors new ways to fool us. That's been true since Alexander Graham Bell came up with the telephone. For example, the media are always on the lookout for "characters" who can convey information with power and clarity. All the better if they're experts in their chosen subject. In 2012, the Portuguese media thought it had discovered a new economics pundit. Artur Baptista da Silva had impressive credentials—a social economics professor who worked for the United Nations. He appeared in televised debates and interviews denouncing the Portuguese government's austerity policy. Then on December 27, the United Nations issued a press statement saying that da Silva didn't work for them and was not authorized to speak on their behalf. He disappeared from Portugal's TV screens as suddenly as he'd appeared.

Impostors have also taken advantage of the possibilities offered by email, Twitter, and other digital social media. And then there's the mass imposture of the flash mob—ordinary people masquerading as equally ordinary people who aren't themselves simply for the fun of it.

This miscellany of mimics features a few of those tales, from a Chinese magician and famous movie director to a military doppelganger and terrorist commander.

One impostor whose motive was clear was a Japanese man arrested for impersonating his own son. In 2009, the fifty-four-year-old man was caught trying to stand in for his twenty-year-old son in an exam. The father ran a medicine distribution company and wanted his son to work with him, but the son needed a license. So, without telling his son, he curled his hair and left his glasses at home to look more like his son's photo and took the exam himself. But he didn't convince the examiners!

A BOY NAMED SOO

On the night of March 23, 1918, a famous Chinese magician named Chung Ling Soo was coming to the end of his act in the Wood Green Empire, a theater in north London. As usual, he performed in silence, apparently unable to speak English. On rare occasions, he performed one of the most dangerous tricks of all, and on that night, the audience was in luck. Chung Ling Soo was going to perform the bullet-catching trick.

At least half a dozen magicians had already been killed while performing this trick. Normally, a gun was fired straight at the magician, who caught the bullet in his teeth. Chung Ling Soo made it even more difficult and dangerous. Two assistants loaded two rifles with bullets that had been marked by members of the audience. Then both rifles were fired at him. He caught the two bullets in his teeth and dropped them onto a porcelain plate he held in front of his chest. The markings

One of Soo's assistants explained to the audience that what they were about to see was a reenactment of the time when Soo was arrested during the Boxer Rebellion in China and condemned to death but survived by catching the firing squad's bullets in midair before they could harm him.

on the bullets proved that they were the same bullets that had just been loaded into the rifle and fired at him.

At 10:45 p.m. on that March night in 1918, the rifles were leveled at Chung Ling Soo, and he prepared himself to catch the bullets. At a signal, the rifles were fired. The magician dropped the plate, which smashed to pieces on the floor. Then he stumbled backward and collapsed. The audience gasped. Everyone waited for him to get up and produce the bullets to uproarious applause, but he stayed down. His assistants noticed an ominous dark stain on the front of his costume. They rushed forward to him. It was clear that something was wrong. A white screen was lowered at the front of the stage, and a newsreel film was projected onto it. Meanwhile, behind the screen, Chung Ling Soo was bleeding heavily from a gunshot wound to his chest. He was rushed to the hospital but died a few hours later. The bullet-catching trick had claimed yet another victim.

Fans reeling from the shock news of Chung Ling Soo's death soon had another surprise when it was revealed that he was not Chinese at all. He was American, a Brooklyn-born Vaudeville entertainer named William Ellsworth Robinson.

Creating Chung Ling Soo

Robinson had worked for years as a magician's assistant, but when he tried to take center stage with his own magic act, he failed. He didn't have the gift of the gab. He couldn't master the patter that stage magicians commonly used in their acts to entertain the audience and distract them during tricks.

At that time, a genuine Chinese magician named Ching Ling Foo was very popular in the United States. He offered $1,000 to anyone who could replicate one of his tricks, called the water trick. It involved producing a large, heavy bowl full of water from under an apparently empty cloth. Robinson offered to perform the trick, but Foo declined to accept his offer. The challenge was simply a publicity stunt.

Then Robinson had the idea of performing as a Chinese magician who couldn't speak English, thus creating an exotic stage persona and also solving his patter problem. Once he adopted his new identity as Chung Ling Soo, he stayed in character offstage too. William Ellsworth Robinson ceased to exist.

In 1905, the two Chinese magicians were performing at London theaters just a stone's throw apart. Foo issued a challenge. If Soo could do ten of Foo's tricks or if Foo was unable to do even one of Soo's tricks, Foo would pay $1,000. The world-famous escapologist Harry Houdini volunteered to judge the contest. Each magician branded the other an impostor, but when the agreed time for the contest arrived, Foo didn't turn up. Soo was triumphant.

Ironically, Robinson became so well known, so convincing, and so popular in Britain as Chung Ling Soo, "The Original Chinese Conjurer," that the real Chinese magician, Ching Ling Foo, was accused of being a copycat fake when he arrived in Britain to tour the theaters!

He continued performing sellout shows until the night he died onstage.

Trick Rifles

An investigation discovered what had happened. Soo's wife, who was onstage with him on the night he was fatally shot, explained how the trick worked. People seated in the audience selected two bullets and marked them. These bullets had no further part in the trick. They were secretly switched for two bullets that had previously been marked by Soo. These bullets were given to two more audience members onstage to examine, noting the markings on them. Then they were loaded into the rifles. By now, Soo had secreted two more (spent) bullets with identical markings in his mouth.

The rifles were specially adapted so that when the trigger was pulled, a gunpowder charge in a chamber below the barrel fired instead of the live round. The rifles looked and sounded as if they had been fired, but actually the bullets never left their barrels. Soo then pretended to catch the bullets and spat them out onto the plate. When they were examined by the volunteers onstage, they appeared to be the same two bullets that had just been loaded into the rifles. However, on the night when Soo died, one of the rifles had become so worn that some of the hot gases from the gunpowder charge leaked into the live chamber and fired the bullet there. The verdict of the inquest was accidental death.

MONTY'S DOUBLE

Leading political and military figures have occasionally found it useful to employ a double to appear in their place. One of the most famous and successful decoys was Clifton James, who impersonated Field Marshal Montgomery during World War II.

In 1944, Allied forces were preparing to invade continental Europe from Britain. It was to be the biggest amphibious invasion ever attempted, involving 12,000 aircraft, 7,000 ships, and nearly 160,000 troops. It was vital that German forces were wrong-footed as much as possible. Plans were put in place to give the impression that the Allies were preparing to invade Norway, the Pas-de-Calais, and southern France when in fact the main invasion force would land on the Normandy coast. The Germans were intensely interested in the whereabouts of senior military officers, as this gave important clues about Allied plans.

An invasion of southern France could be mounted from North Africa, so to convince the Germans that this was indeed part of the Allied invasion plan, the commander of Allied ground forces, Field Marshal Montgomery, made a trip to Gibraltar and Algiers. But in fact, the man visiting Gibraltar and Algiers was not Montgomery, who was busy with plans for the Normandy landings, but a double named Clifton James.

A Class Act

James was born in Perth, Australia, and then moved to England. During World War I, he served with the Royal Fusiliers and saw action at the Battle of the Somme. After the war, he became an actor.

In the weeks before the Normandy landings, an officer saw a photograph of Clifton James in a newspaper and noted how much he resembled Montgomery. In fact, he had already appeared as Montgomery in a play. The information was passed to military intelligence. Soon afterward, James was contacted by an officer named David Niven, who worked for the army's film unit. (Niven would later become a Hollywood star actor.) He invited James to come to London to try out for a part in an army film. After a brief interview, James was surprised to be invited to sign the Official Secrets Act. Then he was told the truth. He was asked if he would be willing to take on the most important acting job of his life—impersonating Monty, as Montgomery was known, to mislead the enemy. The exercise was code-named Operation Copperhead. He accepted without hesitation.

When World War II broke out, James tried to join ENSA, the organization that entertained troops, but was sent to the Pay Corps instead. Determined to continue acting, he joined the Pay Corps Drama and Variety Group.

James was assigned to Monty's staff as a sergeant in the Intelligence Corps so that he could observe Monty at close quarters and learn his mannerisms. He was taken to a camp near Portsmouth, where Monty was working. He watched Monty dealing with officers and talking to his men. He watched how Monty moved, talked, saluted, and waved. He memorized details of Monty's life. Then he was taken for some trial flights to check that he didn't get airsick. They couldn't have an airsick "Monty"!

He rehearsed acting as Monty with intelligence officers. Then he was given a copy of Monty's battle-dress, complete with all the correct medal ribbons, badges, and red tabs. James had lost a finger in World War I, so a prosthetic was hastily made for him in case a particularly observant German spy spotted the missing digit. He was taken out in a car to see how people reacted. They waved to him, convinced they were looking at Monty.

Next, James was flown to Gibraltar in Prime Minister Winston Churchill's plane. At Government House, he deliberately "lost" his handkerchief, which was embroidered with Monty's initials, to confirm news of his presence. He also made sure that workers renovating the house saw him. As he chatted with guests at a reception, he made sure to mention "Plan 303," a scheme to invade southern France. As intended, German intelligence got wind of it and the misleading information was relayed to Berlin. By the time he returned to the airfield, news of his presence had spread and Spanish workers had gathered to catch a glimpse of the famous British officer. Then he was flown to Algiers for more appearances that German intelligence would pick up on. Finally, he was spirited away to Cairo, where he was hidden until the Normandy landings were under way.

> James was schooled in Monty's preferences—he didn't eat eggs or any product of a pig. And he didn't smoke, which was a problem for James, who had to give up smoking!

Operation Copperhead was part of a larger campaign of misinformation called Operation Fortitude that involved bogus radio messages, double agents, dummy aircraft on airfields, and appearances of military leaders in key locations. It was successful. The Germans held back large forces to deal with the expected invasions across the Dover Strait and from North Africa. Meanwhile, the main invasion force landed in Normandy.

After his starring role, James returned to his old job in the Regimental Pay Office in Leicester. He was flown back to Gibraltar by a pilot who hadn't slept for three days. The bleary-eyed flier thought they'd probably make the journey okay, but if not, he reminded the passengers that there was a dinghy stowed in the plane's tail! James received the thanks of officers at MI5 for a job well done and was given a general's pay for every day he impersonated Monty.

His impersonation of Monty was the high point of his life, but it destroyed his acting career. Apart from *I Was Monty's Double*, he couldn't find other work as an actor after the war and fell on hard times. He had to queue up with other unemployed workers and draw the dole (unemployment benefit payments). Theater managers and producers were keen to meet him and audition him, but they wouldn't employ him because they thought audiences would come to see Monty's famous double, not their play. He died on May 8, 1963, in Worthing, England.

James wrote a series of articles about his exploits for the *Sydney Morning Herald* in 1946, followed by a book in 1954 called *I Was Monty's Double* (*The Counterfeit General Montgomery* in the United States). It was adapted for the big screen in 1958. The film, also called *I Was Monty's Double*, starred James, playing both Monty and himself.

THE CASE OF THE TWO MARTIN GUERRES

When Martin Guerre turned up eight years after his unexplained disappearance, his wife and family were delighted. But then a second Martin Guerre arrived! One of them was an impostor, but which one?

In 1548, Martin Guerre was living in the village of Artigat in southwestern France with his twenty-two-year-old wife, Bertrande, and their son, Sanxi. His family owned a tileworks. They also grew crops and raised sheep. Life was good. Then Martin did something unforgivable. He stole some grain from his father. Theft within the family was unacceptable then as now. Without warning, Martin Guerre disappeared. He simply vanished. Nothing was heard from him for years. It left his family in a terrible position. His marriage had been made as an alliance between two families, and his disappearance brought shame on his family. His wife was forbidden from remarrying unless she could prove that he was dead, but she simply didn't know what had happened to him.

Then in 1556, news reached Artigat that Martin Guerre was back.

He had been seen in a nearby village. When his four sisters heard the news, they rushed to find him. Then they came back to collect his wife, Bertrande. When she saw him, she wasn't sure it was really him. A bushy beard had changed his appearance, but he convinced her that he was indeed her husband. His uncle Pierre was suspicious too, but the man seemed to know things about their shared past that only Martin Guerre would know, so Pierre eventually accepted him too. He explained that while he was away, he had served with the French army in Spain. In time, his life with Bertrande and the rest of the wider family returned to normal. Over the next three years, they had two more children, daughters.

However, tensions began to build up within the family business. Martin suspected his uncle Pierre of withholding money from the business. Pierre responded with questions about Martin's identity. If he really was Martine Guerre, how could he have forgotten common Basque words and phrases that he used to know? Why did he no longer show any interest in the swordplay he'd previously enjoyed? Pierre began to wonder if this man who would inherit the family's wealth and business really was Martin Guerre. He convinced some of the family that this Martin Guerre was an impostor, but Bertrande steadfastly stood by him.

The family and indeed the whole village were divided on the issue of Martin Guerre's identity. It was a stalemate. Then in 1559, a soldier arrived in Artigat. He claimed to have known Martin Guerre and fought alongside him in Flanders. He said the man could not be the Martin Guerre he had known, because that Martin Guerre had been badly wounded during the siege of Saint-Quentin and had lost a leg.

Pierre Guerre was now convinced that the man in the midst of his family was an impostor, and so he set out to find out who the man really was. One name suggested to him was Arnaud du Tilh. Nicknamed Pansette, meaning "the belly," he came from a nearby village. Now that Pierre had a name for him, he wanted to have a formal inquiry opened by the court. However, the law stipulated that only the wronged wife could set the legal process in motion. As Bertrande refused to believe that the man wasn't her husband, Pierre lied to the court. He said he was acting on Bertrande's instructions. She was eventually persuaded to support the case. Pierre and his sons-in-law armed themselves, seized Martin early one morning, and took him to prison, where he was held while the inquiry proceeded. The case was heard in the court at a nearby village, Rieux.

> Impersonating someone to defraud a family in those days was a very serious offense. The stakes were high. If the accused man was found guilty, he could be sentenced to death.

A Second Martin Guerre

The judge listened to about 150 witnesses, some speaking in favor of Martin Guerre, others denouncing him as a fraud. The case took several months. Then the judge announced his decision. He found that the man claiming to be Martin Guerre was guilty and sentenced him to death by beheading. Guerre immediately appealed and was taken to Toulouse, where the appeal would be heard. Martin's statement to the court was so confident and compelling that the judge had Pierre and Bertrande imprisoned as false accusers. Some of the witnesses from the first trial were heard again. The judge gave greater weight to those most closely related to Martin Guerre. As the judge prepared to give his verdict, which was in favor of Martin Guerre and against his uncle, a man with a wooden leg arrived and claimed that *he* was Martin Guerre!

The second Martin Guerre said that when he had left Artigat, he crossed the Pyrenees into Spain and worked for Francisco de Mendoza, a Roman Catholic cardinal in Castile. Then he served in the army under Francisco's brother, Pedro. He was sent to Flanders to fight the French at Saint-Quentin. On August 10, 1557, he was shot in the leg. The wound was so serious that his leg had to be amputated. No one knows why he returned home three years later during the appeal.

The two men were interviewed at length by the court. Then a sort of medieval identity parade was held. The newcomer was lined up with several other men, and Pierre Guerre was asked to identify his nephew, which he did without hesitation. Then Martin Guerre's sisters identified the newcomer as their brother. Finally, Bertrande identified him as her husband. The appeal was lost, and the defendant was found guilty of imposture and adultery. He was forced to issue an apology and was sentenced to death by hanging. He finally admitted that he was Arnaud du Tilh. The idea for his imposture came to him when he was mistaken for Martin Guerre while passing through a village near Artigat. When du Tilh discovered that Martin Guerre was in line for a large inheritance, he hatched the plot to impersonate him. He found out everything he could about Martin Guerre. But it all ended in failure. On September 16, 1560, Arnaud du Tilh made his public apology at the church in Artigat. Then he was taken to a gibbet built in front of Martin Guerre's house and hanged.

> The story of an impostor so successful that even the man's own wife fails to detect him had a lasting appeal. The film *Sommersby* (1993), starring Jodie Foster and Richard Gere, and the stage musical *Martin Guerre* (1996) are adaptations of the story.

WASHINGTON'S NURSE

Joice Heth was exhibited by the American showman P. T. Barnum, who claimed she was the 161-year-old nurse who had looked after President George Washington. When she died, Barnum had her publicly autopsied to confirm her age!

According to a pamphlet about Joice Heth published in 1835, she was born in Madagascar in 1674. At the age of only fifteen, she was taken as a slave to America, where she was bought by Thomas Buckner, a Virginia planter. Several years later, she went to work for the Washington family. When George Washington was born in 1732, she became his nurse or nanny.

When she was fifty-four years old, she was sold to a Mrs. Atwood. When Mrs. Atwood died, Heth was inherited by one of her heirs, a

Mr. Bowling. When he moved to Kentucky, he took Heth with him. He appears to have been the first person to exhibit her as President George Washington's nurse.

In 1835, she was sold to a pair of showmen named Coley Bartram and R. W. Lindsay. They continued to promote her as George Washington's nurse but had little success, so they sold her to a grocery shop owner named Phineas Taylor Barnum for $1,000. He had more success with her. She entertained visitors to Mr. Niblo's dwelling house by telling stories about the former president, or "dear little George" as she called him. Barnum toured New England with her, exhibiting her to fascinated spectators. She was on display for up to twelve hours a day, six days a week.

When interest in Heth started to fade, Barnum wrote anonymous letters to local newspapers claiming that she wasn't a person at all but a cleverly constructed machine, an automaton. People came back and paid again to see if they could tell whether she was human.

Given that her claimed birth year was 1674, by the time Barnum started exhibiting her in 1835, she would have been 161 years old. Some people doubted that she could possibly be so old. When she died in 1836, Barnum hired a surgeon, David L. Rogers, to perform a public autopsy of her body in front of 1,500 spectators—Barnum charged each of them 50 cents admission! However, the surgeon's opinion was that Heth was no more than about eighty years old. So she would have been born around 1756, by which time George Washington was twenty-four years old and no longer in need of a nurse to look after him! Heth could not possibly have been George Washington's nurse as Barnum had been led to believe.

Despite the deception, Joice Heth gave Barnum a taste for show business that he never lost. P. T. Barnum and his circus would later become one of the most famous showmen and shows the world has ever seen.

PRICKING POMPOSITY

In the 1920s, the art establishment buzzed with the discovery of a new talent, a Russian artist named Pavel Jerdanowitch. But who was he?

In 1924, Paul Jordan-Smith, a journalist, author, and editor from Los Angeles, was incensed by harsh criticism of a painting by his wife, Sarah. When it was exhibited at Claremont, California, critics described it as being "distinctly of the old school." He set out to show that the critics didn't know what they were talking about, and he did it in a delightfully creative and deliciously underhanded way. He created a fictitious Russian artist named Pavel Jerdanowitch and, as Jerdanowitch, produced his own paintings in an "ultra-impressionistic" style. He even invented a name for this new school of painting—disumbrationism.

Smith was the first to admit that he hadn't the slightest knowledge of painting. He produced a crude painting of a native woman holding something above her head. He insisted that it was supposed to be a starfish, but it ended up looking like a banana skin. That's as far as Smith's painting ambitions went for the time being. The painting served as a fire screen until a visitor said it looked a bit like a work by Paul Gaugin, famous for his South Sea island paintings. It was then that Smith decided to see if it might fool art critics.

In 1925, he entered the "banana" painting by the fictitious Pavel Jerdanowitch in the Exhibition of the Independents in New York's Waldorf-Astoria hotel. His masterpiece, now rather grandly called *Exaltation*, attracted international interest. A French art magazine wrote to him asking for more information about the unknown artist and complimenting the work. Smith furnished them with a fictitious biography and a photograph of himself as Jerdanowitch together with a pretentious description of the meaning of the painting. He claimed that it showed a woman celebrating her freedom after killing a missionary and eating a banana, which was forbidden in her culture, representing breaking the shackles of womanhood.

His first painting was such a success that he was invited to exhibit more of his work. Another painting was exhibited in Chicago. His picture of a woman doing her washing in a large tub while looking up at a rooster sitting on top of a pole was equally well received. Smith was on a roll. He produced more pictures, and the critics loved them.

In 1927, Smith finally revealed the hoax to the *Los Angeles Times*. In his view, it proved that the current fashion in the art world was "poppycock" praised by critics who knew nothing about art. Surprisingly, that wasn't the end of Pavel Jerdanowitch. His work was exhibited again in a gallery in Boston in 1931, and Smith's hoax inspired the "International Pavel Jerdanowitch Painting Contest," an annual competition for bad art that has been running since 2006.

The Genetics of Rudeness

In 2001, an actor used a similar technique to deal with rudeness among professionals. Highly qualified people, specialists in their field, can sometimes be so super confident in their own abilities and so resistant to criticism or challenge that they can be insensitive, unyielding, or even rude to others. On occasion, impostors have adopted false identities to highlight this sort of rudeness or prick the pomposity of professionals.

All actors are impostors to some extent, some more convincing than others. Normally, the thing that separates actors from other impostors is that an actor's pretense is not hidden from the audience, who willingly collude in it.

When we watch a play or a movie, we know we're watching actors at work. We know Daniel Craig isn't really James Bond and Arnold Schwarzenegger isn't really a robot from the future—no, really, he isn't. We suspend our disbelief in return, we hope, for an hour or two of diversion and entertainment. Prank television shows like *Candid Camera* and all the similar shows that followed it used actors to fool victims who had been lured into bizarre situations while audiences watched the fun, but some pranksters are so convincing that they fool everyone, even those watching.

In May 2001, doctors and lawyers at a conference held by the

California Medical Association (CMA) in San Francisco were treated to a lunchtime talk by Dr. Albin Avgher. Avgher, a geneticist, explained that doctors, lawyers, and other highly educated professionals are genetically predisposed to being insensitive to their patients and clients. In other words, they can't help being rude—it's in their genes. Avgher said that these professionals are more likely to have a chromosomal defect that dulls their ability to process what other people are saying to them. The effect is that they are more likely to interrupt someone talking to them, stray off their subject in conversation, and give evasive or vague

> One of the conference organizers said, "It just goes to show that if you can walk the walk, talk the talk, and throw in the right statistics, you can sell almost anything to anybody"—something impostors have known for centuries.

answers to questions. He cited studies and statistics, dazzled the audience with overhead projector slides, and talked about the genetic basis for the theory. The audience of physicians, ophthalmologists, anesthesiologists, and other high-powered "-ologists" was spellbound. Some of them took notes.

However, Dr. Albin Avgher wasn't a geneticist. In fact, he didn't exist at all. He was actually actor and playwright Charlie Varon. Varon enlisted the help of Jonathan Karpf, a professor at San Jose State University who teaches genetics, to come up with a believable and totally fictional scientific theory. And then he played the role of a typical conference speaker—lame jokes, engaging anecdotes, smug persona, the lot. He became the sort of person he was talking about. The audience swallowed it hook, line, and sinker. When they discovered that they'd been spoofed, they were suitably impressed.

BEING STANLEY KUBRICK

By the 1990s, the reclusive American film director Stanley Kubrick had been out of the public eye for so long that few people knew what he looked like any more. If Kubrick wasn't going to play the celebrity game himself, it wasn't long before someone else would think of taking his place.

In 1991, the Playhouse Theatre in London was enjoying a successful run of Tennessee Williams's play *The Rose Tattoo*, with actress Julie Walters in the leading role. Alan Conway was keen to see it,

> Conway didn't look anything like Kubrick and he was English, whereas Kubrick was American, but the theater management and actors readily accepted him as the famous director.

but the theater was sold out. He wondered if someone famous would be turned away from the box office as quickly as he had been. He tried again, but this time he claimed to be Stanley Kubrick. Miraculously, a seat was found for him, and he was even invited to go backstage after the show to meet the cast.

A Rich Encounter

In 1993, the *New York Times*'s theater critic, Frank Rich, was having supper at a restaurant in London's Covent Garden with his wife and friends when a man at the next table introduced himself as Stanley Kubrick. It was Conway. Rich and his guests weren't altogether certain that the man really was Kubrick. When the influential film critic of the *London Evening Standard*, Alexander Walker, heard of the encounter, he was suspicious enough to ring Kubrick and ask him about it. As he thought, the man at the restaurant wasn't Kubrick. Then a couple of weeks later, Walker received a phone call from Kubrick...except that it wasn't Kubrick. It was Conway. Walker listened with interest and noted that Conway got all the details of Kubrick's life and work wrong.

Then Conway turned up in Bournemouth, a resort on England's south coast, where a popular singer named Joe Longthorne was performing. Longthorne was keen to follow in the footsteps of other British entertainers like Tom Jones and Engelbert Humperdink, who had made it big in the United States. He wanted a season in Las Vegas. Conway, masquerading as Kubrick, met Longthorne and said he'd help him. He told Longthorne he was in Bournemouth looking for locations for a new film. Longthorne put him up in an expensive hotel and made a Rolls-Royce available to him.

However, Longthorne's tour manager, Zeb White, became suspicious. He'd heard that Kubrick rarely left home. He managed to get a phone number for Kubrick from Pinewood Studios and found out that he wasn't in Bournemouth scouting locations and that he knew about an impostor who had been impersonating him for several years. He'd first heard about the impostor while he was making *Eyes Wide Shut*. Kubrick's assistant, Tony Frewin, started receiving calls and letters from people claiming that Kubrick owed them money or had promised them parts in films. Of course, Kubrick knew nothing about any of these people or the promises he was supposed to have made them. It was all Conway's doing. The impostor's activities were reported to the police, but the case never came to court because the people who had been duped were reluctant to come forward and give evidence. They didn't want the publicity.

Inquiries revealed that Conway was a former travel agent with a string of convictions for theft, deception, and indecency. He was born as Eddie Alan Jablowsky in Whitechapel, London, in 1934.

Zeb White set out to find out who the mystery man was. He arranged to have a meal with him in a London restaurant and made sure that the bogus Kubrick paid the bill. Then, after they left the restaurant, White went back and asked to see the credit card slip...and there was the name—not Stanley Kubrick, but Alan Conway.

Alan Conway died from a heart attack on December 5, 1998, just a few months before Kubrick himself died, also from a heart attack. Tony Frewin thought the story was so good that he used it as the basis of a screenplay. It was made into a film called *Color Me Kubrick*, starring John Malkovich as Alan Conway.

A SURVIVOR'S TALE?

In the mid-1990s, a book called *Fragments: Memories of a Wartime Childhood* told the heartbreaking story of a young Jewish child incarcerated in Nazi concentration camps during World War II. It received almost universal praise, but within five

> The U.S. Holocaust Memorial Museum invited Wilkomirski to the United States for a speaking tour.

years, publishers started withdrawing it from sale after disturbing discoveries about the author.

Fragments won a host of prizes and rave reviews. Its author, Binjamin Wilkomirski, was in great demand for interviews and talks. His personal appearances attracted large audiences.

He was contacted by an American family descended from Wilkomirskis in Riga, Latvia, where Binjamin had lived before the war. They were keen to find out if they were related to him.

When he came to the United States in 1997, he met the family and they swapped memories. Binjamin's recollections were fragmentary, and not all of them confirmed the facts the family knew, but this could perhaps be explained by his age—he said he was taken to Majdanek concentration camp at the age of only three or four, so perhaps it isn't surprising that his memories were patchy. They couldn't figure out exactly how they were related, and Wilkomirski declined to take a DNA test. Doubts about his story began to surface. Readers noticed factual errors in his story, but memory can be faulty, especially after fifty years. However, questions continued to be raised.

In 1998, Daniel Ganzfried, a journalist, was invited to write a piece

> One problem with Wilkomirski's story is that it was composed of "recovered memories" revealed with the help of a therapist. This technique is based on the theory that traumatic memories may be repressed and forgotten. With interviews and perhaps the use of hypnosis and/or drugs, these lost memories can be recovered. However, the technique is controversial because of the risk of creating false memories that seem amazingly real.

about Wilkomirski for a Swiss Arts Council publication. Ganzfried delved a bit deeper than others who had written about him and turned up some surprising information. He found that Wilkomirski wasn't born in Latvia in 1939 as he claimed. He wasn't even Jewish. Records appeared to show that he was born Bruno Grosjean in Biel, Switzerland, in 1941 and placed in an orphanage by his unmarried mother, Yvonne. When Yvonne died in 1981, he received part of her estate. In 1945, he was fostered by a family named Dössekker, who adopted him in 1957. His natural father paid child support until he was adopted. The inheritance and child support suggest that Bruno Grosjean and the boy adopted by the Dössekker family were one and the same. And it was Bruno Dössekker who was claiming to be concentration camp survivor Binjamin Wilkomirski. It seemed that Wilkomirski had never been in the Majdanek or Auschwitz camps as he'd claimed. The memoir that had broken hearts and won prizes appeared to be a work of fiction. In the end, Ganzfried's article wasn't published by the Arts Council. Instead, it appeared in *Die Weltwoche* (*The World Week*), a Swiss newspaper. Wilkomirski explained Ganzfried's discoveries by claiming that officials had obliterated his Jewish childhood history and substituted Grosjean's details.

In February 1999, the CBS program *60 Minutes* featured Wilkomirski. When he described events he said he had witnessed in Poland after World War II, they produced evidence showing that he was in Switzerland at the same time. They also posed the question that if Wilkomirski had not started his life as Bruno Grosjean, but Bruno Grosjean had demonstrably existed, then what had become of Bruno Grosjean? Where was he?

Wilkomirski still insisted that he was telling the truth, and he gained some credibility when a Holocaust survivor named Laura Grabowski claimed to remember him from one of the camps she had been imprisoned in. However, when Grabowski's story was investigated, she herself was exposed as a fraud. Her real name was Laurel Rose Willson. After her claims to have suffered satanic ritual abuse were debunked, she changed her name to Lauren Stratford and then adopted the false identity of Holocaust survivor Laura Grabowski.

Blake Eskin, who is related to Wilkomirskis from Riga, Latvia, and wondered if he might be related to Binjamin, investigated his past. He went to Riga and asked the director of a Jewish archive there about Wilkomirski's account. He told Eskin that the Latvian part of Wilkomirski's story could not be true. Eskin went on to describe his investigation of Wilkomirski in a book called *A Life in Pieces*.

In 1999, Wilkomirski's literary agent asked historian Stefan Maechler to investigate the writer. Maechler's report confirmed Ganzfried's findings and filled in more of Bruno Grosjean/Dössekker's childhood details. He wrote his own book about the investigation, called *The Wilkomirski Affair: A Study in Biographical Truth*. As a result of Maechler's investigative work, publishers started withdrawing *Fragments* from sale and most of the organizations that awarded prizes to its author revoked them.

Wilkomirski isn't the only person to have written stories about the Holocaust that later proved to be untrue. In 2008, Misha Defonseca, the author of a 1997 book called *Misha: A Mémoire of the Holocaust Years'* admitted that her story of walking across Europe at the age of six in search of her parents who had been taken to Auschwitz was false. The author, whose real name is Monique de Wael, claimed to have been rescued by a pack of wolves at one point.

In 2009, the publication of a book called *Angel at the Fence*, telling the story of Holocaust survivor Herman Rosenblat, was canceled when the publisher learned that some of the story was untrue. Rosenblat really was a Holocaust survivor, having been held at the Buchenwald-Schlieben camp, but he added some false details to his story. He claimed that while he was in the camp, a Jewish girl hiding in the nearby town used to throw food over the fence to him. Years later, he went on a blind date in New York with a girl and claimed to recognize her as the same girl who had thrown food to him during the war. He proposed on the spot, and they married in 1958. However, it wasn't true. Faced with accusations from historians that this and other elements of the story were false, he finally admitted that he'd invented it.

THE TALIBAN COMMANDER

When talks were held between the Taliban and Afghan officials in 2010, news that a senior Taliban commander was going to take part was welcomed.

In 2010, it was nine years since a U.S.-led coalition had invaded Afghanistan, aided by the Afghan Northern Alliance, to unseat the country's Taliban government. Afghanistan had become the home of the al-Qaeda terrorist organization, which had mounted the September 11, 2001, attacks on the United States. Nearly 3,000 people died, and more than 6,000 were injured.

When the Taliban government had been ousted from Afghanistan, the invasion force was replaced by a NATO-led coalition called ISAF (the International Security Assistance Force). More than forty countries contributed troops to ISAF. While the Taliban had been driven from government, they had not been eliminated. Taliban fighters began an insurgency characterized by terrorist attacks on ISAF, other Western agencies, and anyone who helped them. At the beginning of 2010, the Afghan president, Hamid Karzai, announced that he intended to hold peace talks with the Taliban leadership in an attempt to bring their insurgency to an end.

Holding Talks

An Afghan go-between with contacts in both the government and the Taliban arranged meetings between the two sides. A man named Mullah Akhtar Muhammad Mansour, one of the Taliban's most senior commanders, attended the meetings. Mansour had been the Minister for Civil Aviation in the Taliban government and had risen to number two in the Afghan Taliban early in 2010 after his predecessor, Abdul Ghani Baradar, was arrested in Pakistan.

The talks went on for months. However, it seems that the man negotiating on behalf of the Taliban was not Akhtar Muhammad Mansour at all. According to some accounts, he was a shopkeeper from the Pakistani city of Quetta. Doubts about his identity surfaced when one of the meetings was attended by someone who had known

Mansour but didn't recognize the man. Officials then confirmed that the man was not Mansour.

It's difficult to disentangle the web of stories about who did or said what and when and where they did or said it. Local politicians, officials, the CIA, and MI6 blamed each other, but it seems that an Afghan insurgent bought his release from capture by agreeing to introduce the man to the Afghan Interior Minister for talks. The deal is said to have been approved by U.S. military leaders. British MI6 agents were then brought in to make the arrangements.

Despite concerns about his identity, there was so much enthusiasm for talks that might lead to a negotiated settlement that more cautious voices were drowned out. The man is said to have taken part in at least three meetings with officials and was flown to Kabul in NATO aircraft. He may even have attended a meeting with President Karzai himself, although Karzai has denied this. He is also said to have been paid large sums of money to encourage him to continue with the talks, after which he disappeared. One theory is that the man was a Taliban agent, sent to find out if the talks were genuine or a trap. Another theory contends that the fake Taliban commander was sent to assassinate President Karzai.

Yet another theory points the finger at the Pakistani intelligence service, the ISI. Whatever the motive and whoever was behind the plan, the man's true identity remains unknown.

A body double for Mansour was said to have been chosen, because Mansour was known to be a large man and a large man was easier to hide a suicide bomb on. The first few contacts were made to gain the confidence of Western and Afghan officials before the bombing, but the plan unraveled before the final deadly meeting could be arranged.

THE STRANGE CASE OF GU KAILAI

On August 20, 2012, a Chinese woman stood in a court and waited to hear her sentence for murder. However, some people believe that the woman in the dock was not the accused but an impostor.

Early in 2012, the Chinese government was moving smoothly toward one of its once-in-a-generation changes of leadership. One figure expected to be promoted was a high-flying and unusually charismatic politician named Bo Xilai. However, his career crashed suddenly in March as a result of a scandal surrounding the death of a British businessman, Neil Heywood.

Mr. Heywood had been found dead in his hotel room in Chongqing on November 15, 2011. Without bothering to have an autopsy carried out, the authorities decided he had died of alcohol poisoning. Heywood's friends were suspicious, as he wasn't known to be a heavy drinker, but by then his body had been cremated.

Rumors began to circulate that the death was not accidental. Then Wang Lijun, the head of police in Chongqing and an ally of Bo Xilai, was arrested following a mysterious visit to the U.S. Consulate in Chengdu on February 7, 2012. He is said to have made allegations about Gu Kailai's involvement in Heywood's death—Gu Kailai was Bo's wife. On March 26, the British government asked China to reinvestigate Mr. Heywood's death. Then on April 10, the Chinese announced that Gu Kailai was in custody. More arrests followed, and Bo Xilai himself was placed under house arrest, ending his hope of joining China's political elite. Then on July 26, Gu was sensationally charged with Heywood's murder. The motive for the crime was said to be a disagreement over money and fear that Heywood might spill the beans about financial irregularities in one of China's leading political families.

Despite the complexity of the case, Gu's trial lasted only one day and she did not contest the charge. Eleven days later, on August 20, she was given a suspended death sentence.

Soon after the announcement of the verdict was broadcast from the court, messages started appearing online claiming that the woman in the dock was not the accused, Gu Kailai. Reports named the woman in the dock as Zhao Tianshao or Zhao Tianyun, from Langfang in northern China, and suggested that she had read out a scripted confession. Reports claimed that the double was used to prevent Gu from making awkward or embarrassing allegations about other officials in open court. Web pages relating to the case were also censored by the authorities.

If true, it doesn't appear to be unique. The practice of paying body doubles to replace defendants in court, and even to serve prison sentences in their place, is reported to have occurred in other cases. However, security and identity specialists are divided on whether the woman was an impostor, and the Chinese authorities have vigorously denied that the practice of using body doubles in court, called *ding zui*, exists at all. Wang Lijun, the police chief who triggered the scandal, was found guilty of a string of offenses, including abuse of power, taking bribes, and defection and was sentenced to fifteen years in prison.

> Suspended death sentences in China are usually commuted to life imprisonment.

TELEPHONE TRICKSTERS

When you pick up the phone, how can you be sure that the person on the other end really is calling from your bank or insurance company or local police? Can you be sure it really is the president asking you for your vote? No, you can't.

When we communicate with someone, more than half of the information we receive comes from nonverbal cues—body language, clothes, facial expressions, and so on. We're denied all of this information in a phone call, so it's easier for an impostor to seem plausible and sincere.

On October 16, 2003, the ESPN cable television network was broadcasting the 6:00 p.m. edition of its daily sports news program *SportsCenter*. They were keen to talk to Chicago Cubs fan Steve Bartman. He had incurred the wrath of other fans by reaching out to catch a ball during Game Six of the National League Championship Series at Wrigley Field. In doing so, he prevented outfielder Moises Alou from catching it, leading to the Cubs' defeat. The station learned that Bartman was on the phone and wanted to talk. They put him on the air straightaway. The interview went well until "Bartman" suddenly made an inappropriate comment about shock jock Howard Stern. The interview was instantly terminated. The caller wasn't Bartman. In fact, he was a prankster named Captain Janks, real name Thomas Cipriano.

Janks struck again in 2010. When the Philadelphia Eagles let injury-plagued running back Brian Westbrook go, SportsCenter was keen to talk to him. They got a call from Westbrook's manager agreeing to an interview, but only if it went out live. Twenty minutes later, Westbrook was on the line live with presenter Scott Van Pelt. It wasn't long before Howard Stern cropped up in the conversation and the interview was stopped. The calls from Westbrook's manager and Westbrook himself were both made by Janks.

Even heads of state, with all the security and outer office staff who surround them and screen their calls, can be spoofed by impostors on the line. In 1990, eight U.S. citizens and up to ten other nationals were being held hostage in Lebanon. President Bush had repeatedly said he would talk to anyone who might be able to help secure the hostages' release. The National Security Council received a phone call from someone claiming to represent the Iranian government. He said the Iranian president, Hashemi Rafsanjani, wanted to speak to the U.S. president about the hostage issue. A time and date for the call was agreed. However, when the man called and was put through to President Bush, it was soon clear that he was not the Iranian president after all. Bush said he was aware that it could be a prank, but if there was the smallest chance that it might be a genuine call and might help secure the hostages' release, it was worth taking it.

Spoof phone calls have been made by comedy performers and presenters for years, and they're usually no more than

In January 2003, Venezuelan President Hugo Chavez took a call from Cuban leader Fidel Castro, but it was actually Miami radio station Radio El Zol on the line. A few months later, they turned the prank around and called Fidel Castro pretending to be Chavez.

a bit of a joke or a nuisance. However, in 2012, a spoof call had tragic consequences.

At 5:30 a.m. on the morning of December 4, 2012, the King Edward VII hospital in London, England, received a phone call from Queen Elizabeth II and Prince Charles. While most people would instantly be suspicious of someone on the phone claiming to be the queen, it wasn't so hard to believe in this case, because the Duchess of Cambridge, wife of Prince William, had been admitted to the hospital suffering from extreme morning sickness during her first pregnancy.

In 1995, Queen Elizabeth II chatted for more than fifteen minutes with a caller she thought was the Canadian prime minister, Jean Chretien, but it was actually Canadian radio DJ Pierre Brassard. The palace was said to be irritated by the prank, which is typically understated British code for—they went ballistic!

As it was the middle of the night, there was no receptionist on duty. The call was taken by a nurse, Jacintha Saldanha. She put the call through to the nurse looking after the duchess. Both nurses failed to detect an Australian accent in the voices on the line. The callers weren't the queen and Prince Charles. They were Australian radio presenters Mel Greig and Michael Christian. The two presenters said later that they never expected to be put through to anyone. They assumed the phone would be put down on them because of their unconvincing English accents. The recording of the call was then submitted to the normal vetting process at the station, 2Day FM, and, inexplicably, was approved for broadcast. It went around the world in no time. Saldanha, who by all accounts was a conscientious and caring nurse, appears to have been terribly distressed by what happened. She was found dead in the hospital's nurses' quarters three days later, having committed suicide. The DJs received an avalanche of hate messages. They had simply done what other DJs have done scores of times over the years and will probably continue doing—they'd made a silly prank call. The real mystery was why the station's managers or lawyers approved the recording to be broadcast.

FRAUD ALERT: FLASH, BANG, WALLOP

You could find yourself surrounded by hundreds of impostors in any public place today. You might think the people around you are shoppers or travelers until they suddenly burst into song or start dancing. You're in the middle of a flash mob.

Flash mobs began in Manhattan in 2003 when hundreds of shoppers turned up at the same shop to buy the same rug. At first, flash mobs involved large numbers of people collecting somewhere and doing something pointless, like clapping, pillow fighting, or just standing still for a short time and then dispersing. Political activists have also used flash mobs to muster groups for public protests and demonstrations. Then the "mad men" of the advertising industry hit on the idea of using them to promote their clients. It's even got a name—flash mob marketing.

- Pop concerts and television programs have been publicized by flash mobs. On a chilly April morning in 2009 in Piccadilly Circus, London, one hundred single ladies dropped their coats to reveal black leotards (and goose bumps) and danced to Beyoncé's "Single Ladies" to publicize her forthcoming gig at London's O2 arena.
- Fans of the television series *Glee* hold flash mob events. The biggest, with upward of one thousand fans taking part, is held every year in Seattle. Flash mobs usually surprise the people around them, but one of the 2012 *Glee* flash mobbers got the surprise of her life when the music suddenly stopped in the middle of a routine and her boyfriend stood up with a microphone and proposed to her. Dozens more lovestruck guys caught the same bug in 2012 and proposed during flash mobs. Girls, you have been warned!

- In 2009, a film of a flash mob won the television ad of the year award in Britain. At 11:00 a.m. on January 15, rail passengers at London's Liverpool Street Station were surprised to hear loud music booming across the concourse. They were even more surprised when "travelers" standing among them started dancing. The dancers started in twos and threes until four hundred synchronized dancers were doing their stuff. Ten hidden cameras captured the reactions of members of the public, from befuddlement to delight. Three minutes later, the music and dancing suddenly stopped and the performers melted away into the crowds, leaving bemused travelers wondering what had just happened. Film of the event was used to advertise a mobile phone company on television.

- On March 23, 2009, commuters in Antwerp's Central Station in Belgium were surprised to hear their train announcements interrupted by Julie Andrews singing "Do Re Mi" from *The Sound of Music,* and then some of the "travelers" started dancing. Eventually two hundred synchronized dancers were performing to the amusement and amazement of onlookers. It was a stunt for a Belgian television program looking for someone to play the leading role in a musical version of *The Sound of Music*.

- On May 27, 2010, a group that promotes a healthy lifestyle organized a flash mob at Sydney's Central Station in Australia.

CONCLUSION

Impostors have been taking on false identities throughout recorded history to steal everything from cash to kingdoms, trade a dull existence for a glamorous life, evade the consequences of crimes, or break the rules imposed by society. And there's no sign of them becoming an endangered species any time soon. While new technology has consigned some forms of imposture to the history books, or at least made them more difficult to carry off successfully, it has also created brand new opportunities for switching identities. There may not be any more Perkin Warbecks or Anna Andersons claiming royal heritage, but another Victor Lustig could be selling the Statue of Liberty or the Leaning Tower of Pisa to a gullible buyer right now, another John List could be leading a false life to escape a prison sentence, and another David Hampton could be conning people out of money, meals, and a place to sleep by claiming to be the son of a famous movie star. For as long as the lure of the four E's exists—envy, ego, escape, and espionage—impostors will be among us, trading on our trust for their benefit.

RECOMMENDED READING

Abagnale, Frank. *Catch Me If You Can: The True Story of a Real Fake*. New York: Pocket Books, 1990.

Abagnale, Frank and Stan Redding. *Catch Me If You Can: The Amazing True Story of the Most Extraordinary Liar in the History of Fun and Profit*. New York: Grosset & Dunlap, 1980.

Billinghurst, Jane. *Grey Owl: The Many Faces of Archie Belaney*. Vancouver, BC: Greystone Books, 1999.

Bondeson, Jan. *The Great Pretenders: The True Stories Behind Famous Historical Mysteries*. New York: W. W. Norton & Co., 2005.

Bricmont, Jean. *Intellectual Impostures*. London: Profile Books, 2003.

Burton, Sarah. *Impostors: Six Kinds of Liar—True Tales of Deception*. New York: Viking Books, 2001.

Chatterjee, Partha. *A Princely Impostor? The Strange and Universal History of the Kumar of Bhawal*. Princeton, NJ: Princeton University Press, 2002.

Cheesman, Clive and Jonathan Williams. *Rebels, Pretenders and Impostors*. London: St. Martin's Press, 2000.

Crichton, Robert. *The Great Imposter: The Amazing Careers of Ferdinand Waldo Demara*. New York: Random House, 1959.

Davis, Natalie Zemon. *The Return of Martin Guerre*. Cambridge, MA: Harvard University Press, 1983.

Dickson, Lovat. *Wilderness Man: The Amazing True Story of Grey Owl*. New York: Pocket Books, 1999.

Gordon, Irene Ternier. *Grey Owl: The Curious Life of Archie Belaney*. Canmore, AB: Altitude Publishing, 2004.

Gray, Geoffrey. *Skyjack: The Hunt for D. B. Cooper*. New York: Crown Publishing, 2011.

Hill, Fern J. *Charley's Choice: The Life and Times of Charley Parkhurst*. West Conshohocken, PA: Infinity Publishing, 2008.

Howard, Rod. *The Fabulist: The Incredible Story of Louis De Rougemont*. Sydney: Random House Australia, 2006.

Hume, Robert. *Perkin Warbeck: The Boy Who Would Be King*. London: Short Books, 2005.

Keay, Julia. *The Spy Who Never Was: Life and Loves of Mata Hari*. London: Michael Joseph, 1987.

Kurth, Peter. *Anastasia: The Life of Anna Anderson*. London: Fontana, 1985.

———. *Anastasia: The Riddle of Anna Anderson*. Boston: Little, Brown, and Co., 1983.

MacIntyre, Ben. *Operation Mincemeat*. London: Bloomsbury, 2010.

McWilliam, Rohan. *The Tichborne Claimant: A Victorian Sensation*. London: Hambledon Continuum, 2007.

Middlebrook, Diane Wood. *Suits Me: The Double Life of Billy Tipton*. Boston: Houghton Mifflin, 1998.

Murphy, Yannick. *Signed, Mata Hari*. Boston: Little, Brown, and Co., 2007.

Olson, Kay Melchisedech. *The D. B. Cooper Hijacking: Vanishing Act*. Mankato, MN: Compass Point Books, 2010.

Raison, Jennifer and Michael Goldie. *Caraboo: The Real Story of a Grand Hoax*. The Windrush Press, 1994.

Ruffo, Armand Garnet. *Grey Owl: The Mystery of Archie Belaney*. Regina, SK: Coteau Books, 1996.

Seal, Mark. *The Man in the Rockefeller Suit: The Astonishing Rise and Spectacular Fall of a Serial Impostor*. New York: Viking, 2011.

Shipman, Pat. *Femme Fatale—Love, Lies, and the Unknown Life of Mata Hari*. New York: William Morrow, 2007.

Sparrow, Judge Gerald. *The Great Impostors*. London: John Long, 1962.

Steinmeyer, Jim. *The Glorious Deception: The Double Life of William Robinson, aka Chung Ling Soo*. New York: Carroll & Graf, 2005.

Sullivan, George. *Great Imposters*. New York: Scholastic, 1982.

Wade, Carlson. *Great Hoaxes and Famous Imposters*. Middle Village, NY: Jonathan David, 1976.

Welch, Frances. *A Romanov Fantasy: Life at the Court of Anna Anderson*. New York: W. W. Norton & Co., 2007.

Wells, John. *Princess Caraboo: Her True Story*. London: Pan Books, 1994.

West, Nigel. *Counterfeit Spies: Genuine or Bogus? An Astonishing Investigation into Secret Agents of the Second World War*. Boston: Little, Brown, and Co., 1999.

Wheen, Francis. *The Irresistible Con: The Bizarre Life of a Fraudulent Genius*. London: Short Books, 2004.

———. *Who Was Dr. Charlotte Bach?* London; Short Books, 2002.

Woodruff, Douglas. *The Tichborne Claimant: A Victorian Mystery*. London: Hollis and Carter, 1957.

BIBLIOGRAPHY

Chapter 1: Serial Offenders
THE ROGUE ROCKEFELLER (CHRISTIAN KARL GERHARTSREITER)

Blankstein, Andrew, and Richard Winton. "Elusive 'Clark Rockefeller' figure charged in 1980s' slaying of San Marino man." *Los Angeles Times*, March 15, 2011.

Cramer, Maria. "Murder trial date set for man known as Rockefeller." *Boston Globe*, January 10, 2013.

Deutsch, Linda. "Christian Gerhartsreiter guilty: Rockefeller impostor convicted in cold case." *Huffington Post*, April 11, 2013. www.huffingtonpost. com/2013/04/11/christian-gerhartsreiter-rockefeller-impostor-cha-rade-over_n_3059925.html.

———. "Clark Rockefeller trial: Christian Gerhartsreiter used pseudonym and allegedly committed murder." *Huffington Post*, January 18, 2012. www. huffingtonpost.com/2012/01/18/clark-rockefeller-trial-c_n_1212606.html.

Dillon, Nancy. "Wannabe Rockefeller found guilty of 1985 California murder." *New York Daily News*, April 10, 2013.

———. "Wannabe Rockefeller tried to sell blood-stained rug for cash after two land-lords went missing, witness testifies." *New York Daily News*, January 24, 2012.

Feuer, Alan, and Charlie LeDuff. "Hunted man is no Rockefeller, but plays one in Hamptons, the police say." *The New York Times*, October 3, 2000.

Fisher, Greg. "Rockefeller impostor's murder trial: Ex-wife of Christian Gerhartsreiter next to testify." *CBSNews.com*, April 1, 2013. www.cbsnews.com/8301-504083_162-57577348-504083/rockefeller-impostors-murder-trial-ex-wife-of-christian-gerhartsreiter-next-to-testify/.

———. "Rockefeller impostor's murder trial: Lawyer points finger at victim's wife in 1985 Calif. killing." *CBSNews.com*, March 19, 2013. www.cbsnews.com/8301-504083_162-57575111-504083/rockefeller-impostors-murder-trial-lawyer-points-finger-at-victims-wife-in-1985-calif-killing/.

Girardot, Frank C. "Fake Rockefeller to stand trial in 1985 killing." *Silicon Valley Mercury News*, January 10, 2013.

———. "Judge rules fake Rockefeller must stand trial in death of San Marino man." *Pasadena Star-News*, January 24, 2012.

———. "March trial set for fake Rockefeller." *Whittier Daily News*, January 9, 2013.

———. "Missing couple in fake Rockefeller case disappeared 27 years ago." *San Gabriel Valley Tribune*, February 7, 2012.

Kim, Victoria. "Rockefeller impostor ordered to stand trial in 1985 killing." *Los Angeles Times*, January 25, 2012.

Martinez, Michael. "Rockefeller impersonator ordered to stand trial for murder." *CNN.com*, January 25, 2012. www.cnn.com/2012/01/25/justice/california-gerhartsreiter-rockefeller.

McPhee, Michele. "Fresh details on mystery man Clark Rockefeller as trial opens." *ABCNews.com*, May 26, 2009. http://abcnews.go.com/News/story?id=7672617&page=1.

"Rockefeller imposter and convicted felon born." The History Channel. www.history.com/this-day-in-history/rockefeller-imposter-and-convicted-felon-born.

Schoetz, David, Michele McPhee, and Sharon Alfonsi. "Back to Boston for con-man kidnap suspect." *ABCNews.com*, August 5, 2008. http://abcnews.go.com/TheLaw/story?id=5516705&page=1.

Schultz, Zac. "Kidnapping suspect—Madison connection." *NBC15.com*, January 18, 2012. www.nbc15.com/home/headlines/26841999.html.

Seal, Mark. *The Man in the Rockefeller Suit: The Astonishing Rise and Spectacular Fall of a Serial Impostor.* New York: Viking, 2011.

A RUNNER TRIPS UP (JAMES HOGUE)

Barron, James. "Tracing a devious path to the Ivy League." *The New York Times,* March 4, 1991.

Goodman, Mark. "Bright and Athletic, He Seemed Perfect for Princeton, but This Paper Tiger's Stripes Came from the Jailhouse." *People,* March 18, 1991. www.people.com/people/archive/article/0,,20114695,00.html.

Samuels, David. *The Runner: A True Account of the Amazing Lies and Fantastical Adventurers of the Ivy League Impostor James Hogue.* New York: The New Press, 2008.

Tarbell, Marta. "Four caches of stolen property 5,000-plus stolen items, worth an estimated $100,000." *Telluride Watch,* January 26, 2006.

THE CHAMELEON'S TALE (FRÉDÉRIC BOURDIN)

Grann, David. "The Chameleon." *The New Yorker,* August 11, 2008.

———. *The Devil and Sherlock Holmes: Tales of Murder, Madness, and Obsession.* New York: Doubleday, 2010.

O'Brien, Liam. "Page 3 profile: Frederic Bourdin, serial imposter." *London Independent,* August 23, 2012.

Samuel, Henry. "'Chameleon' caught pretending to be boy." *London Telegraph,* June 13, 2005.

THE MAN WHO WAS NEVER BORED (STANLEY CLIFFORD WEYMAN/STANLEY JACOB WEINBERG)

"Afghan princess and 3 sons arrive." *New York Times,* July 9, 1921.

"Amir's envoy waits answer from Hughes." *New York Times,* July 18, 1921.

"Dr. Lorenz's aid proves an impostor." *New York Times,* December 3, 1921.

"Fabulous imposter dies a hero." *Eugene (OR) Register Guard,* August 28, 1960.

"Jeweler sues princess." *New York Times,* December 21, 1921.

"Princess Fatima not a smuggler; sails for Kabul." *Schenectady Gazette,* March 15, 1922.

"A Talented Phony is Again Unmasked." *Life*, May 7, 1951.

Burton, Sarah. *Impostors: Six Kinds of Liar—True Tales of Deception*. New York: Viking Books, 2001.

Grenier, Richard. "Woody Allen on the American Character." *Commentary Magazine*, November 1983. www.commentarymagazine.com/article/ woody-allen-on-the-american-character/.

Hynd, Alan. "Fabulous fraud from Brooklyn." *Montreal Gazette*, March 28, 1956.

———. "Grand deception—'Fabulous fraud from Brooklyn.'" *Spokane Daily Chronicle*, April 13, 1956.

Maeder, Jay. "Not wholly symmetrical Stanley Weyman." *New York Daily News*, January 2, 2002.

McKelway, St. Clair. *Reporting at Wit's End: Tales from the* New Yorker. New York: Bloomsbury, 2010.

Sparrow, Judge Gerald. *The Great Impostors*. London: John Long, 1962.

DRIVEN TO TEACH (MARVIN HEWITT)

"Borrowed name causes teacher's downfall." *Quebec Chronicle*, March 9, 1954.

"'Brilliant' high school grad poses as university physicist." *Daytona Beach Morning Journal*, March 6, 1954.

"Scientist who never attended college taught higher physics at university." *New London (CT) Day*, March 6, 1954.

Brean, Herbert. "Marvin Hewitt, Ph(ony) D." *Life*, April 12, 1954.

Burton, Sarah. *Impostors: Six Kinds of Liar—True Tales of Deception*. New York: Viking Books, 2001.

THE QUEEN OF OHIO (CASSIE CHADWICK)

"Cassie L. Chadwick." Women in History. www.womeninhistoryohio.com/ cassie-l-chadwick.html.

CBC Documentaries. "Great Canadian Liars." *CBC.ca.* www.cbc.ca/documentaries/ doczone/2009/truthaboutliars/canada.html.

THE GREAT IMPOSTOR (FERDINAND DEMARA)

Burton, Sarah. *Impostors: Six Kinds of Liar—True Tales of Deception.* New York: Viking Books, 2001.

CBC Documentaries. "Great Canadian Liars." *CBC.ca.* www.cbc.ca/documentaries/ doczone/2009/truthaboutliars/canada.html.

Crichton, Robert. *The Great Impostor: The Amazing Careers of Ferdinand Waldo Demara.* New York: Random House, 1959.

THE SKYWAYMAN (FRANK ABAGNALE)

"Frank Abagnale." The Biography Channel. www.biography.com/people/ frank-abagnale-20657335.

Abagnale, Frank, and Stan Redding. *Catch Me If You Can: The Amazing True Story of the Most Extraordinary Liar in the History of Fun and Profit.* New York: Grosset & Dunlap, 1980.

Bell, Rachael. "Skywayman: The Story of Frank W. Abagnale Jr." Tru TV Crime Library. www.trutv.com/library/crime/criminal_mind/scams/frank_ abagnale/index.html.

FRAUD ALERT: BRAZEN BLUFFERS

Barry Bremen

"Barry Bremen dies at 64; prankster crashed All-Star games, Emmys." *Los Angeles Times*, July 7, 2001.

Karoub, Jeff. "Mich. man who crashed Emmys, All-Star games dies." *Yahoo! News*, July 7, 2011. http://news.yahoo.com/mich-man-crashed-emmys-star-games- dies-211930874.html.

Schrock, Cliff. "Barry Bremen: The Impostor who crashed the U.S. Open." *Golf Digest*, July 8, 2011.

Jerry Allen Whittredge

"Bogus astronaut." *ABCNews* space page via James Oberg's website, June 8, 1998. www.jamesoberg.com/98jun08-abc-bogus_astronaut.pdf.

Byars, Carlos. "Astronaut impersonator found fit to stand trial." *Houston Chronicle*, December 12, 1998.

Dyer, R. A., Kevin Moran, and Ruth Rendon. "Friends describe bogus astronaut as down-to-earth." *Houston Chronicle*, June 4, 1998.

Tedford, Deborah. "Astronaut impostor allegedly incompetent." *Houston Chronicle*, June 13, 1998.

Chapter 2: Gender Benders
ALL THAT JAZZ (BILLY TIPTON)

"Tipton, Billy (1914-1989): Spokane's Secretive Jazzman." The Free Online Encyclopedia of Washington State History. www.historylink.org/index. cfm?DisplayPage=output.cfm&file_id=7456.

Burton, Sarah. *Impostors: Six Kinds of Liar—True Tales of Deception*. New York: Viking Books, 2001.

Ellingwood, Brook. "Writing his own tune: Billy Tipton's secret surprised even those who knew him best." *KCTS9.org*, February 24, 2012. http://kcts9.org/ im-not-les/writing-his-own-tune-billy-tipton-secret-surprise.

Middlebrook, Diane Wood. *Suits Me: The Double Life of Billy Tipton*. Boston: Houghton Mifflin, 1998.

Smith, Dinitia. "One false note in a musician's life; Billy Tipton is remembered with love, even by those who were deceived." *New York Times*, June 2, 1998.

THE SURGEON'S SECRET (JAMES BARRY)

"Encyclopedia of World Biography: James Barry." www.notablebiographies.com/ supp/Supplement-A-Bu-and-Obituaries/Barry-James.html.

Allen, Brooke. "All of the people some of the time." *New York Times*, February 2, 2003.

Burton, Sarah. *Impostors: Six Kinds of Liar—True Tales of Deception*. New York: Viking Books, 2001.

Fleming, Nick. "Revealed: Army surgeon actually a woman." *London Telegraph*, March 5, 2008.

Moore, Victoria. "Dr. Barry's deathbed secret sex secret: The extraordinary truth about a great war hero and medical pioneer." *London Daily Mail*, March 10, 2008.

THE INFANTRYMEN WHO WEREN'T

Albert Cashier

"An Irish Cailín Goes to War: Jennie Hodgers, Private, Co. G, 95th Illinois Infantry." Civil-War-Irish. http://homepages.rootsweb.ancestry.com/~cwirish/Cashier. html.

"Jennie Hodgers: The Irishwoman Who Fought as a Man in the Union Army." Irish in the American Civil War, August 17, 2011. http://irishamericancivilwar.com/ 2011/08/17/jennie-hodgers-the-irishwoman-who-fought-as-a-man-in-the- union-army/.

Blanton, DeAnne. "Women Soldiers of the Civil War." *Prologue Magazine*, Vol. 25, No. 1, Spring 1993. www.archives.gov/publications/prologue/1993/spring/ women-in-the-civil-war-1.html.

Hall, Andy. "The Uneasy Remembrance of Private Albert Cashier." Dead Confederates, September 2, 2011. http://deadconfederates.com/2011/09/02/ saunemin-illinois-remembers-private-albert-cashier/.

Hicks-Bartlett, Alani. "When Jennie Comes Marchin' Home." Illinois Periodicals Online, February 1994. www.lib.niu.edu/1994/ihy940230.html.

Paul, Linda. "In Civil War, woman fought like a man for freedom." *NPR.org*, May 24, 2009. www.npr.org/templates/story/story.php?storyId=104452266.

———. "Jennie's house: Part of a Civil War secret." *WBEZ.org*, September 2, 2011. www.wbez.org/story/jennies-house-preserving-part-civil-war-secret-91446.

Frances Clalin/Jack Williams

Blanton, DeAnne. "Women Soldiers of the Civil War." *Prologue Magazine*, Vol. 25, No. 1, Spring 1993. www.archives.gov/publications/prologue/1993/spring/ women-in-the-civil-war-1.html.

Sarah/Sam Blalock

"Women in the Ranks: Concealed Identities in Civil War Era North Carolina." North Carolina Civil War Sesquicentennial. www.nccivilwar150.com/features/ women/women.htm.

Harry T. Buford/Loreta Janeta Velázquez

"Loreta Janeta Velazquez." Civil War Trust. www.civilwar.org/education/history/
biographies/loreta-janeta-velazquez.html.

"Loreta Velazquez." Know Southern History. www.knowsouthernhistory.net/
Biographies/Loreta_Velazquez/.

Van Ostrand, Maggie. "A Confederate Soldier in Texas: Full Metal Corset." Texas
Escapes. www.texasescapes.com/MaggieVanOstrand/Confederate-Soldier-in-
Texas-Full-Metal-Corset.htm.

THE SAPPER WITH A SECRET (PRIVATE DENIS SMITH/DOROTHY LAWRENCE)

Lawrence, Dorothy. *Sapper Dorothy Lawrence: The Only English Woman Soldier, Late
Royal Engineers, 51st Division, 179th Tunnelling Company, B. E. F.* London: J.
Lane, 1919.

Newby, Jen. "Dorothy Lawrence: The Woman Who Fought at the Front." Writing
Women's History, July 28, 2012. http://writingwomenshistory.blogspot.
co.uk/2012/07/dorothy-lawrence-woman-who-fought-at.html.

A SAILOR'S LIFE FOR ME

Hannah Snell

"Hannah Snell (1723–1792)." Royal Berkshire History. www.berkshirehistory.com/
bios/hsnell.html.

"Hannah Snell (James Grey) 1723–1792." The Royal Regiment of Fusiliers Museum.
www.warwickfusiliers.co.uk/pages/pg-50-hannah_snell_james_grey_1723_-_
1792/.

"Unravelling the Story." The Hannah Snell Homepage. www.hannahsnell.com/
biography.htm.

Burton, Sarah. *Impostors: Six Kinds of Liar—True Tales of Deception.* New York: Viking
Books, 2001.

Snell, Hannah, and Anonymous. *The Female Soldier, or The Surprising Life and Adventures
of Hannah Snell.* London: n.p., 1750.

Stark, Suzanne J. *Female Tars: Women Aboard Ship in the Age of Sail*. Annapolis, MD: Naval Institute Press, 1996.

Mary Anne Talbot

BBC History Trails—Wars and Conflict. Fact Files. www.bbc.co.uk/history/trail/ wars_conflict/home_front/women_at_war_fact_file.shtml.

Burton, Sarah. *Impostors: Six Kinds of Liar—True Tales of Deception*. New York: Viking Books, 2001.

Stark, Suzanne J. *Female Tars: Women Aboard Ship in the Age of Sail*. Annapolis, MD: Naval Institute Press, 1998.

THE LIEUTENANT NUN (CATALINA DE ERAUSO)

"Lieutenant Nun." Sparknotes. www.sparknotes.com/lit/lieutenantnun/context.html.

Brown, Roberta. "Catalina de Erauso." The Women of Action Network. www.woa. tv/articles/hi_deerausoc.html.

Rapp, Linda. "Erauso, Catalina de." Encyclopedia of Gay, Lesbian, Bisexual, Transgender and Queer Culture. www.glbtq.com/literature/erauso_c.html.

THE PETTICOAT CAVALRYMAN (CHEVALIER D'ÉON)

"Charles, chevalier d'Éon de Beaumont." *Encyclopedia Britannica*.

"George Dance, Chevalier D'Eon, Graphite with watercolour, bodycolour and red stump." British Museum. www.britishmuseum.org/explore/highlights/ highlight_objects/pd/g/george_dance,_chevalier_deon.aspx.

Conlin, Jonathan. "The Strange Case of Chevalier d'Eon." *History Today*, Vol. 60, Issue 4, 2010.

Danielle. "Charles-Genevieve Deon De Beaumont." Beaumont Society. www. beaumontsociety.org.uk/about_us/Public%20information/Biography.pdf.

Lang, Andrew. "The Chevalier d'Eon." The Literature Network. www.online-literature.com/andrew_lang/historical-mysteries/11/.

Langan, Michael. "The Patron Saint of Transvestites." *Polari Magazine*, April 21, 2012.

THE BRICKIE IN THE TOP HAT (HARRY STOKES)

"The remarkable man-woman 'Harry' Stokes." *Whitehaven News*, October 27, 1859.

Burton, Sarah. *Impostors: Six Kinds of Liar—True Tales of Deception*. New York: Viking
    Books, 2001.

ONE-EYED CHARLEY (CHARLEY PARKHURST)

"Rough, Tough Charley Parkhurst—Stagecoach Driver." www.mcguiresplace.net/
    Rough%2C%20Tough%20Charlie%20Parkhurst/.

"The strange life and times of Charley Parkhurst." *Metro Santa Cruz*, March 5–12, 2003.

Barriga, Joan. "Survival with Style: The Women of the Santa Cruz Mountains."
    Mountain News Network. www.mnn.net/cparkhur.htm.

Burton, Sarah. *Impostors: Six Kinds of Liar—True Tales of Deception*. New York: Viking
    Books, 2001.

Righetti, Don. "1970: Charley Darkey Parkhurst had a secret." *Santa Cruz Sentinel*,
    October 8, 2006.

Sams, Ed. *The Real Mountain Charley*. Ben Lomond, CA: Yellow Tulip Press, 1995.

A THOUSAND MILES TO FREEDOM (WILLIAM AND ELLEN CRAFT)

Holmes, Marian Smith. "The Great Escape From Slavery of Ellen and William Craft."
    Smithsonian Magazine, June 17, 2010.

Magnusson, Magnus. *Fakes, Forgers & Phoneys: Famous Scams and Scamps*. Edinburgh:
    Mainstream Publishing Company, 2006.

McCaskill, Barbara. "William and Ellen Craft." New Georgia Encyclopedia. www.
    newgeorgiaencyclopedia.com/nge/Article.jsp?id=h-622.

THE NEW DARWIN? (DR. CHARLOTTE BACH/KAROLY HAJDU)

Wheen, Francis. *Who Was Dr. Charlotte Bach?* London: Short Books, 2002.

FRAUD ALERT: MILITARY MAIDENS

Ulrika Stålhammar/Vilhelm Edstedt

International Institute of Sexual and Gender Diversity—A Gay a Day Archives Page 3.
    www.iisgd.org/A_Gay_a_Day_Archives_3.html.

Transitioning FTM in Australia—Timeline. February 2, 2012. www.ftmaustralia.org/
publications/timeline.

Ann Mills

Dyer, T. F. Thiselton. "Strange Pages from Family Papers." The Echo Library, 2007.

Felsenstein, Frank. "Unravelling Ann Mills: Some Notes on Gender Construction and
Naval Heroism." *Eighteenth Century Fiction,* Vol. 19, Issue 1, Article 24, 2006.

Pennell, C. R. (ed.). *Bandits at Sea: A Pirates Reader.* New York: New York University
Press, 2001.

Deborah Sampson/Robert Shurtliff

"Deborah Sampson." Utah State University Adele and Dale Young Education
Technology Center (YETC) and Emma Eccles Jones College of Education
and Human Services. http://teacherlink.ed.usu.edu/tlresources/units/
byrnes-famous/sampson.htm.

Burton, Sarah. *Impostors: Six Kinds of Liar—True Tales of Deception.* New York: Viking
Books, 2001.

Nadezhda Durova/Alexander Sokolov

Brown, Rita Mae. "*The Womanly Ways of War: The Cavalry Maiden* by Nadezhda
Durova; translation, introduction, and notes by Mary Fleming Zirin." *Los
Angeles Times,* December 18, 1988.

Kamenir, Victor. "Nadezhda Durova: Russian Cavalry Maiden in the Napoleonic
Wars." *Military History,* June 12, 2006.

Chapter 3: False Heirs
A PRINCE AMONG MEN (THE SECOND KUMAR OF BHAWAL)

Chatterjee, Partha. *A Princely Impostor? The Strange and Universal History of the Kumar of
Bhawal.* Princeton, NJ: Princeton University Press, 2002.

THE LOST DAUPHIN (KARL WILHELM NAUNDORFF)

"Descendants of Maria-Theresa." The Learning Center. www.genebase.com/learning/
article/72.

"Identification of the Son of Louis XVI and Marie-Antoinette." Enotes. www.enotes .com/identification-son-louis-xvi-marie-antoinette-reference/identification-son-louis-xvi-marie-antoinette.

"The Mystery of Louis XVII!" *PBS.org*. www.pbs.org/wgbh/masterpiece/lostprince/ insider_louis.html.

Bondeson, Jan. *The Great Pretenders: The True Stories Behind Famous Historical Mysteries.* New York: W. W. Norton & Co., 2005.

Burton, Sarah. *Impostors: Six Kinds of Liar—True Tales of Deception.* New York: Viking Books, 2001.

Center for Human Genetics, University of Leuven, Institut for Rechtsmedizin, Universität Münster, press conference, April 19, 2000. http://louis17.chez. com/english.htm.

Cheesman, Clive, and Jonathan Williams. *Rebels, Pretenders and Impostors.* London: St. Martin's Press, 2000.

KINGMAKERS' PUPPETS

Lambert Simnel

Burton, Sarah. *Impostors: Six Kinds of Liar—True Tales of Deception.* New York: Viking Books, 2001.

Cheesman, Clive, and Jonathan Williams. *Rebels, Pretenders and Impostors.* London: St. Martin's Press, 2000.

Sparrow, Judge Gerald. *The Great Impostors.* London: John Long, 1962.

Perkin Warbeck

Burton, Sarah. *Impostors: Six Kinds of Liar—True Tales of Deception.* New York: Viking Books, 2001.

Cheesman, Clive, and Jonathan Williams. *Rebels, Pretenders and Impostors.* London: St. Martin's Press, 2000.

Sparrow, Judge Gerald. *The Great Impostors.* London: John Long, 1962.

THE FALSE DMITRYS

"False Dmitri." http://everything2.com/index.pl?node_id=1399476.

Burton, Sarah. *Impostors: Six Kinds of Liar—True Tales of Deception*. New York: Viking Books, 2001.

Dunning, Chester, Norman Davies, Pawel Jasienica, Jerzy Malec, and Andrzej Nowak. "Polish-Muscovite War (1605-1618)." www.conflicts.rem33.com/images/Poland/Polish_Moscovite_wars_1605_18.htm.

Naumov, Evgeny. "On the Anniversary of the Time of Troubles." Russkiy Mir Foundation, October 20, 2009. www.russkiymir.ru/russkiymir/en/publications/articles/article0022.html.

THE PRINCESS PAINTER (OLIVIA SERRES)

Bondeson, Jan. *The Great Pretenders: The True Stories Behind Famous Historical Mysteries*. New York: W. W. Norton & Co., 2005.

Reynolds, K. D. "Serres, Olivia." Oxford Dictionary of National Biography. www.oxforddnb.com/view/article/25106.

THE TROUBLE WITH ANNA (ANNA ANDERSON)

"Anastasia arrives in the United States." The History Channel. www.history.com/this-day-in-history/anastasia-arrives-in-the-united-states.

"Discovery solves mystery of last Czar's family." *CNN.com*, April 30, 2008. http://edition.cnn.com/2008/WORLD/europe/04/30/russia.czar/.

Burton, Sarah. *Impostors: Six Kinds of Liars—True Tales of Deception*. New York: Viking Books, 2001.

Magnusson, Magnus. *Fakers, Forgers & Phoneys: Famous Scams and Scamps*. London: Random House UK, 2007.

Tucker, William O. "Jack & Anna: Remembering the czar of Charlottesville eccentrics." *Charlottesville (VA) Hook*, July 5, 2007. www.readthehook.com/86004/cover-jack-amp-anna-remembering-czar-charlottesville-eccentrics.

FRAUD ALERT: CUNNING CLAIMANTS

The Tichborne Claimant

"The Tichborne Archive." Hantsweb. http://www3.hants.gov.uk/community-history/tichborne-claimant.htm.

Annear, Robyn. *The Man Who Lost Himself: The Fabulous Story of the Tichborne Claimant.* London. Robinson, 2003.

Bondeson, Jan. *The Great Pretenders: The True Stories Behind Famous Historical Mysteries.* London: W. W. Norton & Co., 2005.

Burton, Sarah. *Impostors: Six Kinds of Liar—True Tales of Deception.* New York: Viking Books, 2001.

Magnusson, Magnus. *Fakers, Forgers & Phoneys: Famous Scams and Scamps.* London: Random House UK, 2007.

Sparrow, Judge Gerald. *The Great Impostors.* London: John Long. 1962.

Eugenio Lascorz

Sainty, Guy Stair. "The pseudo Lascaris princes and their fantastic claims." Almanach de la Cour. www.chivalricorders.org/royalty/fantasy/lascaris.htm.

Harry Domela

Burton, Sarah. *Impostors: Six Kinds of Liar—True Tales of Deception.* New York: Viking Books, 2001.

Alexis Brimeyer

"I am the son an heir." July 28, 2006. London: Metro. http://metro.co.uk/2006/07/28/i-am-the-son-and-heir-196881.

Sainty, Guy Stair. Jan 25, 2005. "Heraldry and Nobility in the American Context." New York Genealogical & Biographical Society. www.newyorkfamilyhistory.org/research-discover/research-tools/heraldry-and-nobility-american-context.

Chapter 4: Fugitives from Justice

James (Whitey) Bulger

"James (Whitey) Bulger." *New York Times*, November 11, 2012.

"Revealed: The fake ID cards James 'Whitey' Bulger used to evade capture for 16 years." *London Daily Mail*, August 18, 2011.

"Whitey Bulger's stash revealed: cash, guns & fake IDs." *Huffington Post*, July 15, 2011. www.huffingtonpost.com/2011/07/15/whitey-bulgers-stash-reve_n_900019.html#s309554.

CHASING DR. CRIPPEN (HAWLEY HARVEY CRIPPEN)

Dr. Crippen website. http://drcrippen.co.uk/index.html.

"History of the Metropolitan Police—Dr. Crippen." Metropolitan Police. www.met.
police.uk/history/dr_crippen.htm.

"Was Dr. Crippen innocent of his wife's murder?" *BBC News*, July 29, 2010. www.
bbc.co.uk/news/magazine-10802059.

DAN THE SKYJACK MAN (DAN COOPER)

"A Byte out of History—The D. B. Cooper Mystery." FBI, November 24, 2006.
www.fbi.gov/news/stories/2006/november/dbcooper_112406.

"D. B. Cooper Redux—Help Us Solve the Enduring Mystery." FBI, December 31,
2007. www.fbi.gov/news/stories/2007/december/dbcooper_123107.

"In Search of D. B. Cooper—New Developments in the Unsolved Case." FBI, March
17, 2009. www.fbi.gov/news/stories/2009/march/dbcooper_031709.

Beck, Kathrine. "Dan Cooper parachutes from skyjacked airliner on November 24,
1971." Historylink, August 30, 2011. www.historylink.org/index.cfm?
DisplayPage=output.cfm&File_Id=1997.

Pasternak, Douglas. "Skyjacker at Large." U.S. News Mysteries of History. www.
usnews.com/usnews/doubleissue/mysteries/cooper.htm.

Stevens, John. "Is the mystery of D. B. Cooper about to be solved? FBI reveals it has
new suspect 40 years after America's most elusive fugitive parachuted from a
hijacked plane." *London Daily Mail*, July 31, 2011.

THE BREEZE KNOLL MURDERS (JOHN LIST)

"Killer John List, one of 'America's Most Wanted,' dies behind bars." *New York Daily
News*, March 24, 2008.

"A Sunday school teacher murders his family and goes undercover for 18 years." The
History Channel. www.history.com/this-day-in-history/a-sunday-school-
teacher-murders-his-family-and-goes-undercover-for-18-years.

McCracken, Elizabeth. "Wanted—John List." *New York Times Magazine*, December
23, 2008.

Ramsland, Katherine. "John List." Tru TV Crime Library. www.trutv.com/library/
crime/notorious_murders/family/list/1.html.

Stout, David. "John E. List, 82, killer of 5 family members, dies." *New York Times*, March 25, 2008.

Sullivan, Joseph F. "Concern over 'moral values' led to family murders, lawyer says." *New York Times*, April 3, 1990.

THE COPYCAT JACKAL (JOHN STONEHOUSE)

"1974: 'Drowned' Stonehouse found alive." BBC On This Day. http://news.bbc.co.uk/onthisday/hi/dates/stories/december/24/newsid_2540000/2540557.stm.

"1979: Disgraced ex-MP released from jail." BBC On This Day. http://news.bbc.co.uk/onthisday/hi/dates/stories/august/14/newsid_2534000/2534073.stm.

"John Stonehouse 'shed his guilt by adopting a new identity.'" *London Telegraph*, December 29, 2005.

Martin, Arthur. "Former Labour minister who faked his own death was Communist spy." *London Daily Mail*, October 6, 2009.

Milmo, Cahal. "British political scandal: The man who faked his death." *London Independent*, December 29, 2005.

A MURDERER IN OUR MIDST (RENO TREVOR HOGG/GEORGE MITCHELL ALLGOOD)

Henderson, Paul J. "Allgood case now in court." *Chilliwack Times*, September 13, 2012.

————. "B.C. man living under fake identity charged with Saskatoon murder." *Chilliwack Times*, December 20, 2010.

FRAUD ALERT: FELONIOUS FLIERS

2007 Chinese Pilot

"Chinese man fakes it as a pilot." *BBC News*, June 7, 2007. http://news.bbc.co.uk/1/hi/world/asia-pacific/6730783.stm.

2010 Swedish Pilot

"Bogus pilot arrested just before take-off." *Orange News*, March 5, 2010. http://web.orange.co.uk/article/quirkies/Bogus_pilot_arrested_just_before_take_off.

"Fake pilot arrested moments before take-off." *BBC News*, March 4, 2010. http://
news.bbc.co.uk/1/hi/world/europe/8549954.stm.

2012 Italian Pilot

McKenna, Josephine. "Man fakes pilot credentials to fly for free." *London Telegraph*,
September 23, 2012.

Pisa, Nick. "'Fake pilot who joined cabin crew in cockpit' is arrested in plot mirroring
Spielberg's hit film 'Catch Me If You Can.'" *London Daily Mail*, September
23, 2012.

Chapter 5: Frauds and Freebooters

Lewis Morgan

"Morgan pleads guilty to charges." *Kokomo Tribune*, March 14, 1998.

Boulware, Jack. "Fake it to the limit." *SF Weekly News*, April 29, 1998.

O'Brien, Payton. "Randy Meisner Imposter Still Conning at Super Bowl in Vegas."
Gambling 911, February 4, 2009. www.gambling911.com/gambling-news/
randy-meisner-imposter-still-conning-super-bowl-vegas-020409.html.

Van Derbeken, Jaxon. "Impostor still touring as ex-Eagles guitarist." *San Francisco
Chronicle*, November 21, 1997.

THE MAN WHO SOLD THE EIFFEL TOWER...TWICE! (VICTOR LUSTIG)

"Eiffel, Marconi & Count Victor Lustig." ABC—The Science Show, April 6, 2002.
www.abc.net.au/radionational/programs/scienceshow/eiffel-marconi-count-
victor-lustig/3508902#transcript.

"The Smoothest Con Man Who Ever Lived." *Smithsonian Magazine*, August 22, 2012.

"Victor Lustig." The Biography Channel. www.biography.com/people/
victor-lustig-20657385.

Sakalauskas, Tony. "The Man Who Sold the Eiffel Tower." 3 AM Publishing.
www.3ammagazine.com/short_stories/non-fict/truetales/eiffeltower.html.

Vellinger, Jan. "Victor Lustig—the man who (could have) sold the world."
Radio Praha, October 15, 2003. www.radio.cz/en/section/czechs/
victor-lustig-the-man-who-could-have-sold-the-world.

LEAVING BUFFALO (DAVID HAMPTON)

"David Hampton." *London Telegraph*, July 22, 2003.

"Teenager who posed as Poitier 'son' guilty." *New York Times*, November 20, 1983.

Barry, Dan. "About New York; He conned the society crowd but died alone." *New York Times*, July 19, 2003.

Burton, Sarah. *Impostors: Six Kinds of Liar—True Tales of Deception*. New York: Viking Books, 2001.

Fowler, Glenn. "Suspect in hoax is arrested here in rendezvous." *New York Times*, October 19, 1983.

Jones, Kenneth. "David Hampton, Con-Man Whose Exploits Inspired *Six Degrees*, Dead at 39." Playbill, July 20, 2003. www.playbill.com/news/article/80762-David-Hampton-Con-Man-Whose-Exploits-Inspired-Six-Degrees-Dead-at-39.

Kasindorf, Jeanie. "Six Degrees of Impersonation." *New York*, March 25, 1991.

Wadler, Joyce. "His Story Is a Hit on Broadway, but This Con Man Is in Trouble Again." *People*, March 18, 1991. www.people.com/people/archive/article/0,,20114700,00.html.

Witchel, Alex. "Impersonator wants to portray still others, this time, onstage." *New York Times*, July 31, 1990.

THE FRENCH ROCKEFELLER (CHRISTOPHE ROCANCOURT)

"Conman Rocancourt in Cannes with supermodel." *CTVNews.ca*, May 23, 2008. www.ctvnews.ca/conman-rocancourt-in-cannes-with-supermodel-1.297655.

Bean, Matt. "Faux Rockefeller: 'I misled people.'" *CNN.com*, May 20, 2003. http://edition.cnn.com/2003/LAW/05/20/ctv.rocancourt/.

Burrough, Bryan. "The Counterfeit Rockefeller." *Vanity Fair*, January 2001.

Leung, Rebecca. "The counterfeit Rockefeller." *CBSNews.com*, February 11, 2009. www.cbsnews.com/8301-18560_162-550070.html.

Morton, Brian. "$150,000 fraud nets 1-day sentence." *Vancouver Sun*, June 15, 2002.

A REAL MOLL FLANDERS (MARY CARLETON)

"Mary Carleton, the German princess." The Newgate Calendar. www.exclassics.com/newgate/ng34.htm.

Lilley, Kate. "Mary Carleton's false additions: the case of the 'German princess.'"
Humanities Research, Vol. XVI, No., 2010.

THE CAZIQUE OF POYAIS (GREGOR MACGREGOR)

"Gregor MacGregor." Venezuela Tuya. www.venezuelatuya.com/biografias/gregor_
macgregor.htm.

"The Prince of Poyais." Clan Gregor website. (www.clangregor.org.Poyais—no longer
available).

THE CAPTAIN FROM KÖPENICK (FRIEDRICH WILHELM VOIGT)

"16.10.1906: The Captain from Köpenick." Today in History. www.today-in-history
.de/index.php?what=thmanu&manu_id=1614&tag=16&monat=10&year
=2012&dayisset=1&lang=en.

"Der Hauptmann von Koepenick." h2g2, December 5, 2008. www.h2g2.com/
approved_entry/A44196375.

"The Greatest Heist in History? The Captain of Kopenick." Strange History.
www.strangehistory.net/2012/11/07/the-greatest-heist-in-history-the-
captain-of-kopenick/.

Burton, Sarah. *Impostors: Six Kinds of Liar—True Tales of Deception.* New York: Viking
Books, 2001.

FRAUD ALERT: TRUST ME, I'M A DOCTOR!

Vitomir Zepinic

Caterson, Simon. "Hoaxes, lies and surgical tape." *Sydney Morning Herald*, October 16, 2010.

McClymont, Kate. "Fake doctor conned his way into a job at a top medical school."
Sydney Morning Herald, September 27, 2010.

Balaji Varatharaju

Hainke, Nadja, and Fiona McWhirter. "'Fake doctor' Balaji Varatharaju treated
over 400 patients." *News.com.au*, February 28, 2010. www.news.com.au/
national-news/fake-doctor-balaji-varatharaju-treated-over-400-patients/
story-e6frfkvr-1225835255318.

South African Sex Worker

Medley, Laea. "Bogus doctor sentenced." *Iol News*, September 7, 2012. www.iol.co.za/
    news/crime-courts/bogus-doctor-sentenced-1.1378229.

Conrad de Souza

"Bogus doctor: Lewisham PCT's Conrad de Souza jailed." *BBC News*, October 24,
    2011. www.bbc.co.uk/news/uk-england-london-15438332.

O'Doherty, Niamh. "Bogus doctor told to pay back £270,000 he 'earned' over 10
    years while pretending to be a GP." *London Daily Mail*, December 11, 2012.

Sears, Nick, and Jack Doyle. "Bogus doctor's web of deceit: Married love cheat faked
    DNA test so he could deny girlfriend's child was his." *London Daily Mail*,
    October 25, 2011.

Chapter 6: Imitation Indians

Chief Jay Strongbow

Mooneyham, Mike. "Pro wrestling great Chief Jay Strongbow dead at 83." *Charleston
    (SC) Post and Courier*, April 4, 2012.

Oliver, Greg. "Chief Jay Strongbow dies." *Slam! Sports*, April 3, 2012. http://slam.
    canoe.ca/Slam/Wrestling/2011/12/12/19113886.html.

Slotnik, Daniel E. "Joe Scarpa, who gained wrestling fame as Chief Jay Strongbow,
    dies." *New York Times*, April 5, 2012.

LONG LANCE (SYLVESTER LONG)

Burton, Sarah. *Impostors: Six Kinds of Liar—True Tales of Deception*. New York: Viking
    Books, 2001.

Smith, Donald B. *Long Lance: The True Story of an Impostor*. Toronto: Macmillan of
    Canada, 1982.

HE WHO FLIES BY NIGHT (GREY OWL)

"Grey Owl." Parks Canada. www.pc.gc.ca/eng/pn-np/sk/princealbert/natcul/
    natcul1/c.aspx.

Brower, Kenneth. "Grey Owl." *The Atlantic*, January 1990.

Burton, Sarah. *Impostors: Six Kinds of Liar—True Tales of Deception.* New York: Viking Books, 2001.

Dickson, Lovat. *Wilderness Man: The Amazing True Story of Grey Owl.* New York: Pocket Books, 1999.

Smith, Cathy. "Canada: The long, strange flight of Grey Owl." *London Telegraph*, November 13, 1999.

THE CRYING INDIAN (IRON EYES CODY)

"Pollution Prevention. Keep America Beautiful—Iron Eyes Cody (1961–1983)." Advertising Educational Foundation. www.aef.com/exhibits/social _responsibility/ad_council/2278.

De Las Casas, Chadd. "Playing Indian: The Iron Eyes Cody Story." *Yahoo Voices*, October 15, 2007. http://voices.yahoo.com/playing-indian-iron-eyes-cody-story-588177.html.

Florio, Gwen. "Creator of 'crying Indian' Keep America Beautiful ad dies at 84." *Buffalo Post*, October 6, 2009.

THE HERBAL CHIEF (CHIEF TWO MOON MERIDAS)

"Chief Two Moon Meridas." National Heritage Museum, December 9, 2010. http://nationalheritagemuseum.typepad.com/library_and_archives/2010/12/chief-two-moon-meridas.html.

Durrett, Deanne. "Meridas, Chief Two Moon." *American Indian Lives: Healers*. New York: Facts on File, 1997.

FRAUD ALERT: BOGUS BRAVES

Forrest/Asa Earl Carter

"Asa Carter." PBS People & Events. www.pbs.org/wgbh/amex/wallace/peopleevents/pande01.html.

"The Artful Reinvention of Klansman Asa Earl Carter." NPR Radio Diaries, April 20, 2012. www.npr.org/2012/04/20/151037079/the-artful-reinvention-of-klansman-asa-earl-carter.

Carter, Dan T. "The transformation of a Klansman." *New York Times*, October 4, 1991.

Nasdijj/Timothy Patrick Barrus

"Nasdijj the Not-So-Real Navajo." *Time.* www.time.com/time/specials/packages/
    article/0,28804,1868982_1868981_1868974,00.html.

Alexie, Sherman. "When the Story Stolen Is Your Own." *Time*, January 29, 2006.

Chaikivsky, Andrew. "Nasdijj." *Esquire*, April 30, 2006.

Fleischer, Matthew. "Navahoax." *LA Weekly*, January 23, 2006.

Margaret B. Jones/Margaret Seltzer

"Less Love, More Consequences." *Time.* www.time.com/time/specials/packages/
    article/0,28804,1868982_1868981_1868979,00.html.

Pool, Bob, and Rebecca Trounson. "Memoir a fake, author says." *Los Angeles Times*,
    March 4, 2008.

Treuer, David. "Going Native. Why do writers pretend to be Indians?" *Slate*, March 7,
    2008. www.slate.com/articles/arts/culturebox/2008/03/going_native.html.

Chapter 7: Fabulous Fantasists
THE GREATEST LIAR ON EARTH (LOUIS DE ROUGEMONT/HENRI LOUIS GRIN)

Andrews, B. G. "de Rougemont, Louis." Australian Dictionary of Biography. http://
    adb.anu.edu.au/biography/de-rougemont-louis-5961.

Burton, Sarah. *Impostors: Six Kinds of Liar—True Tales of Deception*. New York: Viking
    Books, 2001.

de Rougemont, Louis. *The Adventures of Louis de Rougemont As Told by Himself*.
    London: George Newnes, 1899.

Howard, Rod. *The Fabulist: The Incredible Story of Louis de Rougemont*. Sydney: Random
    House Australia, 2006.

DEAD MAN WALKING (LORD CHRISTOPHER BUCKINGHAM/ CHARLES ALBERT STOPFORD)

Falconer, Bruce. "Escape from America." *LOST Magazine*, No. 31, March 2009.

Freedland, Jonathan. "The talented Mr. Stopford." *London Guardian*, May 12, 2006.

Laville, Sarah. "He lived as a bogus peer for 22 years. Now he's in jail. But who is he?"
    London Guardian, November 9, 2005.

Sapsted, David. "Dilemma over fake aristocrat." *London Telegraph*, April 3, 2006.

Sapsted, David, and Anil Dawar. "Bogus lord who stole baby's identity is former US seaman." *London Telegraph*, May 6, 2006.

THE FAKE FORMOSAN (GEORGE PSALMANAZAR)

"George Psalmanazar." The Biography Channel. www.biography.com/people/ george-psalmanazar-20649983.

"George Psalmanazar the Celebrated Native of Formosa." University of Delaware Library. www.lib.udel.edu/ud/spec/exhibits/forgery/psalm.htm

"The Native of Formosa." Museum of Hoaxes. www.museumofhoaxes.com/formosa. html.

Burton, Sarah. *Impostors: Six Kinds of Liar—True Tales of Deception*. New York: Viking Books, 2001.

Keevak, Michael. *The Pretended Asian: George Psalmanazar's Eighteenth-Century Formosan Hoax*. Detroit, MI: Wayne State University Press, 2004.

THE FANTASY PRINCESS (PRINCESS CARABOO/MARY WILLCOCKS)

Burton, Sarah. *Impostors: Six Kinds of Liar—True Tales of Deception*. New York: Viking Books, 2001.

Haughton, Brian. "Bristol's Princess Caraboo." BBC Legacies. www.bbc.co.uk/ legacies/myths_legends/england/bristol/article_1.shtml.

Raison, Jennifer and Michael Goldie. *The Servant Girl Princess Caraboo: The Real Story of a Grand Hoax*. The Windrush Press, 1994.

Wells, John. *Princess Caraboo: Her True Story*. London: Pan Books, 1994.

THOM'S LAST BATTLE (JOHN NICHOLS THOM)

"Thomas Mears and Others: The Canterbury Rioters, 31st May 1838." The Newgate Calendar. www.exclassics.com/newgate/ng623.htm.

FRAUD ALERT: RANK OUTSIDERS

Joseph A. Cafasso

Rutenberg, Jim. "At Fox News, the colonel who wasn't." *New York Times*, April 29, 2012.

Douglas R. Stringfellow

"The controversial career of Representative Douglas Stringfellow of Utah". Office of
the Clerk of the U.S. House of Representatives. http://history.house.gov/
HistoricalHighlight/Detail/36418.

"Douglas R. Stringfellow, 1954." Museum of Hoaxes. www.museumofhoaxes.com/
hoax/archive/permalink/douglas_r._stringfellow/.

Glass, Andrew. "Rep. Douglas Stringfellow is born, September 24, 1922." Politico,
September 24, 2010. www.politico.com/news/stories/0910/42633.html.

Seegmiller, Janet Burton. "McCarthyism, Granger, and Stringfellow." Utah Historical
Quarterly, 67 Fall. http://historytogo.utah.gov/utah_chapters/utah_today/
mccarthyismgrangerandstringfellow.html.

Lafayette Keaton

"Bogus war hero pleads guilty." KATU.com, September 8, 2010. www.katu.com/
news/local/102490654.html.

Tilkin, Dan. "War hero impostor falls to the facts." KATU.com, March 11, 2010.
www.katu.com/news/local/87413287.html.

Walter Carlson

"Man arrested for wearing military attire released on $10,000 bond." Arlington
National Cemetery, April 23, 2004. http://arlingtoncemetery.net/
wkcarlson-imposter.htm.

Chozick, Amy. "Veterans' web sites expose pseudo heroes, phony honors." Wall Street
Journal, May 6, 2005.

Roger D. Edwards

Jontz, Sandra. "Navy Captain Found Guilty of Wearing Unearned Medals." Military.
com, August 2, 2004. www.military.com/NewContent/0,13190,SS_080204_
Medals,00.html.

Chapter 8: Spooks and Cops

Larry Lee Risser

"Fake CIA agent admits conning 2 out of $20,000." *NBCNews.com*, December 23,
    2007. www.nbcnews.com/id/22373749/ns/us_news-weird_news/t/
    fake-cia-agent-admits-conning-out/#.UY5UIIIj7v4.

"Ventura county man pleads guilty to federal charges of impersonating CIA agent."
    U.S. Attorney's Office, Central District of California press release, December
    21, 2007. www.justice.gov/usao/cac/Pressroom/pr2007/171.html.

Glover, Scott. "Phony CIA 'operative' faces prison." *Los Angeles Times*, December 22,
    2007.

Anders Behring Breivik

"Timeline: How Norway's terror attacks unfolded." April 17, 2012. BBC News
    Online. www.bbc.co.uk/news/world-europe-14260297.

Fake London Police Blogger

Davenport, Justin. "Fake inspector conned real police officers and 3,000 Twitter fol-
    lowers." *London Evening Standard*, July 13, 2012.

Kevin Balfour

"Warren Man Accused of Posing as FBI Agent." *myfoxdetroit.com*, January 22, 2010.
        www.myfoxdetroit.com/story/18498461/warren-man-accused-of-posing-as-
        fbi-agent

"Warren man gets three years for impersonating FBI agent." *Oakland Press*, October
    19, 2010.

Cook, Jameson. "Impersonation case stemmed from New Baltimore tip." *Macomb
    Daily*, April 11, 2012.

Perth Watch House Police Impostor

Wynne, Grant. "Fake police officer works undetected." *ABCNews.au*, June 5, 2012.
        www.abc.net.au/news/2012-06-04/security-breach-at-perth-watch-house/
        4051748.

THE EYE OF THE DAY (MATA HARI/MARGARETHA ZELLE)

Noe, Denise. "Mata Hari." Tru TV Crime Library. www.trutv.com/library/crime/
terrorists_spies/spies/hari/1.html.

Shipman, Pat. *Femme Fatale—Love, Lies, and the Unknown Life of Mata Hari.* New York:
William Morrow, 2007.

THE SPY WHO CAME IN FROM THE COLD SEA (MAJOR WILLIAM MARTIN/GLYNDWR MICHAEL)

"Operation Mincemeat—The Man Who Never Was." h2g2, January 28, 2005. www.
h2g2.com/approved_entry/A3031949.

Gladwell, Malcolm. "Pandora's Briefcase." *The New Yorker*, May 10, 2010.

Lane, Megan. "Operation Mincemeat: How a dead tramp fooled Hitler." *BBC News
Magazine*, December 3, 2010. www.bbc.co.uk/news/magazine-11887115.

MacIntyre, Ben. "Operation Mincemeat." BBC History. www.bbc.co.uk/history/
topics/operation_mincemeat.

Wansell, Geoffrey. "The dead tramp who won World War II: A new book reveals
the full astonishing story of The Man Who Never Was." *London Daily Mail*,
January 15, 2010.

KING CON (ROBERT HENDY-FREEGARD)

"CPS convicts bogus spy." Crown Prosecution Service press release, June 23, 2005.
www.cps.gov.uk/news/latest_news/129_05/.

"Fake spy guilty of kidnapping con." *BBC News*, June 23, 2005. http://news.bbc.
co.uk/1/hi/england/4114640.stm.

"'It was every schoolboy's fantasy.'" *BBC News*, June 23, 2005. http://news.bbc.
co.uk/1/hi/england/4124244.stm.

"'MI5 agent' conman jailed for life." *London Guardian*, September 6, 2005.

Bennett, Neil. "Conman held victims under spell." *BBC News*, June 23, 2005. http://
news.bbc.co.uk/1/hi/uk/4070306.stm.

Newling, Dan. "Victims in fear as MI5 conman is cleared." *London Daily Mail*, April
26, 2007.

Steele, Jon. "Conman who played with women's lives." *London Telegraph*, June 24, 2005.

Weathers, Helen. "The conman who stole my life." *London Daily Mail*, April 28, 2007.

HIT SQUAD (MOSSAD ASSASSINS)

"Britain expels Israeli diplomat over Dubai passport row." *BBC News*, March 23, 2010.
http://news.bbc.co.uk/1/hi/uk/8582518.stm.

"An eye for an eye: The anatomy of Mossad's Dubai Operation." *Der Spiegel Online*,
January 17, 2011. www.spiegel.de/international/world/an-eye-for-an-eye-
the-anatomy-of-mossad-s-dubai-operation-a-739908.html.

Issa, Wafa. "The movements of the Dubai hit team suspects." *Abu Dhabi National*,
February 17, 2010. www.thenational.ae/news/uae-news/the-movements-
of-the-dubai-hit-team-suspects#full.

THE SECRET CIRCLE'S SECRET SPY (JOSEPHINE BUTLER)

"New mystery about spy hero." *York Press*, March 18, 2000.

Butler, Josephine. *Churchill's Secret Agent*. Ashburton, UK: Blaketon-Hall, 1983.

West, Nigel. Counterfeit Spies: *Genuine or Bogus? An Astonishing Investigation into Secret
Agents of the Second World War*. Boston: Little, Brown, and Co., 1999.

Wiant, Jon A. "The Intelligence Officer's Bookshelf—Intelligence in Recent Public
Literature." Central Intelligence Agency, April 14, 2007. https://www.cia.
gov/library/center-for-the-study-of-intelligence/csi-publications/csi-studies/
studies/vol46no2/article10.html.

BOND LITE (MICHAEL NEWITT)

"Double life of 007 fantasist." *This is Leicestershire*, October 31, 2008.

"James Bond Fantasist Gets 2 Years." *Sky News*, November 1, 2008. http://news.sky.
com/story/644786/james-bond-fantasist-gets-2-years.

Britten, Nick. "Bankrupt posed as James Bond-style secret agent for two years." *London
Telegraph*, October 31, 2008.

Dolan, Andy. "Jailed: The James Bond fantasist who fooled police and wife into thinking he was an MI5 agent." *London Daily Mail*, October 31, 2008.

Soodin, Vince. "Crook Bond's cover is blown." *The Sun*, October 31, 2008.

SPY COP (MARK STONE/MARK KENNEDY)

"Did married police spy use sex to infiltrate climate group? Activist felt 'violated' by
relationship with undercover officer." *London Daily Mail*, January 12, 2011.

Jones, Meirion. "Trial collapses after undercover officer changes sides." *BBC News*, January 10, 2011. www.bbc.co.uk/news/uk-12148753.

Lewis, Paul, and Rob Evans. "Mark Kennedy: A journey from undercover cop to 'bona fide' activist." *London Guardian*, January 10, 2011.

———. "Undercover officer spied on green activists." *London Guardian*, January 9, 2011.

CLEARING UP GERALD (BILL JAKOB)

"Fake cop's drug busts stir Missouri town." *CBSNews.com*, February 11, 2009. www.cbsnews.com/2100-201_162-4227278.html.

Davey, Monica. "Town finds drug agent is really an impostor." *New York Times*, July 1, 2008.

Moore, Matthew. "Fake FBI agent faces up to 105 years in jail." *London Telegraph*, July 18, 2008.

Patrick, Robert. "Court case untangles impostor's web of lies." *St. Louis Post-Dispatch*, September 30, 2008.

———. "Federal jury gives small victories to victims of phony officer." *St. Louis Post-Dispatch*, March 10, 2012.

———. "Man posing as federal agent is given five years in prison." *St. Louis Post-Dispatch*, December 20, 2008.

Zagier, Alan Scher. "Residents outraged over fake cop's antics." *ABCNews.com*, June 24–July 1, 2008. http://abcnews.go.com/TheLaw/wireStory?id=5236713#.UY5HA4Ij7v4.

FRAUD ALERT: CYBER DOUBLES

Admiral James Stavridis Impostor

Lewis, Jason. "How spies used Facebook to steal Nato chiefs' details." *London Telegraph*, March 10, 2012.

Commonwealth Bank of Australia Impostor

Boyd, Tom. "CBA's Twitter nightmare highlights anonymity risk." *Financial Review*, August 28, 2012.

HSBC Singapore Impostor

Tan, Andrea. "HSBC banker sues Yahoo Singapore for impostor's identity." *Bloomberg.
com*, August 13, 2012. www.bloomberg.com/news/2012-08-13/hsbc-banker-
sues-yahoo-singapore-for-impostor-s-identity.html.

Daniel Roche Impostor

"Outnumbered/CBBC star Daniel Roche's Facebook impostor." BBC CBBC
Newsround, February 7, 2011. http://news.bbc.co.uk/cbbcnews/hi/
newsid_9390000/newsid_9390000/9390071.stm.

Leake, Christopher, and Alex Marunchak. "Just William star targeted by stalker on
Facebook…but when parents complained about fake page, internet giant and
Scotland Yard fail to act." *London Daily Mail*, January 20, 2011.

Chapter 9: A Miscellany of Mimics

Japanese Impostor Who Impersonated His Son

"Dad impersonating son in exam arrested." *CNN.com*, January 15, 2009. http://
edition.cnn.com/2009/WORLD/asiapcf/01/15/japan.man.cheating.test/.

"Man caught impersonating son for company entrance exam." *Japan Today*,
January 15, 2009. www.japantoday.com/category/national/view/
man-caught-impersonating-son-for-company-entrance-exam.

Artur Baptista da Silva

"Clarification of alleged UNDP spokesperson in Portugal." United Nations
Development Programme press release, December 27, 2012. www.undp.org/
content/undp/en/home/presscenter/articles/2012/12/27/clarification-of-
alleged-undp-spokesperson-in-portugal.html.

Fotheringham, Alasdair. "The fraudster who fooled a whole nation: Portuguese media
pundit exposed as conman." *London Independent*, January 20, 2013.

A BOY NAMED SOO (CHUNG LING SOO/WILLIAM ELLSWORTH ROBINSON)

"Bullet Catch—the most dangerous feat in magic." Bullet Catch. http://bulletcatch.com/.

"Chung Ling Soo." Magic—The Science of Illusion. www.magicexhibit.org/story/
story_chungLingSoo.html.

Gardner, Lyn. "How not to catch a bullet." *London Guardian*, June 9, 2006.

Steinmeyer, Jim. *The Glorious Deception: The Double Life of William Robinson, aka Chung Ling Soo*. New York: Carroll & Graf, 2005.

MONTY'S DOUBLE (CLIFTON JAMES)

James, Clifton. "The general went home as a lieutenant." *Sydney Morning Herald*,
August 20, 1946.

———. "Gibraltar welcomed a false British commander." *Sydney Morning Herald*,
August 19, 1946.

———. "How I played General 'Monty'—Experiences in Africa." *Melbourne Age*,
September 21, 1946.

———. "How I played General 'Monty'—In the 'limelight of suspicion.'" *Melbourne Age*, August 31, 1946.

———. "How I played General 'Monty'—Official reception at Gibraltar." *Melbourne Age*, September 14, 1946.

———. "How I played General 'Monty'—Rehearsal and departure." *Melbourne Age*,
September 7, 1946.

———. "I doubled for Montgomery." *Sydney Morning Herald*, August 17, 1946.

THE CASE OF THE TWO MARTIN GUERRES (ARNAUD DU TILH)

Burton, Sarah. *Impostors: Six Kinds of Liar—True Tales of Deception*. New York: Viking
Books, 2001.

Davis, Natalie Zemon. *The Return of Martin Guerre*. Cambridge, MA: Harvard
University Press, 1983.

WASHINGTON'S NURSE (JOICE HETH)

"Joice Heth." Museum of Hoaxes. www.museumofhoaxes.com/joiceheth.html.

"The Life of Joice Heth." Documenting the American South. http://docsouth.unc. edu/neh/heth/summary.html.

PRICKING POMPOSITY

Pavel Jordanowitch/Paul Jordan-Smith

"The Disumbrationist School of Art." Museum of Hoaxes. www.museumofhoaxes. com/hoax/archive/permalink/the_disumbrationist_school_of_art.

Dr. Albin Avgher/Charlie Varon

"Creative speechwriting tactic displayed at California conference." Health Care Communication News, August 3, 2007. www.healthcarecommunication. com/Main/Articles/Speechwriters_in_the_News_5072.aspx.

Carroll, John. "Charlie Varon's amusing prank." *San Francisco Chronicle*, May 10, 2001.

———. "The genetic basis of jerkitude." *San Francisco Chronicle*, May 9, 2001.

Varon, Charlie. "Genome Out of the Bottle." www.charlievaron.com/genome.html.

BEING STANLEY KUBRICK (ALAN CONWAY)

"Alan Conway." Biography Channel. www.biography.com/people/alan-conway-20653827.

Anthony, Andrew. "The counterfeit Kubrick." *London Guardian*, March 14, 1999.

A SURVIVOR'S TALE? (BINJAMIN WILKOMIRSKI/BRUNO GROSJEAN)

Eskin, Blake. "Crying wolf—Why did it take so long for a far-fetched Holocaust memoir to be debunked?" *Slate*, February 29, 2008. www.slate.com/articles/ arts/culturebox/2008/02/crying_wolf.html.

Eskin, Blake. *A Life in Pieces: The Making and Unmaking of Binjamin Wilkomirski*. New York: W. W. Norton & Co., 2003.

Herman Rosenblat

"Holocaust 'greatest' love story a hoax." December 30, 2008. CNN.com. http:// edition.cnn.com/2008/US/12/30/holocaust.hoax.love.story.

"Holocaust 'love story' was fake." December 29, 2008. BBC News Online. http://
news.bbc.co.uk/1/hi/7802608.stm.

Misha Defonseca

Shields, Rachel. "Adopted by wolves? Best-selling memoir was a pack of lies." *London
Independent*, March 1, 2008.

THE TALIBAN COMMANDER

"Karzai aide blames British for Taliban impostor." *BBC News*, November 26, 2010.
www.bbc.co.uk/news/world-south-asia-11845217.

Baer, Robert. "Taliban Imposter: The U.S. Doesn't Know Its Enemy." *Time*,
November 28, 2010.

Boone, Jon. "Fake Taliban leader 'dupes Nato negotiators.'" *London Guardian*,
November 23, 2010.

Filkins, Dexter, and Carlotta Gill. "Taliban leader in secret talks was an impostor." *New
York Times*, November 22, 2010.

Gibbons, Fiachra, and Stephen Moss. "Fragments of a fraud." *London Guardian*,
October 15, 1999.

Partlow, Joshua. "Negotiator for Taliban was an impostor, Afghan officials say."
Washington Post, November 23, 2010.

Yousafzai, Sami. "Afghanistan: The Taliban to assassinate Karzai." *Daily Beast*,
December 8, 2012. www.thedailybeast.com/articles/2012/12/08/afghanistan-
the-taliban-plot-to-assassinate-karzai.html.

THE STRANGE CASE OF GU KAILAI

"'Body double' blocked in online searches; Gu Kailai imposter at trial?" *China Daily
Mail*, August 22, 2012.

Davies, Lizzy. "The Gu Kailai trial—timeline." *London Guardian*, August 7, 2012.

Garnaut, John. "Impostor claims in Chinese trial." *Sydney Morning Herald*, August 17, 2012.

Knowles, Hazel. "Wife of Chinese Premier 'hired body double' in Heywood murder
trial because she feared real suspect would reveal damaging secrets about
corruption." *London Daily Mail*, August 26, 2012.

Morse, Felicity. "Neil Heywood Murder: Gu Kailai 'Hired Body Double To Serve Her Prison Sentence.'" *Huffington Post*, August 21, 2012. www.huffingtonpost.co.uk/2012/08/21/gu-kailai-lookalike-murder-body-double-bo-xailai_n_1816468.html.

Urwin, Rosamund. "Seeing double…is that really Gu Kailai?" *London Evening Standard*, August 21, 2012. www.standard.co.uk/lifestyle/london-life/seeing-double-is-that-really-gu-kailai-8069630.html

Wu, Yuwen. "Gu Kailai and the body double debate." *BBC News Magazine*, August 24, 2012. www.bbc.co.uk/news/magazine-19357107.

TELEPHONE TRICKSTERS

Steve Bartman/Brian Westbrook/Captain Janks/Thomas Cipriano

Dougherty, Robert. "Brian Westbrook ESPN Prank Latest Strike by 'Captain Janks.'" *Yahoo! Voices*, February 24, 2010. http://voices.yahoo.com/brian-westbrook-espn-prank-latest-strike-captain-5535211.html?cat=49.

"'SportsCenter' fooled by club fan impostor." *Los Angeles Times*, October 17, 2003.

Hashemi Rafsanjani Impostor

Friedman, Thomas L. "Bush was duped on hostage call, U.S. says." *New York Times*, March 9, 1990.

Ibrahim, Youssef M. "Iranian leader mocks Bush over hoax." *New York Times*, March 10, 1990.

Jean Chretien Impostor/Pierre Brassard

MacKinnon, Ian, and Nick Cohen. "Can the Queen laugh it off?" *London Independent*, October 29, 1995.

Fidel Castro Impostor

"Palin, Chavez, Castro in best radio pranks ever." *Brisbane Courier-Mail*, December 6, 2012.

Mel Greig & Michael Christian

"Royal prank call DJs Mel Greig and Michael Christian will not face charges." *Huffington Post*, January 2, 2013. www.huffingtonpost.co.uk/2013/02/01/royal-prank-call-djs-kate-middleton_n_2597318.html.

"UK considers charges against hoax DJs Mel Greig and Michael Christian." *Brisbane Courier-Mail*, December 23, 2012. www.couriermail.com.au/news/world/uk-considers-charges-against-hoax-djs-mel-greig-and-michael-christian/story-fnd12peo-1226542477413.

Bond, Anthony. "'It was a low, lazy and artless prank': International backlash against sick jokers who boasted as tragedy of suicide nurse unfolded." *London Daily Mail*, December 7, 2012.

Duell, Mark, Emily Andrews, Sam Greenhill, Richard Shears, and Rebecca English. "We're both shattered. My first thought was: Is she a mother? Radio hosts at center of prank give self-pitying interviews." *London Daily Mail*, December 10, 2012.

Evans, Natalie. "Kate Middleton hospital nurse found dead in suspected suicide days after falling for radio prank call." *London Daily Mirror*, December 7, 2012.

Nolan, Steve. "More than two thirds of Australians don't think DJs were to blame for nurse's death, new poll reveals." *London Daily Mail*, December 9, 2012.

FRAUD ALERT: FLASH, BANG, WALLOP

"Flash mob history." Flashmob 101. http://iml.jou.ufl.edu/projects/fall07/Picataggio/history.html.

"What is a flash mob." Wisegeek. www.wisegeek.com/what-is-a-flash-mob.htm.

2009 "Single Ladies" Flash Mob

"100 Single Ladies Flashmob On Piccadilly Circus." BuzzFeed Community, April 29, 2009. www.buzzfeed.com/silvans/100-single-ladies-flashmob-on-piccadilly-circus-7xp.

"Flash Mob 100 Girls Dance in Piccadilly Circus to Beyonce Single Ladies." YouTube, April 29, 2009. www.youtube.com/watch?v=qgguEZCE3Dk.

2012 Glee *Flash Mob*

"Glee Flash Mob 2012." *Seattle Weekly News*, April 23, 2012. www.seattleweekly.com/
slideshow/glee-flash-mob-2012-36642512/.

"Glee Flash Mob & Marriage Proposal (Seattle—2012)." YouTube, April 26, 2012.
www.youtube.com/watch?v=nZqsVk4XYKk.

2009 Liverpool Street Station Flash Mob

"Making of t-mobile dance." YouTube, February 3, 2009. www.youtube.com/
watch?v=xWz9meMpUhs.

Sweney, Mark. "T-Mobile flashmob win TV ad of year." *London Guardian*, March 11, 2010.

"T-Mobile Liverpool St. Flash Mob Dance Advert High Quality." YouTube, January
17, 2009. www.youtube.com/watch?v=6-3kkqXX85c.

Wrenn, Eddie. "Dance of the commuters: 400-strong 'flash mob' gets funky at
Liverpool Street Station." *London Daily Mail*, January 15, 2009.

2009 Antwerp Central Station Flash Mob

"Centraal Station Antwerpen gaat uit zijn dak!" YouTube, March 23, 2009. www.
youtube.com/watch?v=0UE3CNu_rtY.

Leo, Alex. "'Sound of Music' train station dance: Why is it so popular?" *Huffington
Post*, May 13, 2009. www.huffingtonpost.com/2009/04/12/sound-of-music-
train-stat_n_186016.html.

2010 Sydney Central Station Flash Mob

"Flash mob at Central Station Sydney." YouTube, June 28, 2010. www.youtube.com/
watch?v=Jf97asCKfeA.

INDEX

T

U

ABOUT THE AUTHOR

Ian Graham is a British author of popular science, technology, and history books. He was born and raised in Belfast, Northern Ireland, and studied applied physics and journalism at City University, London. He worked as a writer and editor in magazines before making the switch to books. He has worked as a freelance writer for thirty years, specializing in space exploration, aviation, transport, science, history, and military technology.